Leverett Wilson Spring

Kansas

The prelude to the war for the union

Leverett Wilson Spring

Kansas
The prelude to the war for the union

ISBN/EAN: 9783742823076

Manufactured in Europe, USA, Canada, Australia, Japa

Cover: Foto ©Andreas Hilbeck / pixelio.de

Manufactured and distributed by brebook publishing software
(www.brebook.com)

Leverett Wilson Spring

Kansas

American Commonwealths.

EDITED BY

HORACE E. SCUDDER.

KANSAS

TO ACCOMPANY

LEVERETT W. SPRING'S

KANSAS in AMERICAN COMMONWEALTHS.

0 10 20 30 40 50 60 70 80 90 100
Scale of Statute Miles.

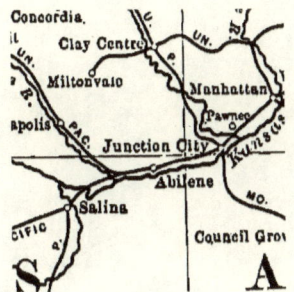

CONTENTS.

CHAPTER I.
PRELIMINARY . . . . PAGE 1

CHAPTER II.
THE FIELD 17

CHAPTER III.
DRIVING DOWN STAKES 24

CHAPTER IV.
LESSONS IN POPULAR SOVEREIGNTY . . 37

CHAPTER V.
COUNTER-MOVES 59

CHAPTER VI.
WAR ON THE WAKARUSA 79

CHAPTER VII.
SOME HEAVY BLOWS 102

CHAPTER VIII.
DUTCH HENRY'S CROSSING, BLACK JACK, AND OSAWATOMIE 137

CHAPTER IX.
PER ASPERA 163

CONTENTS.

CHAPTER X.
THE LECOMPTON STRUGGLE 209

CHAPTER XI.
JAYHAWKING 237

CHAPTER XII.
CLOSE OF THE TERRITORIAL PERIOD . . 257

CHAPTER XIII.
DURING THE WAR FOR THE UNION . 268

CHAPTER XIV.
AD ASTRA 306
BIBLIOGRAPHY 323
INDEX 329

PREFATORY NOTE.

THE limits prescribed for this volume have not permitted a minutely detailed account of the Kansas struggle. I have endeavored to exhibit the logic and spirit of "the first actual national conflict between slaveholding and free-labor immigrants," rather than to attempt an exhaustive collection of facts. Newspaper files, public documents, books, manuscripts that promised to throw light upon the subject have been carefully examined. A large amount of material has been derived from personal intercourse with men of all parties who helped to make the history of Kansas. If my version of it should not prove to be colored with the dyes in vogue twenty-five years ago, I beg the reader to bear in mind that there is too much truth in what Theodore Parker said in 1856, at the anniversary of the Anti-Slavery Society, concerning the Kansas business, — " I know of no transaction in human history which has been covered up with such abundant lying, from the death of Ananias and Sapphira down to the first nomination of Governor Gardner."

The map which accompanies this volume is designed to illustrate the text, rather than to exhibit the Kansas of to-day. It shows the chief places of historic interest, — some of which no longer exist.

L. W. S.

State University, Lawrence, Kansas,
September, 1885.

KANSAS.

CHAPTER I.

PRELIMINARY.

THE eminent Union-savers, who devised and carried through Congress the compromise of 1850, fully expected that it would drive the question of slavery totally and permanently out of national politics. They drained their vocabulary in applauding that wonderful specific which involved the enactment of a stringent fugitive slave law; the admission of California with a free-labor constitution; the organization of Utah and New Mexico as territories on the basis of popular sovereignty; and the removal of slave marts from the District of Columbia. When at last it received the sanction of Congress, Henry Clay, drawn from retirement by the stress of public affairs to undertake a mission of pacification, felicitated the country upon the peace which quickly followed and gave promise of permanence. General Lewis Cass did not believe that "any party could now be built up in relation to the question of slavery."

He even contemplated the extraordinary self-denial of making no more speeches about it. To put the matter beyond recall; to breathe against the great disturber

"The hopeless word of — never to return,"

forty-four members of the thirty-first Congress, including many leading politicians of the South, solemnly and publicly pledged themselves to oppose the candidacy of any man for the office of president, vice-president, congressman, or state legislator who should favor "a renewal of sectional controversy upon the subject of slavery." In 1852 Whig and Democratic conventions struck hands in eulogizing the compromise, and resolved that mankind should be dumb in regard to the wrongs of the negro. The triumphant election of Franklin Pierce as president turned upon the popular conviction, that he was more unqualifiedly in sympathy with the policy and measures of conciliation than his illustrious rival.

But the drowsy syrups of compromise were swallowed in vain. The conflict, which no genius of skillful temporizing could effectually stifle, after a brief and uneasy repose broke out afresh. Slavery, so recently and so impressively banned from the halls of national legislation, returned thither almost before the applause that greeted its exile had died away. In the Senate, December 4th, 1853, A. C. Dodge of Iowa offered a bill, of the usual form and purport, for the organization of

Nebraska — a measure unsuccessfully attempted during the preceding session. After consideration by the Committee on Territories, of which Stephen A. Douglas of Illinois was chairman, the bill reappeared in the Senate January 4th, 1854, variously amended and accompanied by an elaborate disquisition upon the status of slavery in the public domain.

Though Mr. Douglas did not leave his theories in doubt, and insisted that the compromise of 1850 reposed on principles of congressional non-action in the territories, yet he shrank from definite, downright announcement that the compromise of 1820 was at an end. By the terms of that adjustment Missouri came into the Union as a slave state, but all unoccupied portions of the old Louisiana province north of the parallel 36° 30′ were perpetually reserved for freedom. January 16th, Senator Dixon of Kentucky, dissatisfied with the hesitation of the bill, offered an amendment that directly assailed the Missouri restriction. Douglas finally espoused the bolder policy — not without reluctance and uncomfortable augury. "I have become perfectly satisfied," he said to Dixon, "that it is my duty as a fair-minded national statesman to coöperate with you as proposed, in procuring the repeal of the Missouri Compromise restriction. It is due to the South; it is due to the constitution; it is due to that character of consistency which I have heretofore labored to maintain. The repeal, if we can effect it, will produce much stir in the free states of the Union for a season. Every opprobrious epithet will be applied to me. I shall probably be hung in effigy. . . . This proceeding may end my political career. But acting under the sense of duty which actuates me, I am prepared to make the sacrifice."

Douglas recalled the bill, which was subjected to repeated and essential revisions. In its ultimate form, as reported from the workshop of the committee February 7th, it cancelled the Missouri Compromise; cut Nebraska into halves — styling the southern section Kansas and the northern Nebraska; and enunciated the doctrine that citizens of the United States, peopling the territories, have plenary jurisdiction over all their domestic institutions.

The debate which instantly sprang up on the reappearance of the slavery question in Congress — inferior to none of its predecessors in violence or duration of parliamentary noise — fell below the contest of 1850 in freshness of thought and expression. It affords no exhibition of scenical and oratorical tableaux so memorable as when Calhoun, wrecked in health but with intellect and power of will still unbroken, listened to the reading of his last speech, thickly sown with anxieties and ill-boding; as when Daniel Webster on the 7th of March rallied all the splendid forces of his oratory and renown for an assault on the anti-slavery movement — the tendency and outcome of which had been " not to enlarge, but to restrain, not to set free but to bind faster, the slave population of the South."

Douglas did not assume a new rôle by leading the crusade against congressional restriction in the territories. He bore a distinguished part in the compromise of 1850, of which popular sovereignty constituted a prominent if not paramount feature. Alexander H. Stephens, who has given in his " War between the States " interesting details not generally known of its evolution through private conferences between representative men of the North and the South, argues with apparent conclusiveness that popular sovereignty " was the compromise of that year ; " that " the other associated measures all depended upon it." Mr. Douglas, as chairman of the Senate Committee on Territories, introduced bills for the organization of Utah and New Mexico in harmony with the conference adjustments. " A few weeks afterward," he said in a speech March 3d, 1854, " the committee of thirteen took these two bills and put a wafer between them and reported them back to the Senate as one bill, with some slight amendments. One of these amendments was that the territorial legislatures should not legislate upon the subject of African slavery. I objected to that provision upon the ground that it subverted the great principle of self-government upon which the bill had been originally framed by the territorial committee. On the first trial the Senate refused to strike it out, but subsequently did so, after full debate, in order to establish that principle as the rule of action in territorial organizations." William H. Seward, silent on this particular point during the earlier stages of the Kansas struggle, substantially admitted at a later period all that Stephens and Douglas claimed. The pacification of 1850, he repeatedly conceded, secured for Utah and New Mexico "the right to choose freedom or slavery when ripened into states."

While Douglas possessed some capital qualifications for leadership; while his resources embraced remarkable endowments of rude, boisterous, half-educated force, of invincible self-assertion, of insolent and unsurpassed dexterity in the practices of forensic gladiatorship, yet he was weak in those essential qualities and inspirations that spring out of a profound ethical conviction. In regard to the moral aspects of slavery, which stirred the conscience of the civilized world, he affected a phlegmatic, nonchalant sentiment — an indifference whether it was voted up or down in the territories.

Southern congressmen, reinforced by liberal Democratic contingents from the North, rallied with enthusiasm in support of popular sovereignty.

This doctrine had been uncordially received by all parties on its appearance in the arena of politics. "Well do I remember," said Thomas H. Benton in the House of Representatives, April 25th, 1854, "the day when it was first shown in the Senate. Mark Antony did not better remember the day when Cæsar first put on that mantle through which he was afterwards pierced with three and twenty envious stabs. It was in the Senate in 1848, and was received . . . as the quintessence of nonsense." In 1854 Southern political sentiment blew from an opposite quarter. Then Southern leaders accepted popular sovereignty with enthusiasm as a providential expedient for the defense and extension of their social institutions. They argued that Congress had no legitimate competency to draw lines of restriction across the public domain, which excluded one half of the country from fair and equal occupancy of it; that the Missouri Compromise was in no sense a compact, as it lacked every element of state and party consent; that the principle of popular sovereignty, the right of communities, state and territorial, to legislate for themselves, is distinctly and emphatically an American doctrine; that it was the issue at stake in the colonial struggle with Great Britain and in the crisis of 1850; that the much-quoted anti-slavery sentimentalities of the fathers of the republic carry little weight because notable advances in sociology have been made since their day, because the domestic institutions of the South, tested by a wider experience, are seen to embody and define the great race-subordinations of nature. Besides, the geographical makeshift failed to tranquillize sectional disturbances, as it furnished abolitionists a precedent for intermeddling. "It is a disunion line," said Representative Caskie of Virginia. "No, sir," exclaimed Senator Butler of South Carolina, "instead of Peace standing on the Missouri line with healing in her wings and olive-branches in her hands, it has been Electra with snakes hissing from her head and the torch of discord in her hand."

The champions of popular sovereignty disagreed as to the time when the inhabitants of a territory might constitutionally exercise the right "to form and regulate their domestic institutions in their own way." Current Southern constructions, which the Supreme Court afterwards confirmed, maintained that nothing could be done previous to the formation of a state constitution. Douglas insisted, on the contrary, that the people could act legally and effectively whenever they pleased. Among the questions propounded to him by Abraham Lincoln in the joint debates of 1858, there was one which touched this point. Douglas replied that as slavery could not exist a day nor an hour anywhere, unless supported by local police regulations which the territorial legislature must establish, the people need only elect

CHAPTER II.

THE FIELD.

THE territory of Kansas extended westward from Missouri to the summit of the Rocky Mountains and northward from the thirty-seventh to the fortieth parallel, embracing an area of about one hundred and twenty-six thousand square miles. The history of this vast, mid-continent region belongs mainly to yesterday. Barely the life-period of a single generation has elapsed since civilization touched it otherwise than casually and fugitively.

Francisco Vasquez de Coronado is reputed to be the first European who visited Kansas. In 1540 he set out from Mexico with a small army of Spaniards and Indians to seize Cibola, a province situated somewhere in New Mexico, and rumored to abound in magnificent cities which the prose of actual investigation discredited into a few wretched hamlets.

Coronado's disappointments did not end at Cibola. Notwithstanding that dissuasive experience, he fell into the toils of a smooth-tongued fabling Indian nicknamed the Turk, "on account of his resemblance to the people of that nation," a rascal who vapored about a country of remarkable wealth and splendor lying far eastward across the plains and called Quivera.

In the spring of 1541 the credulous Spaniard broke camp at Tiguex, a province of the Rio Grande valley, near the mouth of the Puerco, to which he retired after a bootless exploration of Cibola, and began a new quest. In thirty-seven days he reached the Arkansas. Here provisions began to fail, and the bulk of the expedition retraced its steps to New Mexico. The route of Coronado, who pushed on with a few picked men, is bestead with uncertainties. Nothing better can be offered in regard to it than conjectures more or less plausible. He appears to have advanced from southwestern Kansas " through mighty plains and sandy heaths, smooth and wearisome and bare of wood. . . . All that way the plains are as full of crook back oxen as the mountain Serena in Spain is of sheep. . . . They were a great succor for the hunger and want of bread which our people stood in. One day it rained in that plain a great shower of hail, as big as oranges, which caused many tears, weaknesses, and vows." The expedition probably called a halt in northeastern Kansas near the Nebraska line. One point only is absolutely clear — Coronado had been duped again. No rich spoils, no flamboyant fervors of architecture, were discovered; no imperial cities

> "Such as vision
> Builds from the purple crags and silver towers
> Of battlemented cloud, as in derision
> Of kingliest masonry."

It is doubtful whether any single feature of the expedition afforded the Spaniards more retrospective satisfaction than the fate of the tricky Turk. Confessing that he had lured them into the desert to accomplish their ruin, he was promptly and it may be presumed enthusiastically strangled. This first reconnaissance of civilization upon Kansas achieved nothing of practical importance.

After the departure of Coronado no Europeans visited Kansas for an interval of more than a hundred and seventy-five years. Meanwhile Louisiana, a vast territory vaguely denominated as the region drained by the Mississippi and its affluents, passed into the possession of France. Of this enormous tract Kansas, with the exception of some unimportant territorial additions from the Texas cession of 1850, formed a portion. It was not until 1719 that Frenchmen found their way thither. In that year M. du Tissenet, acting under orders of M. de Bienville, governor of Louisiana, made a hasty tour of exploration, found the country "beautiful and well timbered," native warriors "stout, well made and great," lead mines "abundant, . . . and erected a column with the arms of the king placed upon it 27th of September, 1719."

This cursory and inconsequential visit alarmed

the Spaniards. In New Mexico there was a movement to save Kansas from the Frenchmen. An armed caravan left Santa Fé in 1721 on this errand, but it was ill-managed, and blundered into total destruction.

To guard against danger from New Mexico in the future, the French erected in 1722-23 a fortification called Fort Orleans, upon an island in the Missouri River near the mouth of the Osage, and M. de Bourgmont was put in command. During the following year Bourgmont made an extended tour in Kansas. With the various Indian tribes who inhabited the region he assiduously cultivated pacific relations. There were receptions, speeches, pipe-smokings, distributions of presents, peace-dances, and general assurances of profound and mutual regard. It is singular that the finale of this much-protesting intercourse should have been a tragedy of utter completeness and atrocity, but such is the case. In 1725 Fort Orleans was captured by Kansas savages and the garrison slaughtered. Details are wholly unknown, as not a white man survived to recount the story, and the stolid, close-mouthed Indian never broke silence.

The massacre effectually blighted the enthusiasm of Frenchmen for explorations in Kansas. Indeed, from 1725 until the United States purchased it of Napoleon Bonaparte, in 1803, the territory dropped almost completely out of the knowledge of mankind — glided back into the blankness and vacuity of a *terra incognita*. The expeditions of Lewis and Clark in 1804-06, and of Lieutenant Z. M. Pike in 1806-07, furnish almost the earliest scientific and trustworthy information. A portion of it was traversed in 1819-20 by a detachment of Major S. H. Long's party. To these early American explorers Kansas hardly presented an attractive or promising appearance. The beautiful prairies of the eastern border,

"Billowy bays of grass ever rolling in shadow and sunshine,"

kindled their enthusiasm, but in the interior and to the westward they found a hopeless reach of desert, well enough for Indians — for white men untenantable. Lieutenant Pike considered " the borders of the Arkansaw river . . . the paradise (terrestrial) of our territories for the wandering savages. . . . I believe there are buffalo, elk, and deer sufficient on the banks of the Arkansaw alone, if used without waste, to feed all the savages in the United States territory one century." But the region could not support white men in large numbers even along " the rivers Kanses, La Platte, Arkansaw and their branches. . . . The wood now in the country would not be sufficient for a moderate share of population more than fifteen years, and then it would be out of the question to think of using any of it in manufactories, consequently their houses would be built entirely of mud-brick (like those of New Spain) or of the brick manufactured with fire. But possibly time may make discoveries of coal mines, which would render the country habitable."

With the establishment of American occupancy an era of migration set in through Kansas toward the Pacific slope — a migration at first slender, capricious, and without system, but acquiring ultimately volume, method, and persistence sufficient to imprint clear-cut trails sheer across the mighty plains. Traders, eager to seize upon new and inviting avenues of commerce; travelers, ambitious to compel the half unknown world beyond the Missouri to yield up its secrets; Kearney's soldiers, with greedy eyes fixed on New Mexico; Mormons, fleeing into the wilderness before the wrath of civilization; gold-hunters, aflame with visions of sudden wealth among the mines of California, — such was the heterogeneous, intermittent mob that trooped across Kansas during the years immediately preceding the Kansas-Nebraska legislation.

At the time of organization the territory was an Indian reservation, inhabited by about a score of native and imported tribes, among which a white population of six or seven hundred civilians had drifted, who congregated mainly around the military stations, the trading posts, and the half dozen denominational mission schools. The Kansas-Nebraska bill ejected the Indians from their homes and sent them elsewhere. This consideration was not overlooked by its opponents. Edward Everett protested in polished phrase. Senator Bell of Tennessee denounced federal unfaith in the matter of Indian treaties, which " set aside at our discretion and trample under foot the most explicit and solemn guarantees." General Sam Houston made an impassioned plea in behalf of Indian rights, but the spoliating measure could not be arrested. The aborigines were successfully bargained out of the way. Some of them removed at once, and others more leisurely.

Thus in the heart of the nation there was staked off a great territory for experiments in popular sovereignty as a Union-saving expedient, a territory substantially unhistoried, with no intrusive, meddlesome past that could mar the trial. Thither hurried partisans of the North and South — representatives of incompatible civilizations — to take a hand in the impending struggle. It was a crosspurposed and variorum migration, — hirelings, adventurers, blatherskites, fanatics, reformers, philanthropists, patriots. That such a medley of humanity, recruited from Moosehead Lake to the Rio Grande, responsive to all the sectional animosities which distracted and imperiled the country, conscious after some vague sort that great destinies might hinge upon their mission, would transform the wilderness of Kansas into an immediate Utopia was hardly to be anticipated.

" So foul a sky clears not without a storm."

CHAPTER III.

DRIVING DOWN STAKES.

WESTERN Missouri, containing in 1854 fifty thousand slaves, worth at a moderate valuation twenty-five millions of dollars, was fully awake to the momentous social and political perils that lurked in the compromise of 1820. Throughout that region an uneasy, apprehensive, feverish state of affairs existed. The declaration of a large and representative pro-slavery convention at Lexington, Missouri, in July, 1855, that "the enforcement of the restriction in the settlement of Kansas was virtually the abolition of slavery in Missouri," gave formal expression to convictions that had gradually become general.

Leadership in these graver exigencies fell mainly upon David R. Atchison, senator from Missouri during the years 1841-55, a man of commanding presence, social, generous, passionate, a stump orator of no mean order. " Senator Atchison . . . may be considered the exponent of Southern opinion," said " Lynceus " in " Letters for the People on the Present Crisis," writing at St. Louis, September 7, 1853. " In speeches he has been making in various portions of the State he is reported as taking the ground . . . that he will fight the admission of Nebraska unless it . . . shall come in as a slave territory, or, at least, with the question left open and all done to foster slavery that is possible." Atchison denounced the restriction, and painted with a heavy brush the calamities that would follow if abolitionists should get a footing in Kansas. On this point the Lexington convention faithfully echoed his sentiments — "a horde of our western savages with avowed purposes of destruction would be less formidable neighbors." Atchison thought that the interests of Missouri required nothing beyond formal repeal of the offensive legislation which laid restrictions upon slavery. In that event Missouri would be able to take care of herself, and of Kansas also.

The Missouri border abounded in igneous and explosive materials. Typical Southern folk of the better grade, intelligent, hospitable, courteous, high-minded, were not wanting. Yet other sorts of humanity had large representation: numerous and unhappy varieties of "white trash," demoralized veterans of the Mexican war, adventurers graduated from the plains or the mountains of Colorado or the mining camps of the Pacific coast, — thoughtless, passionate, whiskey-guzzling, guffawing, unconventional men

"Who meeting Cæsar's self, would slap his back,
Call him ' Old horse ' and challenge to a drink."

The border experienced a boisterous revival of pro-slaveryism, and the reputation of abolitionists, never very high thereabouts, sank into utter discredit.

No sooner had President Pierce signed the Kansas-Nebraska bill than companies of Missourians pushed into Kansas and seized upon extensive tracts of the best lands, not waiting, in some cases, for the Indians to get out of the way. A convenient simplicity marked their proceedings. The laws of preëmption, literally interpreted, required the erection of cabins and periods of actual residence: but exigencies are unfriendly to restrictive and dilatory technicalities. At all events, they must not be allowed to imperil great public interests. That the squatter should simply notch a few trees in evidence of occupancy, or arrange half-a-dozen rails upon the ground and call it a cabin, or post a scrawl claiming proprietorship and threatening to shoot intermeddlers at sight, seems to have been all that was considered absolutely essential. These energetic first-comers were mostly amateur immigrants, — men who bestirred themselves in the interest of slavery rather than at the solicitation of personal concerns, who proposed to reside in Missouri, but to vote and fight in Kansas should necessity arise for such duality.

On the 10th of June, 1854, more than six weeks before the arrival of the earliest New England colony, though disquieting rumors of invasion from the East had begun to be rife, there was a convention of pro-slavery men at Salt Creek Valley to discuss territorial affairs. The sentiments of this initial Kansas convention, — forerunner of an enormous brood of partisan meetings, — sentiments loudly chorused by the whole pack of border newspapers, took form in a series of twelve resolutions which, in addition to considerable frank advice for the benefit of abolitionists, announced that slavery already existed in Kansas, and urged its friends to lose no time in strengthening and extending it to the utmost.

Missouri leaders perceived the necessity and the expediency of immediately flooding Kansas with slaves. They believed at that time and still believe, that this strategy, courageously and persistently prosecuted, would have won the day. During the winter of 1854–55, B. F. Stringfellow visited Washington in the interest of an extensive slave-colonization. He unfolded the project in a conference of prominent Southern congressmen, and showed that servile labor could not be less successful in Kansas than in Missouri, a notably prosperous commonwealth; that the territorial crisis called as loudly for negroes as for voters. "Two thousand slaves," urged Stringfellow, "actually lodged in Kansas will make a slave state out of it. Once fairly there, nobody will disturb them." This not unpromising scheme elicited ample pledges of coöperation, not one of which was ever redeemed.

Several pro-slavery towns sprang up in the territory, situated principally on the Missouri River between Kansas City and the Nebraska line: Kickapoo, a savage, implacable little burg, containing in its palmiest days twenty-five or thirty cabins, now utterly collapsed; Atchison, christened in honor of the Missouri senator, second only to Kickapoo in political venom, but unlike that almost expunged hamlet surviving its early mistakes and growing into the most important town in northeastern Kansas; Leavenworth, ruled mainly though not wholly by Southern sentiment, which more than once maddened into deeds of brutal violence, surpassing all Kansas rivals, during the first quarter century of its history, in population and commercial importance; Lecompton, somewhat inland, political headquarters of the pro-slavery party, blighted in its downfall, rudely awakened from brilliant dreams to the realities of a ragged, straggling frontier village.

Early in the summer of 1854, rumors that powerful capitalized societies were forming in New England for the purpose of sending anti-slavery colonies to Kansas alarmed the people of western Missouri, and suggested doubts whether the repeal of the old restrictive compromise legislation would eventually prove as fortunate for their interests as they dreamed. They had looked upon Kansas as an easy, inevitable prey, a likelihood almost universally conceded throughout the Northern States. "The fate of Kansas was sealed," said "The Liberator" of July 13th, 1855, "the very moment the Missouri Compromise was repealed."

In the midst of general despondency it occurred to Eli Thayer, of Worcester, Massachusetts, that the public had misread the situation; that apparent disasters were only successes disguised; that the calamities befallen the anti-slavery cause in Congress might be retrieved by tactics of organized emigration, — a contest in which the Southern oligarchy, much-cumbered and heavily shod, could not cope with freedom in its nimbler movements. While the congressional struggle was in progress, before the fate of the Kansas-Nebraska bill had been settled, he wrote out a constitution for the " Massachusetts Emigrant Aid Company " and procured a legislative charter. Thayer originally contemplated a formidable corporation, with a capital of five millions of dollars, by which he expected to control migration — the vast westering flux of natives as well as foreigners — in the interest of liberty; to marshal it against the aggressions of the South; to secure the territories in the first place, and then turn his revolutionizing agencies upon the slave states themselves.

The public declined to embark in this wholesale and magnificent project. Abolitionists repudiated expedients of colonization as "false in principle," and able to compass at best only "a transplanted Massachusetts," — a futile and unworthy consummation, since even "the original Massachusetts has been tried and found wanting," — while the general skepticism took practical and disastrous shape in failure of contributions. The enterprise was verging toward financial collapse when Amos A. Lawrence, of Boston, came to the rescue and advanced out of his own pocket the funds necessary to put life into it.

No organization was ever effected under the first charter. It saddled objectionable monetary liabilities upon the individuals who might associate under it, and was abandoned. The whole business then passed into the hands of Thayer, Lawrence, and J. M. S. Williams, who were constituted trustees, and managed affairs in a half personal fashion until February, 1855, when a second charter was obtained and an association formed early in March with slightly rephrased title — "The New England Emigrant Aid Company" — and with John Carter Brown, of Providence, Rhode Island, as president. In the conduct of the company, the trustees who bridged the interval between the first and second charters continued to be a chief directive and inspirational force. Mr. Thayer preached the gospel of organized emigration with tireless and successful enthusiasm, while Mr. Lawrence discharged the burdensome but all-important duties of treasurer. Among the twenty original directors were Dr. Samuel Cabot, Jr., John Lowell, and William B. Spooner, Boston; J. P.

Williston, Northampton; Charles H. Bigelow, Lawrence, and Nathan Durfee, Fall River. The list of directors was subsequently enlarged to thirty-eight, and included the additional names of Dr. S. G. Howe, Rev. Edward Everett Hale, Boston; George L. Stearns, Medford; Horace Bushnell, Hartford, Connecticut; Prof. Benj. Silliman, Sr., New Haven, Connecticut; and Moses H. Grinnell, New York. The company in its reorganized shape receded, at least temporarily, from all wholesale projects, and devoted itself to the problem of planting free-labor towns in Kansas.

The facilities offered by the Boston organization, in addition to the obvious advantages of associated effort, were reduction in cost of transportation, oversight by competent conductors, investments of capital in mills, hotels, and other improvements which would mitigate and abbreviate the hardships of pioneering. Though the design of the organization was frankly avowed, yet anybody, whether in sympathy with its mission or not, might freely avail himself of its advantages. The obligations of the emigrants who went to Kansas under its wing were wholly implied and informal. Assuredly it offered no premium for extremer types of anti-slavery men. On the contrary, a Hunkerish strain of conservatism prevailed among the colonists which naturally provoked criticism. "The Liberator" of June 1st, 1855, speaking of the *personnel* of the companies already sent on to Kansas, remarked that "hardly a single abolitionist can be found among all who have migrated to that country.... Before they emigrated they gave little or no countenance to the anti-slavery cause at home.... If they had no pluck here what could rationally be expected of them in the immediate presence of the demoniacal spirit of slavery? ... To place any reliance on their anti-slavery zeal or courage is to lean upon a broken staff."

The number of colonists who reached Kansas over the lines of the Emigrant Aid Company was not large. During the summer and autumn of 1854 five companies were dispatched, which comprised a total of seven hundred and fifty souls. From the opening of navigation on the Missouri River in 1855 until July as many more companies were fitted out, though the numbers fell off to six hundred and thirty-five. About one hundred and forty thousand dollars were expended first and last in prosecution of Kansas colonization.

But the work of the Boston organization cannot be adequately exhibited by arithmetical computations. A vital, capital part of it lay in spheres where mathematics are ineffectual — lay in its alighting upon a feasible method, which was copied far and wide, of dealing with a grave political emergency, and in the backing of social and monetary prestige that it secured for the unknown pioneers at the front.

If volume and bitterness of criticism afford any trustworthy standard by which its efficiency may be tested, the Emigrant Aid Company played no subordinate part in the Kansas struggle. Douglas declared that popular sovereignty was struck down "by unholy combinations in New England." In the opinion of Senator J. A. Bayard, of Delaware, "whatever evil or loss or suffering or injury may result to Kansas, or to the United States at large, is attributable as a primary cause to the action of the Emigrant Aid Society of Massachusetts." Senator Green, of Missouri, said in 1861, long after the Kansas question had been practically settled, that "but for the hot-bed plants that have been planted in Kansas through the instrumentality of the Emigrant Aid Society, Kansas would have been with Missouri this day."

The principal representative of the Massachusetts corporation in Kansas — the man who sustained toward it the most intimate and confidential relations, and who mainly shaped its politico-financial policy in the territory — was Dr. Charles Robinson, of Fitchburg, Massachusetts. To him Kansas was not wholly an unknown region when the Emigrant Aid Company commissioned him as its agent. In 1849 he passed across it on an overland trip to California, and was favorably impressed with the possibilities of the country. He participated rather prominently in the stormy experiences through which California passed in

1849–51 — experiences which Kansas subsequently repeated in many of their salient features. Both contests sprang up on the border, abounded in anomalies and expedients for which little precedent could be cited, and exhibited all the lawless, blustering, open-throated peculiarities that distinguish such events. Not only were the types and sorts of humanity involved substantially identical, but also, in a degree worthy of passing notice, there was repetition among the actors. Missourians in particular returned betimes from the Pacific coast to mingle in a fray nearer home. Robinson learned an effective lesson in the California school for the Kansas epoch.

The Emigrant Aid Company planted a handful of towns in the territory — Hampden, which disappeared after a little, Wabaunsee, Osawatomie, Manhattan, Topeka, and Lawrence. Of these anti-slavery villages the oldest, and for a time the chief, was Lawrence. Upon the first day of August, 1854, the pioneer party, twenty-nine in number, sent out by the Boston society, reached the spot where that town was afterwards built. The directions given to C. H. Branscomb, conductor of the company, were, " proceed through the Shawnee Reservation and select the first eligible site on the south side of the Kansas River." Six weeks later a second expedition of one hundred and fourteen members arrived. In its earliest and rudimentary stage the village was merely a little collection of tents. Then followed, in due time, queer, grass-thatched huts, copied apparently from African kraal village models, and rude, squat, mud-plastered log-cabins, beyond which the line of territorial architecture advanced slowly and with difficulty.

What the new village should be called was a matter of some discussion. For a while it had various names — Wakarusa, New Boston, Yankee Town. Citizens of Worcester, Massachusetts, offered a library if it should be christened Worcester. The name Lawrence was finally agreed upon in honor of the treasurer of the Emigrant Aid Company. "I think I was the first to suggest your name for the city," Dr. Robinson wrote Mr. Lawrence October 16th, 1854; "though I have never urged it at all, as I wished every person to be satisfied in his own mind. . . . Most of our people are very much attached to it, and after I explained your course in connection with the enterprise . . . there was much enthusiasm manifested. . . . A committee has been chosen to give a formal notice of the naming of the city."

It was unavoidable that a portion of the immigrants fetched from New England to the outposts of civilization, set down amidst the privations and discomforts of pioneering and in the neighborhood of powerful pro-slavery communities — mutterings of great social disturbances singing in the upper air and threatening to add unknown elements of peril to the hardships of the wilderness — should give way to homesickness and despair. They had dipped their hopes in the magic dyes of the imagination, had pictured to themselves some restored paradise on the wonderland plains of Kansas; and when the raw, crude, belligerent reality dawned upon them, they shook the dust of the territory from their feet and returned, disgusted with the border, to their old homes. But the great majority of colonists, not only from New England but also from other Northern States, — men and women little given to irresolution, cowardice, or panic, ruled by exacter, less romantic ideas, — were not unprepared to meet the trials of the wilderness and the inevitable hostility of Missouri.

CHAPTER IV.

LESSONS IN POPULAR SOVEREIGNTY.

The first territorial governor of Kansas was Andrew H. Reeder, of Pennsylvania, a mild, easy, rhetorical, admirable man, of good intellectual parts, well reputed as a lawyer, a national democrat, and an enthusiastic advocate of popular sovereignty. A complete assortment of customary officials — judges, secretaries, marshals, surveyors, land commissioners — was fitted out in Washington. One or two gentlemen of leisure, reckoning, though wholly without their host, on a dearth of local candidates, accompanied these dignitaries with design of standing for any desirable office the territory might offer.

Reeder arrived at Fort Leavenworth October 7th, where a public reception — given by pro-slavery partisans, who viewed the new governor as nothing more than their tool — and a wordy, noisy address of welcome awaited him. In responding, Reeder pleasantly referred to the reception as "a foreshadowing of kindness and confidence" which he hoped to receive from citizens of the territory. His talk, however, was not wholly given over to eulogy and congratulation. The spirit of violence which was already beginning to stir he denounced with the fluent boldness and confidence of inexperience. "I pledge you," he said, "that I will crush it out or sacrifice myself in the effort." It was an heroic avowal that failed to kindle any enthusiasm whatever among the auditors.

The governor sensibly prefaced his work in Kansas by a tour of observation which consumed some weeks. He was anxious to get his knowledge at first hand — an ambition that did not favorably impress the gentry concerned in the Leavenworth reception. They regarded themselves as entirely competent and were more than willing to furnish information on any point of Kansas affairs. Then followed a partition of the territory into districts, and the election of a delegate to Congress November 29th, 1854.

This first Kansas election never attained the notoriety of the second, which took place four months afterwards, yet both experiences present the same characteristic features — large and elaborate expeditions from Missouri to stuff territorial ballot-boxes with illegal votes. No defense or apology has ever been put forward for these extraordinary proceedings except the necessitarian plea of fighting the devil with fire. The opinion universally entertained on the border in 1853 and in the earlier months of 1854, that the safety of slavery in Missouri and its ultimate expansion into Kansas would be assured simply by the repeal of restrictive legislation, showed unmistakable signs of weakening in the resolutions adopted at Salt Creek Valley. Subsequent events tended to increase and exasperate the alarm. Rumors now flew thick and fast on evil wings that the Emigrant Aid Company and the kindred organizations, which sprang up with a tropical luxuriance throughout the North, were pushing "military colonies" into Kansas, primarily to protect it from pro-slavery inroads, and secondarily to attack Missouri. It is true that the Boston company, in the enormous breadth of its original scope, mapped out some such prospectus which gave rise to discomposing talk on the border. "Free-state men," said B. F. Stringfellow, "before we resorted to aggressive measures, openly boasted in the streets of Weston that they would drive slavery out of Missouri." Discussions in Congress added fuel to the fire, and as a consequence there was no small stir along the border. "When the people of Missouri," said Mordecai Oliver, defending his constituency in the House of Representatives, "saw these proceedings on the part of these intermeddlers in the affairs of Kansas and in contradiction of the principles of the Kansas-Nebraska Act, they were roused — I confess it and confess it with no spirit of humiliation, but with pride and to the honor of my people — they were roused to an indignation that knew no bounds."

Anger is well enough in its place, but it would have been wise for these furious Missourians to make sure of their ground before proceeding to extremities. A little investigation would have established the fact that the Emigrant Aid Company never bought a firelock or furnished its patrons with warlike equipments of any sort; that it simply opened a western emigrant agency, — a perfectly legitimate transaction which broke none of the commandments ethical, political, or interstate. Though at a later day — after the first two election experiences — members of the corporation in a private, individual way contributed freely toward the purchase of Sharpe's rifles for the use of free-state settlers, the corporation itself religiously held fast, through the whole period of its operations, to the unmilitary functions of an ordinary transportation bureau. Had the Missourians followed the Massachusetts example and poured into Kansas as actual settlers rather than as crusading ballot-box stuffers, their fortunes would have thrived the better.

There was comparatively little at stake in the election of November 29th — nothing more than the choice of a delegate to Congress, and that for a fractional term. Besides, the pro-slavery candidate, J. W. Whitfield, a tall, strongly-made, rather prepossessing but thick-tongued Tennessean, holding the office of Indian agent, was not particularly objectionable. Whatever partisan sentiments he may have cherished were kept out of sight, and unquestionably he would have been elected, had the Missourians stayed at home. But rumor and demagogues roundly abused the ear of the border. Western Missouri was armed and equipped to assail abolitionists in the territory. For this purpose Blue Lodges — a species of semi-secret, counter-Massachusetts societies designed to operate at Kansas elections — had been extensively organized. To allow so much froth and fume, so much stir and alarm, to end in nothing might present an uncomfortable parallel to the historic feat of marching up the hill and then marching down again. The leaders chose to do something superfluous rather than nothing at all. The 29th of November at all events would afford opportunity for a little experimenting to see what seeds of promise lay in the Blue Lodges. So seventeen hundred and twenty-nine Missourians invaded different election districts and cast as many gratuitous ballots for Whitfield, who received his credentials and appeared in Washington as the first congressional delegate from Kansas, but was not allowed to take his seat.

The incursion from Missouri was not the only original suffrage feature of the election. Rumors got abroad that Whitfield designed to impress an aboriginal "Native American" vote into his service. The fact of his being an Indian agent lent plausibility to the canard. Some enterprising

Yankee hit upon an expedient to forestall any advantage that the pro-slavery party might expect from extensions of the franchise in that quarter. Learning that a certain Delaware chief had recently enunciated his views on the relative merits of Yankees and Missourians — " Good man — heap — Yankee town. Missouri — bad — heap — heap — heap ! — d—n um " — it occurred to him that here might possibly be a neglected field of politics worth cultivating. Unfortunately his bright thoughts were somewhat belated. They did not fairly dawn upon him until the evening before election. However, he rode over to the Delaware Reservation in the morning, assembled the braves, and expounded to them their unappreciated political privileges; confidently argued their right to vote, and proposed that they should instantly assert it at the election in progress that very day. The Indians drew off by themselves and entered upon a council over the matter which went on interminably without apparent signs of conclusion. The opportunity for " Native American " or for any other phase of suffrage was rapidly disappearing, and at last the exasperated Yankee, in no very conciliatory or complimentary dialect, demanded some sort of answer. Finally, the oldest chief arose and, appareled in a solemnity never surpassed by the judiciary of Tartarus, said — " Tinkum four days — den vote heap — heap-um ! — sometime — may be ! "

LESSONS IN POPULAR SOVEREIGNTY. 43

But the most astonishing exhibition of popular sovereignty occurred in the spring of 1855. During the preceding February the authorities took a census of the territory, which showed a population of 8,601. There were figured out 2,905 voters, a majority of whom came from slave states. Alexander H. Stephens made effective use of this fact in a speech in the House of Representatives July 31st, 1856. "This census," he said, "gives the name of each resident legal voter in the territory thirty days before the March election. . . . I have counted every name on the census roll and noted the section of country from which the settler migrated, and I find that of those who were registered as legal voters of the territory in February, a month before the election, 1,670 were from Southern States and only 1,018 from the entire North. There were 217 from other countries. . . . The inference which I draw from these facts is that there was a decided majority of anti-Free-Soilérs in the territory . . . in the month of February." Mr. Stephens erred in classing all immigrants from Southern States as pro-slavery in sentiment. A not inconsiderable element among them preferred that Kansas should become a free state.

Both sides appreciated the importance of securing the legislature which was to be elected March 30th. Success in that matter would be a decisive victory. In Missouri the excitement surpassed all foregoing experiences. The orators were abroad in their most tempestuous mood, denouncing abolitionists and Eastern corporations that sought to fang the heart of Missouri as with the tooth of a viper. Voting machineries had been tested and worked to the satisfaction of the experts who devised them. To meet the present emergency, it was only necessary to put on a little higher pressure. Blue Lodges bestirred themselves energetically. There were recruitings, organizations of companies, drills, armings, as if some great military expedition were afoot. Those who could not give personal attention to the preservation of law and the purity of public franchise in Kansas were exhorted to assist in paying the bills. At a meeting in Boonesville, held for the purpose of raising money and enthusiasm, a half-tipsy planter stumbled up to the speaker's table, and, flinging down a thousand dollars, said, — "I've just sold a nigger for that, and I reckon it's about my share towards cleaning out the dog-gauned Yankees."

The Missouri expounders of popular sovereignty marched into Kansas to assist in the election of a territorial legislature — an unkempt, sun-dried, blatant, picturesque mob of five thousand men with guns upon their shoulders, revolvers stuffing their belts, bowie-knives protruding from their boot-tops, and generous rations of whiskey in their wagons.

Six thousand three hundred and seven votes

were polled on this memorable 30th of March election — nearly eighty per cent. of them by Missourians, who, of course, swept the boards. In a military point of view the expedition was managed effectively, and succeeded in distributing pro-slavery voters through the territory in such bulks as were needed to overcome opposition. The invaders did not, as a general rule, molest actual residents unless they showed fight. Judges of election who meekly accepted the situation and received all ballots offered were seldom set aside. In cases where they objected to Missourian theories of suffrage they were promptly removed, and their places supplied by men whose scruples of conscience did not lie in that direction.

At Lawrence there was an illustration of the milder sort of displacement. One of the judges insisted that the first Missourian who presented himself at the polls should swear that he resided in Kansas. The fellow hesitated. He evidently stumbled at the ethics, lately sanctioned by high pro-slavery authority, that in dealing with abolitionists scruples of conscience were an impertinence. The leader of the gang, seeing there promised to be an awkward hitch in the programme, ordered him to retire and presented himself at the polls, that the on-looking crowd might have the benefit of his elucidating and inspiring example. "Are you a resident of Kansas?" asked the election judge. "I am," the

Missourian replied. "Does your family live in Kansas?" persisted the former. "It is none of your business. If you don't keep your impertinence to yourself I'll knock your d—d head from your shoulders." The judge, considering his usefulness gone, retired, and thenceforward everybody voted who felt so disposed.

At Bloomington there was an exceptionally successful Bedlam. The judges exhibited obstinacy which yielded only to an active revolver and bowie-knife treatment. They persisted in theories of suffrage altogether too illiberal and narrow for the times. It was intimated that their resignations would be accepted — a hint which they neglected to act upon. Finally, to expedite affairs, a borderer drew his watch and announced a five minutes' period of grace — then resignations or death. The five minutes expired and nothing had been done. An extension of one minute was allowed, during which the judges decamped.

In the main there was but slight occasion for anything beyond a savage pretense of violence. Numbers, bluster, profanity, and a liberal display of fighting-gear completely cowed opposition. The visiting voters returned to Missouri, feverish with triumph — "We've made a clean sweep this time." Border newspapers rioted in extravagances of felicitation. "Abolitionism is rebuked," one of them screamed, "her fortress stormed, her flag draggling in the dust." But dashing into the territory with a braggart, rub-a-dub publicity, and casting four thousand nine hundred and eight votes in a total of six thousand three hundred and seven, turned out to be a ruinously expensive victory.

In Western Missouri the policy of invasion received a practically unanimous support. Dissent meant trouble for the dissenter. It drew suspicion and unpopularity upon him if nothing worse. The " Parkville Luminary," venturing to question distantly and mildly the expediency of forcing slavery upon Kansas, was summarily quenched in the Missouri River. Now and then an intrepid, outspoken man, with clearer, less jaundiced vision than his neighbors, made head against the universal frenzy. One person of this stamp, old Tom Thorpe, of Platte County, Missouri (a remarkable specimen of frontier independence), appeared before the Congressional Investigating Committee in 1856. "Whenever there was an election in the territory," Mr. Thorpe testified, "they were fussin' roun' an' gettin' up companies to go, an' gettin' hosses an' wagins. They come to me to subscribe, but I tole 'em that I was down on this thing of votin' over in the territory, an' that Tom Thorpe did n't subscribe to no such fixins. They jawed me too about it — they did; but I reckon they found old Tom Thorpe could give as good as he got. They tole the boys they wanted to make Kansas a slave state; an' they tole 'em the abolitionists war a commin' in; an' that the Emigrant Aid Society Company & Co. war pitchin' in; an' they 'd better too. You see they took the boys over, an' they got plenty liquor, an' plenty to eat, an' they got over free ferry. Lots an' slivers on 'em went. A heap o' respectable folks went with them. There's Dr. Tibbs, lives over in Platte, he used to go, an' you see they 'lected him. The boys tole me one time when they come back — says they 'We've 'lected Dr. Tibbs to the legislature;' an' says I 'Is it the state or the territory?' An' says they 'The territory.' Says I, 'Boys, ain't this a puttin' it on too thick? It's a darned sight too mean enough to go over there and vote for them fellers, but to put in a man who don't live there is all-fired outrageous.' There's my own nephew — he come all the way up from Howard County to vote. He come over to see me an' our folks as he went along. I says to him — says I, 'Jim Thorpe, hain't you nothin' better to do than to come way up to vote in the territory?' Well he tole me that they want buisy at home, an' that they got a dollar a day an' liquor; an' says I, 'Stop, Jim Thorpe, that's enough; you can't stay here in my house to-night an' nobody can that goes for votin' in the territory. I tell you what, boy, I've always been down on that kind o' thing. I ain't no abolitionist neither. I tell you I'm pro-slave. I'm dyed in the wool an' can't make a free-soiler; but mind what I say, if the boys keep a cuttin' up so I'll come over to the territory an' 'nitiate Betsey.'"

The events of March 30th disturbed free-state settlers profoundly, and well they might. Dr. Robinson wrote A. A. Lawrence April 4th — "the election is awful, and will no doubt be set aside. So says the governor, although his life is threatened if he does n't comply with the Missourians' demands. I with others shall act as his body-guard."

But there was no general movement of protest against the irregularities of the election. From six only of the eighteen election districts did remonstrances appear. This was a negligence that the "Democratic Review" energetically rebuked. "What did the Free-Soilers do? Did they protest? Did they deny the legality of the votes? Not a bit. . . . There was an admirable chance for Free-Soilers to prove how much they loved order, law, and regulated freedom. It could hardly be supposed that they would miss so fine a chance to immortalize their law-abiding tendencies. But really and truly they let it slip. They were drowsy over it. Jupiter nodded."

There was some excuse. It lay in the isolation of the little towns, in difficulties of communication necessary to concerted action, and in the hazard that attended the business. One man who was active in pushing a protest got into trouble. William Phillips, a Leavenworth lawyer, prominent in an effort to have the election canceled, because, among other things, "the New Lucy, a boat, on the morning of the day of election started for Leavenworth from Weston with citizens of Missouri," who "did vote at the polls of the sixteenth district, and then immediately returned on said boat to Missouri," was brutally mobbed. As a sequel to tar and feathers, head-shaving, and riding on a rail, a negro sold the unfortunate lawyer at auction — "How much, gentlemen, for a full-blooded abolitionist, dyed in de wool, tar and feathers and all? How much, gentlemen? He'll go at the first bid." This wretched outrage, if we may believe the "Kansas Herald," published at Leavenworth, sent a thrill of delight through the community.

Rumors that Governor Reeder designed to set aside the entire election, or at least to refuse certificates to a large number of candidates whom the judges of elections had declared elected, blasted whatever personal popularity he might still retain among the Missourians. The alienation which began with the reception festivities at Fort Leavenworth had constantly widened and deepened. Now, in the waxing bitterness, pro-slavery men freely coupled threats with denunciations. Some talked of "hemping" the scoundrel, while others felt more like "cutting his throat from ear to ear."

On the 5th of April Governor Reeder heard

protests and canvassed returns. Beweaponed gentry representing both factions thronged the executive office. Free-state men, with their slender list of remonstrances, insisted that the election should be canceled, and another ordered under precautions which would make a second 30th of March impossible. Charges of illegal voting they themselves did not entirely escape, arising mainly from the circumstance that a party of Eastern immigrants reached Lawrence on the day of election, some of whom, it was alleged, voted notwithstanding the brevity of their residence in Kansas. A few of the new-comers, alarmed by the threatening aspect of affairs, immediately fled the territory. It is uncertain whether any of these fugitives went to the polls or not. Yet it is beyond reasonable doubt that the number of anti-slavery ballots cast by men, against whom charges of non-residence could be sustained, was very small. In the shifting, prospecting, to-and-fro situation considerable laxity of suffrage could not be escaped. But neither the Emigrant Aid Company nor any like Northern society ever committed the stupid blunder of sending pseudo-settlers half across the continent simply to vote. The pro-slavery representatives, however, did not find illegal voting a congenial theme. They accentuated the point that the governor could not lawfully go behind the returns — that it only remained for him to authenticate them.

Governor Reeder adopted an intermediate, half-way policy, which failed to satisfy anybody. Stickling unhappily for technicalities, he cast out the mote of eight candidates against whom protests had been filed, and ordered new elections in their districts, but ignored the beam of a great systematic, wholesale fraud. Of the thirty-one members of the legislature twenty-eight were satisfactory to the pro-slavery managers. But they loudly resented the governor's interference, and their curses were almost as violent as might have been expected had it been less ineffectual. The little company of free-state men who went down from Lawrence to Shawnee Mission to act as Reeder's body-guard wished they had allowed him to take care of himself. Dr. Robinson announced that for his part he repudiated both governor and legislature — a declaration prophetic of future free-state movements.

Reeder soon afterwards visited Washington, where his reputation needed attention. President Pierce and Jefferson Davis, secretary of war, disliked the situation in Kansas, the responsibility for which they charged principally upon the governor. Missourians posted to the capital, grew red in the face denouncing him, and would listen to nothing less than his removal. The president intimated that his resignation would be acceptable, and should not fail of suitable reward. Might not the mission to China have attractions for him?

The negotiations failed. Reeder finally declined to present himself as a burnt-offering to the administration and returned to Kansas.

July 2, 1855, the first territorial legislature assembled at Pawnee, a town of the smallest realized attainments, situated inland on the Kansas River about one hundred and forty miles from its mouth. Preparations to accommodate the lawmakers were of a scanty and primitive character. Rev. Thomas Johnson, long time missionary to the Indians at Shawnee Mission Manual Labor School and president of the council, states that "nearly all the members of the legislature had to camp out in the open sun, and do their own cooking without a shade tree to protect them; for there were no boarding-houses in the neighborhood excepting two unfinished shanties." The gentry came prepared for roughing it, as they brought an unprecedented assortment of legislatorial fixtures — pots, kettles, sauce-pans, provisions, and tents.

The supplementary elections ordered by the governor and held May 22d, since the pro-slavery party did not contest them, resulted in a complete free-state victory. At the outset, therefore, the legislature contained twenty-eight pro-slavery and eleven anti-slavery members. As a preliminary move in the policy of repudiation, strong pressure was brought to bear upon the latter to prevent them from taking their seats. These efforts were unsuccessful, except in the case of Martin F. Conway, who was finally induced, after a good deal of reluctance and hesitation, mainly through the insistent if not imperative urgency of Dr. Robinson and Colonel Kersey Coates, of Kansas City, to send in his resignation to the governor as member of the council. Mr. Conway's highly-charged phrases and defiant sentiments show no trace of the dubious, irresolute state of mind that preceded his discussions with Robinson and Coates. "Instead of recognizing this as the legislature of Kansas," he wrote June 30th, 1855, "and participating in its proceedings as such, I utterly repudiate it, and repudiate it as derogatory to the respectability of popular government and insulting to the virtue and intelligence of the age. . . . I am so unfortunate as to have been trained to some crude notions of human rights — some such notions as those for which, in ages past, our foolish ancestry periled their lives on revolutionary fields. . . . Simply as a citizen and a man I shall, therefore, yield no submission to this alien legislature. On the contrary, I am ready to set its assumed authority at defiance, and shall be prompt to spurn and trample under my feet its insolent enactments whenever they conflict with my rights or inclinations."

To the homespun, brown-fisted, doing-its-own work legislature at Pawnee Governor Reeder addressed a sonorous and courtly message. He exhorted the statesmen there convened " to lay aside all selfish and equivocal motives, to discard all unworthy ends, and in the spirit of justice and charity to each other, with pure hearts, tempered feelings, and sober judgments," to enter upon their duties.

The legislature, as soon as an organization had been effected, gave attention to the ten remaining anti-slavery members. Nine were summarily unseated and their places filled by the men to whom Governor Reeder denied certificates. A solitary Free-Soiler — S. D. Houston — kept his place until July 22d, when he retired, as " to retain a seat in such circumstances would be . . . a condescension too inglorious for the spirit of an American freeman," and left the legislature unvexed by political heresy or schism.

At Pawnee the legislature attempted little except the expulsion of obnoxious members. After a session of only four days — reports that cholera had appeared in the neighborhood materially contributing to the discontent — there was an adjournment to Shawnee Mission, where it reassembled July 16th.

It was this adjournment which led Governor Reeder to break with the legislature. Though the members of it had been elected by notorious invasions from Missouri, that scarlet political offense could be absolved; he could still hope that they would escape all unworthy conduct, " save that which springs from the inevitable fallibility of just and upright men;" but when, in the phrase of Toombs of Georgia, "they removed from Reeder's town to somebody else's town," then was there committed a monstrous and unforgivable sin. To be in the wrong place destroyed the constitutionality of the legislature. The circumstance that Governor Reeder was financially interested in the success of Pawnee, which the action of the legislature ruined, furnished his enemies with a convenient text for abusive discourse. Yet the more probable explanation of the matter is that, repenting of his blunder in failing to set aside the March election, he took advantage of the adjournment, which was at the expense of some technicalities, as the most plausible excuse at hand for parting company with the legislature.

Nothing in the work of the legislature at Shawnee Mission has any flavor of originality — unless the slave-code be excepted. A natural instinct led it to transfer to Kansas almost in bulk the statutes of Missouri. That was in harmony with Atchison's frank confession — " I and my friends wish to make Kansas in all respects like Missouri." The pro-slavery managers steeped their slave-code in despotism. Uncertain of the future, confronted by vague, indefinite perils — perils which, like clouds on the horizon no bigger than a man's hand, might dissolve or blacken the heavens with storm — they went nervously to work and ran into absurd extremes of precaution and stringency. In their code two years of imprisonment would expiate the crime of kidnapping and selling into bondage a free colored man, but death was denounced against him who aided in the escape of a slave. To question the right of slave-holding in Kansas might draw upon the querist's head pains of felony. A citizen could be disfranchised should he decline taking oath to support the Fugitive Slave Law — thus impertinently enlarging the area of penalty in a federal enactment. The statesmen at Shawnee Mission succeeded in making "the enunciation of the great and eternal principles of liberty a penitentiary offense." Their code struck at the liberty of the press, at freedom of speech, and the sanctities of the ballot-box. And not the least singular feature of this extraordinary legislation is that according to the official publication of 1855 the territorial governor had no power to pardon offenses against it. In the act of Congress organizing the territory of Kansas it was provided, that the governor " may grant pardons and respites for offenses against the laws of said territory, and reprieves for offenses against the laws of the United States until the decision of the president can be known thereon." In " The Statutes of the Territory of Kansas," printed at Shawnee Mission in 1855, the congressional act of organization is republished, and from design or accident the clause is made to read — the governor " may grant pardons and respites for offenses against the laws of the United States, until the decision of the president can be known thereon." Free-state men charged that the mutilation was intentional, and one of their first measures on getting possession of the legislature was to order the publication of a correct copy of the organic act.

The legislature and its allies successfully prosecuted their quarrel with Governor Reeder, who received notice of his removal from office August 15th. In the fight they had effective aid from the territorial supreme court, which decided the removal of the capital to be constitutional. The grievances, which did duty in public as the cause of Reeder's removal, were charges of delay in reaching the territory and in getting the government under way, of usurpation, lack of sympathy with the people, and land-speculation; but the real difficulty was that he did not submit tamely and obediently to pro-slavery dictation.

Governor Reeder's administration ran its troubled course in less than a year. It achieved no very signal success. That were perhaps impossible in the condition of the territory — hopeless as a child's freak to stamp out a spring bubbling up under stones. Unquestionably it was beyond the reach of a man, without preëminent endowments of insight, adaptation, or executive force — a stranger to border life, suddenly thrust into the wilderness with a commission to smother outbreaks of the irrepressible conflict.

CHAPTER V.

COUNTER-MOVES.

MISSOURIANS felicitated themselves upon the state of affairs in Kansas, upon a legislature unanimously, fanatically pro-slavery, upon a judiciary not at all unfriendly, upon an executive department purged of an obnoxious incumbent. Free-state men certainly found themselves confronted by a very grave question — what course shall be pursued in the emergency? Few and beggarly were the signs of promise visible for them. Their cause seemed to have foundered. Something should be done, but what?

The line of policy adopted — repudiation of the territorial legislature as an illegal, usurping, "bogus" concern, and organization forthwith of a state government and application to Congress for admission to the Union — emanated from Robinson. This scheme, an outgrowth and suggestion in part of the California struggle, began to shape itself in his thoughts on the very day that Reeder handed over the territorial legislature to the Philistines. The rise of a state government, independent of the territorial government, severing all friendly relations with it and aiming to effect its overthrow — like the emergence in the Roman world of a standing army of twenty-five legions from the ruins of the republic — was an event of capital importance in Kansas history.

A preliminary step in the counter-move against Missouri was to secure a supply of Sharpe's rifles. The reputed " military colonies " were practically without weapons. Robinson lost no time in dispatching G. W. Deitzler to New England for arms, ostensibly to protect the polls at the special elections May 22d, but really as the first stroke in the projected scheme of anti-Missouri operations. Sharpe's rifles, he saw, were an absolutely essential preliminary. They would ensure the settlers respect and consideration which they might not otherwise receive. One hundred of these weapons soon reached Lawrence in packages marked " books " — a species of literature that created wide interest on the border. " Sharpe's rifles," said the " Democratic Review," are " the religious tracts of the new Free-Soil system."

Then it would be necessary to establish in place of the disowned territorial government some political organization to serve as a rallying point for the people until the legislature could be captured or admission to the Union secured. To provide for this emergency a state government was decided upon, which would be put into actual service whenever Congress should authenticate it. In the interval the anti-slavery portion of the community proposed to do without laws as best it might. November 1st, 1855, Dr. Robinson wrote A. A. Lawrence, reviewing somewhat in detail the progress of events up to that time. "[We must be] as independent and self-reliant and confident," he said, "as the Missourians are, and never in any instance be cowed into silence or subserviency to their dictation. This course on the part of prominent free-state men is absolutely necessary to inspire the masses with confidence and keep them from going over to the enemy. . . . I have been censured for the defiant tone of my Fourth of July speech, but I was fully convinced that such a course was demanded. The legislature was about sitting and free-state men were about despairing. . . . [A few of us] dared to take a position in defiance of the legislature and meet the consequences. We were convinced that our success depended upon this measure, and the demonstration of the Fourth was to set the ball in motion in connection with Conway's letter to Governor Reeder resigning his seat and repudiating the legislature. For a while we had to contend with opposition from the faint-hearted, but by persevering in our course, by introducing resolutions into conventions and canvassing the territory, repudiation became universal with free-state men. . . . We conceived it important to disown the legislature, if at all, before we knew the character of its laws, believing they would be such as to crush us out if recognized as valid, and believing we should stand on stronger ground if we came out in advance. . . . The 1st of July forms an important epoch in our history. It was about that time that open defiance was shown our enemies. . . . Pro-slavery bullies were daily in the streets and insulted all free-state men whom they supposed would make no resistance. This drove our people into a secret organization of self-defense, and it was not long before they were glad to cry for quarters. A free-state Missourian, a regular California bully, came among us and took them in their own way and frightened every pro-slavery man from the field. His name is David Evans, and if I had a Sharpe's rifle at my disposal I should make him a present of it. . . . To divide into parties before our admission into the Union would be ruinous and give our enemies the advantage."

Between the 8th of June and the 15th of August, 1855, not including the large Fourth of July meeting already mentioned, when Dr. Robinson delivered an address on local and national issues, seven so-called political conventions were held in Lawrence. These conventions — one or two of the first being small, impromptu affairs — were all except one in opposition to the federal administration and its territorial policy. On the evening of June 27th a few Democrats assembled and resolved that " the best interests of Kansas require an early organization of the Democratic party." The master spirit in this convention was James H. Lane, recently from Indiana, where he had obtained some notoriety. He participated in the Mexican war, was elected lieutenant-governor of Indiana in 1848, and appeared in Congress as representative from that state in 1852. For some cause Lane's political fortunes did not thrive in Indiana, and in the spring of 1855 he betook himself to the fresh fields of Kansas, pro-slavery in sentiment, boasting that he would as readily buy a negro as a mule, conceding the legality of the territorial legislature, and accepting it as a foregone conclusion that Kansas would become a slave state if its soil should prove to be adapted to servile labor. But the Democratic venture came to nothing. It touched no responsive chord among the people. Lane's interest in feeble minority parties was very slight, and he soon found his way to the opposition benches.

The various minor assemblies at Lawrence led up to a more pretentious convention which began on the 14th of August, and continued until the following day. The special significance of this convention lies in the fact, that it initiated measures looking toward the formal organization of a political party. It declined to attempt that task itself as being too local and unrepresentative in its make-up, and confided it to a more comprehensive assembly that should meet October 5th at Big Springs, for the purpose of "constructing a national platform upon which all friends of making Kansas a free state may act in concert."

Big Springs in the autumn of 1855 was a place of four or five shake-cabins and log-huts. To that town repaired one hundred delegates and thrice as many spectators, who took quarters out of doors on the prairie. At this convention all the anti-Missouri elements — heretofore unassociated and without definite concert of action — got into a kind of organic connection and denominated themselves the Free-State party.

The platform put forth by the new political clanship emphatically confirmed the declaration of "The Liberator," that no abolitionists had taken passage for Kansas. As a matter of fact, Dr. Robinson was at that time almost the only free-state man of prominence in the territory who avowed himself an abolitionist, and he did not happen to be a member of the convention. And it is a significant fact, which forcibly illustrates the absence of any general and radical sentiment of abolitionism in Kansas, that so late as the year 1858 Missourians hired out slaves at Lawrence, received their wages, and nobody made objection.

Though recently escaped from the stranded Democratic movement, Lane intrigued himself into the chairmanship of a committee of thirteen to which the construction of a platform was intrusted.

The question of slavery brought on an all-night discussion, in which he persuaded the committee to adopt violent anti-negro principles. Only one among the thirteen stood out to the end, — an inexpugnable home missionary, James H. Byrd. The platform branded the charges of abolitionism, so industriously circulated against free-state men, as "stale and ridiculous." With that mischievous and deplorable fanaticism it disavowed all sympathy. "The best interests of Kansas require a population of white men." When the time came for the establishment of a state government, negroes of every stripe, bond and free, should be excluded. The convention adopted the platform without dissent. At Big Springs assuredly the anti-slaveryism was of a diluted milk-and-water type.

The convention appointed a committee to draft resolutions in regard to the territorial legislature. That assembly the committee treated with powerful verbal caustics. Such a course might have been expected in any case, but the fact that Governor Reeder wrote the resolutions made assurance doubly sure. After his removal from office Reeder threw himself heartily and unreservedly into the free-state cause. Widely and favorably known in Eastern States, where his defense of repudiation had great influence in the persuasion of a conservative and law-abiding public that this revolutionary measure must arise out of inexorable necessities, he was an accession of primary importance. National as well as local considerations entered into the problem pressing upon the new free-state party. Unless the country at large could be wakened; unless the few hundred men at the front could be backed by moral and material support from non-slaveholding states, it would be folly to risk a contest with Missouri. Governor Reeder's chief service lay outside of Kansas. No other man in the free-state ranks had anything like a national reputation; no other man could then command a hearing so wide or so effective.

Reeder's aggrieved personal experiences tinctured his resolutions with a tang of wormwood. Five months after fitting out the territorial legislature with certificates, and couching his communications to it in the most courtly phrases of official etiquette, he describes that body as "the monstrous consummation of an act of violence, usurpation, and fraud," — "a contemptible and hypocritical mockery of republicanism," trampling down as with the hoofs of a buffalo the Kansas-Nebraska bill, libeling the Declaration of Independence, and staining the country with indelible disgrace. Whenever "peaceful remedies shall fail, and forcible resistance shall furnish any reasonable prospect of success," — then let the now shrinking and reluctant hostility be pushed to "a bloody issue." The resolutions scourging the legislature evoked a response quite as rapturous as Lane's negrophobia.

The first and only discord that jangled the harmonies at Big Springs occurred when a subject, incidental and subordinate to the special purposes of the convention, was reached — the question of establishing a state government. It was stirring the community — an uppermost theme in the public thought — and could not be ignored. The special committee, that took it under advisement, shrank from pledging the party to the support of so novel and venturesome an experiment. They pronounced it "untimely and inexpedient." But the convention thought differently, and adopted approving resolutions.

As epilogue to the labors of the convention, and as prologue to the opening career of the new party, there was nomination of a delegate for Congress. Only one man received a moment's consideration for this honor — Reeder. The presentation of his name called out tremendous applause. His speech in accepting the candidacy produced a powerful impression. "A steady, unflinching pertinacity of purpose, never-tiring industry, dogged perseverance, and all the abilities with which God has endowed" him — such was the service he pledged to Kansas. Reeder's speech modulated in its closing paragraphs into the belligerent tone of the resolutions on the legislature — " when other resources fail, there still remain to us the steady eye and the strong arm, and we must conquer or mingle the bodies of the oppressors with those of the oppressed upon the soil which the Declaration of Independence no longer protects!"

The convention secured unity and concert among the detached anti-Missouri elements, which merged into a political party as vapor-wreaths combine into the larger cloud. But the convention unfortunately exposed itself to damaging criticism. Lane's "black-law" platform and Reeder's heated declamation gave the enemy aid and comfort. The unlucky "bloody-issue" phrase was worn threadbare in Congress and out of it by the incessant service to which administration speakers put it. Douglas thundered against "the daring and defiant revolutionists in Kansas," who were plotting " to overthrow by force the whole system of laws under which they live." He professed great anxiety lest, through the inefficiency of federal processes, the insurgents should escape the just penalty of their deeds. This government, he remarked, has been " equal to any emergency . . . except the power to hang a traitor!"

If the formation of a political party was a matter of too considerable magnitude for the Lawrence convention of August 14th and 15th to enter upon, reasons still more cogent and conclusive existed why it should shrink from initiating the movement for a state government. The convention met primarily and avowedly in the interest of a new political organization, and therefore could not escape charges of partisanship, whereas it was thought particularly desirable that the state government should have an origin at least technically unpartisan. During the progress of the first convention a petition was circulated and numerously signed, calling a second convention of citizens, without regard to political affiliations, to consider the state-government project. No sooner had the former body adjourned on the 15th than the latter, composed of substantially the same membership, assembled. The recent politicians now became simply citizens, and made brief work of the business before them. The resources of talk had been pretty much exhausted by the first convention, where the discussion took wide range and the expenditure of words was less than usual. Opposition to the experiment of a state organization showed little or no strength. A delegate territorial convention, to meet at Topeka September 19th, was agreed upon.

The Topeka convention subjected the straw which had been violently threshed at Lawrence and Big Springs to a fresh flailing, with no results other than attended earlier experiments. A constitutional convention seemed feasible, delegates to which were elected October 9th. They received in the aggregate twenty-seven hundred and ten votes. On the same day Reeder was elected free-state delegate to Congress and received all the ballots cast — twenty-eight hundred and forty-nine. The territorial legislature had also ordered an election for congressional delegate and selected October 1st as the date. J. W. Whitfield received twenty-seven hundred and twenty-one votes — only seventeen scattering ballots disturbed the unanimity of this election — and secured the governor's certificate. Reeder, backed by protests from thirty-two voting precincts, contested Whitfield's seat, but did not carry his point.

The constitutional convention continued in session at Topeka from October 23d to November 11th. Lane was elected president, and delivered, on taking the chair, a short address that sketched in outline the nobler Kansas of the future. Wide diversities of antecedents appeared among the members of the convention who represented half the states of the Union. Though convened for a purpose that did not lack much of being revolutionary, it was a decidedly conservative assembly. Nineteen of the thirty-four members reported themselves democrats, six registered as whigs, while independents, free-soilers, republicans, free-state men, and nothingarians found representatives among the remaining nine. The incidental debates, which arose during the session on the merits of the Kansas-Nebraska bill, showed that a majority were friendly to it in spite of all that had happened in the territory.

The convention put together a fairly good patchwork constitution, which adopted the boundaries of the Kansas-Nebraska bill, prohibited slavery after the 4th of July, 1857, conferred the right of suffrage on "white male citizens," and on "every civilized male Indian who has adopted the habits of the white man," and located the capital temporarily at Topeka. Lane still advocated the exclusion of negroes, pleading for a free white state, and carried the convention with him. Robinson fought the "black law" iniquity stoutly, but could make no head against it. A portion of the convention wished to incorporate anti-negro discriminations in the constitution, but the whole matter was ultimately referred to the people, who voted by a majority of nearly three to one that colored men should be excluded from the state. December 15th the constitution was ratified at the polls by seventeen hundred and thirty-one affirmative to forty-six negative votes. The election of officers for this tentative, empirical commonwealth took place January 5th, 1856, and resulted in the choice of Charles Robinson as governor. One interesting and noteworthy result followed — whatever the philosophy of it may be — the sudden and final extinction of black-law sentiment in Kansas. Silence fell upon its numerous and active champions with the election of an abolitionist to the governorship. That event in its effect was like some great change of climate which abruptly revolutionizes the life, customs, and habits of a people.

The elections of December 15th and of January 5th excited no general disturbance. Pro-slavery men sneered at them as silly, scarecrow performances. At two points only did anything like the old time violence break out — Leavenworth and Easton. While the election was in progress at Leavenworth, on the 15th of December, a gang of pro-slavery roughs appeared at the polls and demanded the ballot-box on the ground that the election was illegal. Considering the reply unsatisfactory, the leader, followed by the whole brawling rout, crashed through the window where votes were received, and caused a great panic among the judges of election, who did not relish that style of suffrage. "I was not right well afterwards," one of them complained. The raiders captured the ballot-box and bore it away in triumph, reducing consequently the majority in favor of the Topeka constitution by several hundred votes.

Only a single affray of any importance disquieted the January election. In consequence of rumors that the Kickapoo rangers — a pro-slavery military company of bad reputation — were planning an attack, the election at Easton did not take place until the 17th. A few armed free-state men from Leavenworth, led by Captain R. P. Brown, were in attendance to lend their friends any assistance that might be necessary. At night there was a brief skirmish in which one pro-slavery man was killed. Nobody on the free-state side received serious injury. "I found a shot in my scalp a day or two afterwards," said an Easton man, "but I did not know it at the time."

In the morning Brown and his men started for Leavenworth, but were intercepted by the Kickapoos, who had been hastily summoned to Easton and were in a rage to avenge the killing of the preceding night. Their fury burned especially against Brown, whose resolution and activity made him very unpopular among the Kickapoos. "We've got him sure," one of them chuckled. They carried him back to Easton and confined him in a store, while an attempt was being made to organize a court for his trial. But some of the savages could not brook the delays of the rudest, most expeditious judiciary. They dispersed the court and dealt Brown a fatal hatchet-stroke on the head. As he was not killed outright, they bestirred themselves to take him home — a distance of several miles. It was late in the afternoon of one of the bitterest winter days ever known in Kansas before they set forth. "I am very cold," groaned the dying man, who, iced with gore, was flung upon the floor of a farm wagon and jolted homeward for hours over the roughly frozen roads. "Here's Brown," the devils blurted out as they drove up to the door of his cabin.

The state legislature met at Topeka March 4th, and Governor Robinson delivered his message — a strong, sensible, cautious paper. With a mixture of shrewdness, poetry, and bathos, the legislature after a brief session adjourned to the 4th of July. It attempted nothing beyond the passage of a few laws, the appointment of a codifying committee to prepare business for the next session, the election of Reeder and Lane as senators, and the preparation of a memorial praying for admission to the Union under the Topeka constitution. Neither officers nor laws were regarded as having anything more than a conditional, tentative existence, until favorable and validating action could be secured on the part of Congress. The governor was careful to say that he "recommended no course to be taken in opposition to the general government or to the territorial government while it shall remain with the sanction of Congress. Collision with either is to be avoided."

Thus far an unbroken prosperity had attended the counter-move against Missouri, but in Washington it experienced rough weather. April 7th, General Cass presented in the Senate the memorial of the Topeka legislature, asking that the State of Kansas might be admitted to the Union. The appearance of the memorial caused a commotion. "I find," said Douglas, "that the signatures are all in one handwriting. . . . I perceive on inspection various interlineations and erasures. All things are calculated to throw doubt on the genuineness of the document." Senator Pugh thought the memorial appeared " as if some person who had it in charge had watched the progress of discussion in this body, and had stricken out propositions to accommodate it to the present stage of discussion." " Are we not aware," sneered Benjamin, of Louisiana, " that the men whose signatures purport to be attached to this paper are fugitives from justice?" The memorial was ignominiously bundled out of the Senate. " I ask leave to withdraw it," said Cass, " with a view to return it to the gentleman who handed it to me."

The gentleman in question was Lane, who, in no wise abashed, immediately began to plan a second effort for recognition. He resorted to the sanctities of an affidavit which rehearsed the alleged history of the memorial. It was originally the work of a special committee, was accepted by the legislature, and then sent back for revision as the phraseology needed mending. The committee delegated the editorial function to Lane, who attended to it after his arrival in Washington. The " sets of signatures," executed by members of the legislature, having been " unfortunately mislaid," Lane's private secretary came to the rescue and signed the names of these gentlemen to the memorial — such was the substance of the affidavit.

Harlan, of Iowa, presented the memorial with

the explanatory affidavit to the Senate, but the second reception of it was no more friendly than the first. The shabby, deleted, interpolary condition of the document, and the absence of original signatures, neutralized the force of all explanation however adroit and plausible.

Besides, the memorial was silent in reference to the "black law" restrictions, which, though not literally a part of the constitution, would practically have the same effect as if they had been incorporated in it — an omission readily lending color to charges of concealment and disingenuousness. The infelicities of the memorial afforded Senator Douglas opportunities for assailing Lane, which he improved to the utmost. You presented to us, he said in substance, an original document that had no signatures, no mode of authentication, and no date. You attempted to palm upon the Senate an imperfect copy of the constitution of the so-called State of Kansas. You suppressed a material provision of that supreme law. You withheld what you dare not defend — the permanent legislative instructions excluding colored men from the state. In every line of your expurgated and recast memorial evidences of fraud appear!

Lane did not relish the affair, and demanded from Douglas an explanation such as "will remove all imputation upon the integrity of my acts or motives in connection with the memorial," and intimated that a challenge would follow in case his explanation should be inadequate. Douglas replied that no exculpatory facts were within his knowledge, and there the episode ended.

At the close of a long discussion the House of Representatives voted by a majority of two in favor of the admission of Kansas to the Union with the Topeka constitution, but the hostility of the Senate could not be surmounted.

The Topeka movement could show but little backing of precedents. State governments had repeatedly come into existence without enabling acts, but never before in defiance of the territorial authorities. That was the situation in Kansas. Bayard, of Delaware, pronounced the conduct of the free-state party "incipient treason." But if their action touched, it did not cross, the line of treason. Had there been an appeal to force treason would have been committed. If the people of Kansas chose to supplement memorials to Congress with a state constitution under which officers had been provisionally elected and laws provisionally passed — all a dead organism until federal inspiration should breathe into it the breath of life — they were only exercising the primal rights of American citizens.

The Topeka government taking the field against the Missouri legislature — a veritable, though hypothetical Kansas institution warring upon an interloper — was erected, as has been already remarked, with a view to national, as well as domestic uses. It was an emphatic method of publishing the territorial assembly as hopelessly, intolerably bad, and in this way it made an effective appeal to Northern sympathy. Locally it afforded a rallying point for the anti-slavery party, and presented at least a show of aggressive activity which bespoke nerve and vigor in the leadership. The legislature never passed any laws of importance, and never put in force those which it did pass. It was a disguised mass-meeting — a mass-meeting shrewdly and effectively masquerading as a state government. Whatever savage declarations and threats it may have uttered, it took care to do nothing illegal. The crafty scheme drew the pro-slavery fire and held the free-state men together until they could get possession of the legitimate legislature.

CHAPTER VI.

WAR ON THE WAKARUSA.

WILSON SHANNON, of Ohio, the second governor of Kansas, was a lawyer of good repute, with an honorable record as governor of his native state, minister to Mexico, and representative in Congress, genial, companionable, his sympathies and instincts naturally gravitating toward whatever is just and honorable, a tenacious, unwavering Democrat of the old school, but no iron, decisive storm-queller able to rule the anarchy let loose in the territory.

The period immediately preceding and the period immediately following Shannon's advent were not prolific in violence. The political fight — the fence of hostile constitutional expedients, a hypothetical state government matched against a legitimatized territorial legislature — got well under way.

Now and then the underlying ferment broke out into spasmodic acts of personal violence. The fortunes of Rev. Pardee Butler are among the most notable experiences of discomfort during this interval. The divine so far forgot all maxims of policy as to avow free-soil opinions in the pro-slavery town of Atchison. "I intend," said he, "to utter my sentiments where I please." A local bully had recently fallen upon an estrayed abolitionist who ventured into the region, and had soundly thrashed him. Public sentiment applauded the act, and, as it seemed to merit special recognition, a paper was drawn up gratefully recounting the bully's devotion to public interests, the signing of which became a test of political orthodoxy. A bright thought struck the junior editor of the "Squatter Sovereign," a rabid, pro-slavery newspaper published in town. It occurred to him that this paper might be useful in taming the doughty free-soiler, and he presented it to him for his signature, which, of course, was not secured. A mob of considerable size, understanding the game, and gathered in anticipation of the parson's probable decision, then took him in hand and hurried him toward the Missouri River, apparently with the purpose of tossing him into it. After reaching the bank his face was blackened. Then followed a long discussion — the divine being a "target at which were hurled imprecations, curses, arguments, entreaties, accusations, and interrogatories." It was suggested that the ends of justice would be sufficiently served if he should immediately and permanently quit the country. These Atchison fanatics offered to point out the very tree on which he would be gibbeted in case of return, if he felt their discourse needed the illumination of an object-lesson. He stiffly replied that he should certainly return, provided his life were not taken and Providence permitted. The conservators of public peace relented so far as to consent to his remaining in the vicinity with the understanding that he should keep his mouth shut. "I shall speak as I choose," said the incorrigible parson; "I have done no wrong. I have as good a right to come here as you. I am but one man, you are many. Dispose of me as you think best. I ask no favors of you."

The discussion accomplished nothing in the way of compromise. The mob finally came to a vote on the question — what sort of public honors shall be conferred on the divine? and a majority gave their suffrages in favor of hanging — a verdict that undoubtedly would have been executed, had not the teller tampered with the returns in the interest of humanity and misreported the result. A milder sentence took effect. Extemporizing a raft out of cottonwood logs, and placing upon it the clergyman and his baggage — the whole tricked out with derisive placards — the gang thrust the strange craft out into the stream for a down-the-river voyage. After floating five or six miles, escorted a part of the distance by citizens of the town who followed along the banks, the traveler made land and escaped.

This outrage, which happened August 16th,

was afterwards reënacted with variations. The Rev. Mr. Butler, undeterred by past experiences, visited Atchison again some months subsequent to his voyage on the Missouri, and fell into the clutches of a company just arrived from South Carolina, who were determined to put him out of the way. It was with the greatest difficulty that the South Carolinians could be prevailed upon to scale down the penalty from capital punishment to a coat of tar and feathers. They finally yielded, and the coat of tar and feathers was administered.

An elaborate pro-slavery reception awaited Governor Shannon on his arrival at Shawnee Mission September 3d. There was a speech by an orator, unsurpassed and unsurpassable in high-flying sentiment, who welcomed him to a land where "the gentle pressure of the hand attests the cordial welcome of the heart;" where no Catilines abound, "no lank and hungry Italians with their treacherous smiles, no cowards with their stilettos, no assassins of reputations." In this recovered Eden " the morning prayer is heard on every hill, the evening orison is chanted in every valley and glen." Doubtless the governor was glad to learn that rogues were scarce in Kansas, and that the squatters had such a *penchant* for praying. He was in accord with the optimism of the hour. Reported disturbances, like the misfortunes of Rev. Pardee Butler two weeks before, he believed to have been grossly exaggerated for partisan purposes. "There is no state in the Union where persons and property are more secure than in this territory." Whatever irregularities may have attended the election of the legislature, he contended that it has been duly recognized by the territorial executive and the president of the United States, and that its laws must be enforced. "I come amongst you," the governor said, "not as a mere adventurer to better his fortune and then return home, but as one desiring for himself and family a permanent location."

Governor Shannon fell into an unfortunate error at the beginning of his administration — an error which he subsequently strove to correct — in openly and exclusively affiliating with the Missouri party. He found that faction in complete possession of the government. Daniel Woodson, secretary of state, who acted as governor in the interval between Reeder's removal and Shannon's arrival, who signed the notorious laws of the first legislature — a manageable sort of man, easily steered into any port — was in favor with the pro-slavery party. They were indignant because President Pierce did not promote him to the governorship. For a time Shannon wholly resigned himself to Missouri influence and policy. He unwisely consented to preside at a convention of "the lovers of law and order," which assembled at Leavenworth November 14th, to formulate and publish to the world both their principles and their grievances. The conduct of "certain persons professing to be friends of human freedom" was denounced as "practical nullification, rebellion, and treason." The Topeka constitutional convention "would have been a farce if its purposes had not been treasonable." Any instrument which the Topeka government may present to Congress "ought to be scouted from its halls as an insult to its intelligence and an outrage upon our sovereign rights." Governor Shannon made a speech which was received with vociferous enthusiasm. "The president is behind you," he shouted; "the president is behind you." The convention, following the example of the meeting at Big Springs, formed a political party which was called the "law and order" party, and was expected to gather up all the pro-slavery elements of the territory. The 14th of November, said "The Kansas Herald" on the 17th, "will be a day long to be remembered, for the death-knell of the abolition, nullification, and revolutionary party was sounded."

But this mood of exultation soon passed away, and was followed by a sense of disquiet and apprehension. There began to be suspicions before long that no decisive victory had been gained when the legislature and the governor were captured. Free-state men managed to ignore the bulky statutes of Shawnee Mission. They discarded all the civil and legal machineries established by the legislature — courts, justices of the peace, probate judges, registers of deeds — and resorted to some make-shift. In Lawrence, deeds were recorded by a private citizen who acted without authority other than a vague, indefinite public consensus. Then these insurgents were consolidating into the unity of an efficient political organization, and that circumstance began to cloud the pro-slavery sunshine. Besides, there was the audacious Topeka movement, an amateur constitution drawing upon itself the eyes of the nation, rousing intense passions of friendship and hostility, and actually pushing through one house of Congress.

The Missouri border became eager to try more vigorous and summary measures in the treatment of territorial abolitionism than had thus far been prescribed, to substitute for the policy of legislating the Yankees out, the policy of wiping them out. In the indifferent, waning success of those milder expedients which culminated at the polls, and in the compilation of iron-clad statutes, public opinion steadily gravitated toward an aggressive root-and-branch policy as infolding larger buds of promise. Why not disperse the intruders and have a quick end of the foolishness? Lawrence, in particular, as the headquarters of sedition, had acquired an evil name that grew blacker with every turn of affairs favorable to the free-state cause. There came to be a general conviction that nothing less than the destruction of this opprobrious town would give peace and safety to the border, and naturally enough the passion to experiment upon it with the bowie-knife and revolver cure rose to an almost uncontrollable pitch. Only a pretext was needed to precipitate an attack, and the flimsiest would be accepted if nothing better offered.

A fatal claim-dispute, November 21st, 1855, at Hickory Point — a settlement ten miles south of Lawrence — furnished the coveted excuse for an appeal to arms. F. N. Coleman, a pro-slavery squatter, assassinated Charles M. Dow, a young neighbor of free-state proclivities, who made his home with old Jacob Branson. Dow was "a right peaceable man," said Branson; "a man that I thought as much of as any I ever got acquainted with."

Five days after the killing, an excited band of armed free-state men congregated about the spot crimsoned by Dow's blood to discuss under its dark inspiration measures of retribution. The assassin and his friends — implicated more or less directly in the crime — took alarm at the earliest signs of mischief and fled to Shawnee Mission. A proposition to fire their deserted cabins was discussed and rejected, though the adverse decision did not save them from being burnt down at night. The talk of the assembly befitted time and occasion. It was reminiscent, furious, stygian, avengeful, but no plans of practical violence were adopted beyond the appointment of a vigilance committee, with instructions "to ferret out and bring the murderers and their accomplices to condign punishment." The committee exhibited more zeal than marksmanship in the discharge of their duties if Coleman may be credited. "I was not safe in traveling through the territory," he testified before the congressional investigating committee a few months after the homicide. "I had been shot at more than twenty times by men from Lawrence."

Old Branson is described as "an elderly man of most quiet and modest deportment," yet, according to the testimony of pro-slavery neighbors, whose evidence should be received with abatements, the butchery of his friend stirred him to great fluency of sanguinary talk. They report him as swearing mouth-filling oaths that a certain Harrison Buckley, who egged on the murder, "should not breathe the pure air three minutes," if he could once draw a bead upon him. Buckley, in real or simulated alarm for his life, procured a peace warrant for Branson's arrest, which was put into the hands of Samuel J. Jones, lately commissioned sheriff of Douglas County.

Sheriff Jones, a prominent figure in coming events, was a mixture of black and white that fairly represented the good and evil of the border

— a man of great energy, noise, violence, courage, and sincerity. He won his first partisan laurels at Bloomington polls on the 30th of March, when he succeeded in driving off two or three rather mettlesome and plucky election judges. That exploit gave him a very odious reputation in free-state circles.

At a late hour on the night of November 26th a loud, unceremonious thumping saluted Branson's cabin door. "Who's there?" shouted the old man. "Friends," was the reply. So urgent was the haste of these friends that they forced the door before they could be invited to come in. They told Branson to consider himself a prisoner, and to be very careful how he behaved. Slight indiscretions might lead to unfortunate results. Mrs. Branson ventured to inquire of the visitors by what authority they were pouncing upon her husband at dead of night, when her attention was called to a seven-shooter as a warrant singularly effective and constitutional. Jones pulled Branson out of bed, ordered him to put on his coat and trousers, mounted him on a sharp-backed mule, and set off for Lecompton *via* Lawrence.

News of the raid flew swiftly through the neighborhood. There was a hurried rally to overhaul Jones. On reaching Blanton he found Captain J. B. Abbott with fifteen men drawn across the road to dispute his passage. "What's up?" asked the sheriff. "That's what we want to know," Abbott growled. Pistols, squirrel-guns, Sharpe's rifles, were ready for business in a twinkling. One of Abbott's men, in the absence of better armament, provided himself with two large stones and proposed to play the part of a catapult against the enemy. But, notwithstanding the warlike aspect of affairs, volleys of words were the deadliest missiles exchanged. "Come out of that," somebody among the rescuers shouted to Branson, and out of it he came.

Abbott and his men hurried to Lawrence, where they arrived early in the morning. They halted at Dr. Robinson's house on Mt. Oread. "I shall never forget the appearance of the men," Mrs. Robinson wrote, "in simple citizen's dress, some armed and some unarmed, standing in unbroken line, just visible in the breaking light of a November morning. The little band of less than twenty men had . . . walked ten miles since nine o'clock of the previous evening. Mr. Branson, a large man, of fine proportions, stood a little forward of the line, with his head slightly bent, which an old straw hat hardly protected from the cold, looking as though in his hurry of departure from home he took whatever came first."

Now that the rescuers had succeeded in their enterprise, they began to fear that it might lead to serious consequences, and the visit to Dr. Robinson was for explanation and advice. S. N. Wood, who acted as spokesman, narrated the events of the night. "Now what shall we do?" he asked in conclusion. "I am afraid the affair will make mischief," Robinson replied. "The other side will seize upon it as a pretext for invading the territory. Go down to the town and call a meeting at eight o'clock."

The meeting was called, and after the circumstances of the rescue had been set forth by Wood and Branson, Robinson led off in a speech, outlining the policy which was subsequently pursued — disavowal of all responsibility in the matter, dispatch of the men who were implicated out of town without delay, and adoption of a strictly defensive attitude. Conway, G. P. Lowrey, and others followed in the same strain. A committee of safety was appointed and clothed with authority to take such measures of precaution as the emergency might require.

Upon losing his prisoner, Sheriff Jones rode to Franklin distraught betwixt conflicting emotions of rage and exultation. The success of the Yankees exasperated him, yet in that success he foresaw a sure dawn of day for the pro-slavery cause — foresaw the overthrow of Lawrence and the approach of that millennial period when he would "corral all the abolitionists and make pets of them."

Jones hastened to send missives from Franklin to his friends in Missouri calling for help. It soon occurred to him that appeals to Missouri might have a queer look, and couriers were sent to Governor Shannon with an exaggerated account of the troubles. In the judgment of Jones, it would require a force of three thousand men to deal effectually with the traitors of Douglas County and avenge the affronts offered to justice. The governor caught the sheriff's outlaw-crushing furor, and unhesitatingly ordered militia officers to collect as large a force as possible and march at once to Lawrence. Nobody, whether sheriff, militia general, or governor, thought it necessary to communicate with that town, to ask explanations or make demands. It was not a word and a blow, but a blow without the word.

Kansas volunteers did not respond in any large numbers to the governor's summons. The town of Franklin furnished a company led by Captain Leak — a commander with unhappy, though not disqualifying antecedents. "Mr. Leak," in the words of a resident of Franklin, "was a traveling gambler — he told me so himself." Other towns in the territory furnished contingents, but probably the whole number of Kansans did not exceed fifty. The great mass of invaders came from Missouri. They straggled along in detached parties toward Lawrence, armed with every variety of weapons from rusty flint-locks and old-fashioned horse-pistols to modern rifles, until twelve or fifteen hundred of them were concentrated in the vicinity — encamping for the most part on the

Wakarusa, a small affluent of the Kansas River — an unwashed, braggart, volcanic multitude. They laid the surrounding country under contribution, overhauled travelers, rifled cabins, fired hay-stacks, seized horses and cattle — in a word, filled the region with confusion as an overture to letting slip fiercer dogs of war.

The militia generals, who responded to Shannon's call with frolicsome alacrity that befitted a pleasure jaunt, grew sober on reaching Lawrence. It was found that the committee of safety had developed an embarrassing amount of defensive energy. The chief command they intrusted to Dr. Robinson, with the rank of major-general, though he had never seen military service. To Lane they assigned a second rank. His practical war-record would naturally have claimed the first, but the committee, in the grave and critical juncture, did not dare to risk a frothy, pictorial, unballasted leadership. Five small forts covered the approaches to the town, within the lines of which some six hundred men — large reinforcements having arrived from neighboring villages — drilled incessantly. Two hundred of these men were armed with Sharpe's rifles — a vexatious circumstance that gave the Missourians pause. A fresh installment of them — the first reached Lawrence a few weeks after the March election — was received just as hostilities began. "I have only time to thank you and the friends who sent us the

Sharpe's rifles," Dr. Robinson wrote A. A. Lawrence December 4th, "for they . . . will give us the victory without firing a shot."

General Eastin, editor of the pro-slavery "Kansas Herald," reconnoitred Lawrence and advised Governor Shannon that "the outlaws were well fortified," — that an assault upon them would be at heavy cost. He counseled recourse to the federal troops at Fort Leavenworth. His communication excited alarm at Shawnee Mission. Governor Shannon, who had viewed the whole matter as a mere bagatelle, requested permission of the authorities at Washington to employ United States soldiers in the emergency. He also urged Colonel E. V. Sumner, in command at Fort Leavenworth, to march for the scene of disturbance without awaiting orders. This request Sumner declined to comply with, but suggested that the great mob enveloping Lawrence should be made to understand it must confine itself wholly to defensive operations — a hint which was promptly acted on. The War Department placed the garrison of Fort Leavenworth at Shannon's service, but Colonel Sumner refused to move until orders reached him from Washington.

If the besiegers outside of the town found themselves harassed by unexpected and increasing difficulties, the besieged inside of it were not free from perplexities. The influx of reinforcements taxed the commissariat very heavily. Whoever possessed supplies of food or clothing found himself uncomfortably circumstanced. The expression on the faces of tradesmen as they distributed their goods among the soldiery in exchange for worthless scrip was like lamplight glimmering on the wall of a sepulchre. There was a general observance of order and decorum. Most citizens made a virtue of necessity and contributed freely what otherwise must have been rudely confiscated. In a single instance a little outbreak of violence occurred — expending itself in the sack of a small tailor's shop. One night during the siege, according to the story of a clerk, "about twenty men, armed with revolvers," invaded the premises and extinguished the lamp by firing a tobacco-box at it. " Before I could light a candle," the clerk continued, " everything in the store was taken off the shelves and carried away." A young woman who had the misfortune to keep a hotel — the Cincinnati House — in Lawrence during the impecunious era of the siege, wrote a few days after its close: " It looked strange ... to see the streets paraded from morning till night by men in military array; to see them toil day and night throwing up intrenchments; to see them come in to their meals each with his gun in hand and sometimes bringing it to the table. ... How we toiled to feed the multitudes, seldom snatching a moment to look out upon the strange scenes — often asking, 'What are the prospects to-day?' — or at midnight as, worn and weary, we sought the pillow, discussing such themes as these ... — 'There's prospect of an attack to-night.' 'The guard has been doubled, and we are all vigilance.'" ...

The sobriety of affairs in Lawrence induced the committee of safety to open communications with Governor Shannon. G. P. Lowrey and C. W. Babcock set out at one o'clock on the morning of December 6th for Shawnee Mission. Near Franklin they encountered a picket-guard, and were ordered to advance and give the countersign. "We got the *cork* out of the only countersign we had as soon as possible, and that passed us." The commissioners soon stumbled upon another batch of sentinels. "Where are you going?" they demanded. "Things are getting dangerous hereabouts," said Babcock, "and I've made up my mind to scoot for Illinois." "Abolitionists scared in Lawrence, eh? Don't believe we can let you pass." After some discussion it was agreed that the officer in command, who turned out to be the traveling gambler, Captain Leak, should be consulted. This worthy was reported asleep, but it was a sort of sleep which the most energetic shaking, permitted by a very lax military etiquette, could not break, and his valuable advice was inaccessible. The commissioners managed to pacify the guard and worry through the lines. In general, the Missourians were talkative and expressed their opinions unreservedly. Some of them fumed over reports that the Lawrence outlaws had substituted a red flag for the Stars and Stripes. Some gloried in the ruin about to fall on the abolition stronghold — a ruin that would not leave one stone upon another. Others cursed Reeder as the author of all the trouble — "We must have his head even if we have to go to Pennsylvania after it."

Lowrey and Babcock found Governor Shannon in ill humor. He roundly denounced free-state men — charged them with driving from the territory settlers who were politically obnoxious and firing their cabins, and with displaying a startling spirit of insubordination and rebellion by their resistance to territorial officers and their nullification of territorial laws. The delegation from Lawrence contended that the governor had been deceived; that Lawrence was no more responsible for the rescue of Branson than for the precession of the equinoxes; that the question of territorial legislation did not enter into present complications, and that he was beating about in heavy fogs of ignorance and misapprehension concerning the facts out of which they rose. "I shall go to Lawrence," said Shannon, "and insist upon the people agreeing to obey the laws and delivering up their Sharpe's rifles." "We have not resisted the laws," the commissioners retorted. "As to the rifles nobody would be safe in going before our people with any proposition to deliver them up. If you have such an idea you had better stay away and let the fight go on."

For the first time suspicions began to haunt Shannon that he might have been misled by his Missouri advisers. The shrewdness, poise, and quickness to detect an opponent's weak points displayed among the outlaws, whose intelligence he had put at a paltry valuation, astonished Shannon. They ought to have scattered like a flock of affrighted birds at the first rustle of danger instead of digging trenches, learning the manual of arms, and discovering an embarrassing skill in diplomacy.

The governor, on his arrival at the Wakarusa camp, found the militia, excited by whiskey and ignorant of free-state strength, clamoring for permission to attack the town. He spared no efforts to discourage their frenzy. In this movement he was heartily and effectively seconded by Atchison. "But for his mediatorial offices," said Butler, of South Carolina, speaking in the Senate March 5th, 1856, vaguely and imperfectly comprehending the ugly dilemma in which the overhasty Missourians found themselves, "the homes of Lawrence would have been burned and the streets drenched with blood." Senator Butler thought that these kind offices were very inadequately appreciated. But let the ingrates beware. "If ever D. R. Atchison shall pass the line again and say as Cæsar did, 'I have passed the Rubicon and now I draw the sword,' I should dread the contest."

Shannon visited Lawrence December 7th, in company with prominent Missourians, to prosecute negotations for peace. Robinson and Lane received the visitors in behalf of the citizens and of the committee of safety. The interview completely undeceived Shannon. Now the pressing question was not how to disperse free-state outlaws, but how, without an explosion, to disperse the Missourians, whom the governor called "a pack of hyenas." To accomplish this he urged the representatives of Lawrence to be as generous as possible in the matter of concessions. A treaty was concluded, astutely designed to bear more than one interpretation — a treaty in which contradictory phrases shouldered and jostled each other, but which succeeded amidst the confusion in informing the Missourians that the governor "has not called upon persons residents of any other state to aid in the execution of the laws, and such as are here in this territory are here of their own choice."

Governor Shannon called a meeting of the Missouri commanders at Franklin. They were not consulted about the treaty, and knew nothing of its tenor. With the exception of Atchison, who did not relish the pass to which matters had come and declined to attend, the principal military men were present. Shannon insisted that Robinson and Lane should accompany him to Franklin, and assist in sugar-coating the unpalatable treaty. The governor led off in a long talk, and rehearsed the details of the campaign. Lane followed, but had hardly spoken half-a-dozen sentences when some arrogance of manner or impolicy of language gave offense, and the sensitive gentry began to pick up their hats and revolvers. "Wait a minute," Shannon interposed, "and hear what Dr. Robinson has to say." Robinson succeeded in getting the attention of the restless audience, while he expounded the unreason of the demand, so popular among Missourians, that free-state men should surrender their Sharpe's rifles. They had a constitutional right to bear arms. You, gentlemen, in your own case, would not for an instant tolerate the impertinence of such a claim. Further, Lawrence was not a party to the assault upon Jones. What is more, Lawrence has never resisted the service of a legal writ. "Is that so, Mr. Sheriff?" a militia colonel broke in. The sheriff could not deny the statement. "Then we have been damnably deceived," said the colonel.

The inevitable must be accepted, and the baffled Missourians swore with a lighter accent than might have been expected. Sheriff Jones was disgusted at the turn of affairs. Hopes of a future opportunity to settle with the abolitionists gave him a little comfort. "I'll get up another scrape," he said, "if I'm opposed in executing the laws. No old granny shall stop me next time."

Atchison did not remit his efforts for peace. "The position of General Robinson is impregnable," he said in a speech to the disgusted invaders, "not in a military point of view, but his tactics have given him all the advantage as to the cause of quarrel. If you attack Lawrence now, you attack it as a mob, and what would be the result? You would cause the election of an abolition president and the ruin of the Democratic party. Wait a little. You cannot now destroy these people without losing more than you would gain."

Saturday, December 8th, the pleasant weather — so mild that many soldiers on both sides were in summer clothing — suddenly changed into winter. In the evening a tremendous sleet-storm set in and extinguished among the Missourians whatever ardor for fighting may have survived the frosty articles of peace. They retired sullenly, carrying three "dead bodies — one killed by the falling of a tree, one shot by the guard accidentally, and one killed in some sort of a quarrel." The victory of Lawrence was complete — a bloodless victory won by strategy.

A single voice was raised in solemn and public protest against the peace. After the treaty and its stipulations had become known; after speeches of felicitation on the happy subsidence of perils that threatened to engulf the settlement in ruin had been made, an unknown man — tall, slender, angular; his face clean-shaved, sombre, strongly lined, of Puritan tone and configuration; his blue-gray eyes honest, inexorable; strange, unworldly intensities enveloping him like an atmosphere — mounted a dry-goods box and began to denounce the treaty as an attempt to gain by foolish, uncomprehending make-shift what could be compassed only by the shedding of blood. Since that day the name of this unknown man, plucked down from the dry-goods box with his speech mostly unspoken, has filled the post-horns of the world — Old John Brown.

CHAPTER VII.

SOME HEAVY BLOWS.

The winter of 1855-56 in Kansas was of a Siberian character. For a time meteorological woes surpassed all others in the territory. The sleet-tempest that celebrated the close of the Wakarusa war faithfully foretokened the coming months. For the most part the immigrants were very inadequately protected against the sudden and extreme cold. Log huts — the common type of dwelling — had few attractions for winter residence. Ordinarily they were a sorry affair — a floorless pen of half-hewn logs, roughly battened with a filling of stones, sticks, and mud — the whole loosely roofed over, and usually containing a single room. In the absence of anything better, doors and windows were manufactured out of cotton cloth. Into these rickety cabins storms drifted from every quarter — above, beneath, around.

"I failed to complete my log-house before the winter of 1855-56 set in," said Captain Samuel Walker. "The sides were up, roofed, and partly plastered when the Wakarusa war interrupted work. On my return home, after the conclusion of peace, the cold was so severe that nothing more could be done, and we had to shift as best we could until warm weather. Our cabin had no floor, but we were as well off in this particular as most of our neighbors. Chinks and fissures abounded in roof and gables, as the green slabs with which they were covered warped badly. Seven of us made up the family — five children, mostly small. At times, when the winds were bleakest, we actually went to bed as the only escape from freezing. More than once we woke in the morning to find six inches of snow in the cabin. To get up, to make one's toilet under such circumstances, was not a very comfortable performance. Often we had little to eat — the wolf was never very far from our door during that hard winter of 1855-56."

The inhospitalities of Kansas frontier life fell with peculiar severity upon women. "He who has seen the sufferings of men," said Victo Hugo, "has seen nothing. Let him look upon the sufferings of women." Burdened with drudgeries in their most primitive, unrelieved shape, exposed to all the anxieties and perils which a state of anarchy implies, denied the relief of public and aggressive service — their heroic, untrumpeted endurance was not least heroic and worthy among the pioneer services rendered to Kansas.

Severities of winter, that frost-bit the ill-furnished settlers, called a truce to active hostilities. Yet warlike movements, that pointed to future invasions on a more formidable scale than had heretofore been attempted, continued along the border. "We have reliable information," Robinson wrote A. A. Lawrence January 25th, 1856, "that extensive preparations are being made in Missouri for the destruction of Lawrence and all the free-state settlements. You can have no idea of the character of the men with whom we have to deal. We are purchasing ammunition and stores of all kinds for a siege. . . . We have telegraphed to the president and members of Congress and the Northern governors our condition, and sent out six men to raise an army for the defense of Kansas and the Union. . . . I am doing my utmost to conquer without bloodshed, and I believe that if my suggestions are acted upon promptly in the states we shall avoid a war. . . . Our plans are all well laid, and if the states will do their part promptly, I believe but little money will be actually used, and no lives lost."

Among the six men dispatched eastward on a mission of explanation and appeal were J. S. Emery, M. F. Conway, and G. W. Smith. They left Lawrence about the middle of January in a buggy, which they soon found of little service on the snow-clogged roads. Before starting the company held a consultation concerning the safest method of managing their credentials. Should some border-ruffian with a turn for investigation discover these credentials, the party would very likely receive rough usage. In the midst of their perplexities a bright thought struck Smith — " Boys, I 've hit it. In Missouri everybody carries a *jug*. There a jug never excites suspicion. Put the papers in jugs with corncob stoppers and they 'll be safe." The suggestion was greeted with applause and immediately carried into effect. Plodding slowly across the State of Missouri — the journey occupied two weeks — masquerading under various disguises, the travelers safely reached the Mississippi River opposite Quincy, Illinois, over which they walked on the ice. Midway in the river they halted, broke the jugs, and transferred the credentials to their pockets. This delegation, and other delegations that followed, successfully pleaded the free-state cause in the North and East.

There was also stir and excitement at the South, from which bands of armed emigrants reached the territory during the spring and summer of 1856. " Even in my own state," said Senator Butler, of South Carolina, " I perceive parties are being formed to go to Kansas — adventurous young men who will fight anybody." The senator probably had in mind the operations of Major Jefferson Buford, of Alabama, who conducted thither the most notorious company of Southern immigrants. Buford issued a call for three hundred men, promising them by way of inducements transportation, support for a year, a homestead, and the satisfaction of a chance at the abolitionists. He fitted out the expedition largely from his own resources. To reimburse the outlay, it was understood that each member of the company would take up a claim, one half of which should be turned over to Buford. But the venture did not succeed financially, as few of the company became permanent residents of Kansas.

The appearance of Buford on the border encouraged the pro-slavery leaders. "Our hearts have been made glad," said the managers of the Lafayette Emigration Society, — a Missouri organization, — in an appeal to the South, "by the late arrivals of large companies from South Carolina and Alabama. They have responded promptly to our call for help. The noble Buford is already endeared to our hearts; we love him; we will fight for him and die for him and his companions. Who will follow his noble example? We tell you now and tell you frankly, that unless you come quickly and come by thousands we are gone. The election once lost, we are lost forever. Then farewell to our Southern cause and farewell to our glorious Union."

Congress shared inevitably in the disturbances which radiated North and South from Kansas — a word seized upon according to the "Democratic Review" "by the most cunning of modern magicians, the abolitionists, to raise the devil with."

Numerous expedients for allaying these disastrous agitations came to the surface. Senator Crittenden, of Kentucky, proposed unsuccessfully that Lieutenant-General Scott should be sent to Kansas as pacificator, equipped with " the sword in his left hand and in his right hand — peace, gentle peace." Toombs, of Georgia, submitted a plan of adjustment, the terms of which were fair and unpartisan. It contemplated the appointment of five commissioners — men of the highest character and selected from both parties — who should take an accurate census, apportion the territory into districts, and on the 4th of November, 1856, cause an election to be held for delegates to a constitutional convention, at which all male citizens, residents of three months' standing, might vote. December 1st these delegates were to assemble, take under advisement the question of establishing a state government, and, should it be decided affirmatively, enter at once upon the work.

This bill, though energetically combated by anti-slavery senators from distrust of President Pierce, in whose hands the appointment of commissioners was lodged, and from apprehensions that in some way Missouri would again decisively interfere, passed the Senate, but did not survive the opposition of the House. That body originated and sanctioned a measure known as the Dunn bill, the leading features of which were — the election of a new territorial legislature in November, the dismissal of criminal prosecutions for offenses against territorial laws, and the restoration of the Missouri Compromise, though it was stipulated that slaves, already in the territory, should not be disturbed before January, 1858. This scheme failed in the Senate.

Out of the various bills, compromises, substitutes, amendments, which appeared in Congress during the spring and summer of 1856, a single measure only emerged that reached any practical importance — the appointment by the House of Representatives of an investigating committee, the members of which were William A. Howard, of Michigan, John Sherman, of Ohio, and Mordecai Oliver, of Missouri. This committee proceeded to the territory, held its first meeting at Kansas City April 14th, examined three hundred and twenty-three witnesses, who represented every shade of political opinion, and on the 1st and 2d of July presented a report, in which a great mass of facts is accumulated wholly creditable to neither side.

Early in the spring the local campaign showed signs of life. Sheriff Jones, who had a touch of genius for finding quarrel in a straw, led off in the revived operations. He still pursued the policy which barely missed success in the Wakarusa war, fumed about Lawrence with much insolent ado, and attempted without success to arrest S. N. Wood, who, in addition to taking a prominent part in the Branson matter, had made himself still more obnoxious by doing effective free-state service on the stump in Ohio. Jones pursued his efforts to arrest different people at Lawrence, until at last he got a sharp blow in the face from somebody who resented his familiarities. Thereupon he rode to Lecompton and reported to Governor Shannon that he had been assaulted in the discharge of his duties, and demanded a military escort for his protection. April 23d he reappeared in town accompanied by Lieutenant McIntosh and eleven soldiers. He succeeded in arresting six citizens on the charge of "contempt of court," as they declined to assist him in making arrests during former visits. Instead of proceeding to Lecompton with his prisoners, he remained in town, possibly with the hope of exciting an attempt at rescue. Though threats had been freely made against him, he chose to spend the night in McIntosh's tent rather than in less exposed quarters. During the evening Jones and the lieutenant went out to a neighboring water barrel for a drink. While they were there a shot was fired from a little knot of men standing at no great distance. "I believe that was intended for me," said Jones, with a shrug. The lieutenant thought he must be mistaken as several pistols had been discharged, apparently into the air, since night-fall. "That *was* intended for me," said Jones, when they returned to the tent, "for here is the hole in my pants." The lieutenant hurried out to investigate the affair. "I immediately joined the crowd," he reports, "and while speaking to them heard another shot, and at the same time some of my men exclaimed, 'Lieutenant, the sheriff is dead.'" Not many seconds later a young man — J. P. Filer by name — with his pistol still smoking — burst into a cabin hard by where two or three chums were sitting, and said, "Boys, hide this; I've shot Sheriff Jones." After a hasty consultation they decided not to betray the culprit, and pledged themselves by a solemn oath to silence. For a quarter of a century the secret was faithfully kept.

The shooting intensified the general excitement. A public meeting of the citizens of Lawrence on the following day denounced it "as the act of some malicious and evil-disposed individual," for whose arrest they offered a reward of five hundred dollars. The congressional investigating committee were in session at Lawrence, and Whitfield, pro-slavery delegate to Congress, seized upon the unfortunate affair as a plausible pretext for attempting to break down the investigation. He declared himself in fear for his life, expatiated on the unreasonableness of asking witnesses to venture into an assassin's den, and actually fled the town, but crept back in a few days on finding that his absence did not affect the committee. Pro-slavery newspapers eulogized Jones as a noble patriot, "shot down by the thieving paupers of the North." Though the wound did not prove fatal, reports of his death were current and roused fiercer passions upon the border than lay within the compass of any Branson-rescue exploit. " His murder shall be avenged," said the " Squatter Sovereign," " if at the sacrifice of every abolitionist in the territory. . . . We are now in favor of leveling Lawrence and chastising the traitors there congregated, should it result in the total destruction of the Union."

At this juncture the pro-slavery cause was powerfully reinforced by the appearance in the field of the territorial judiciary. Early in May the grand jury of Douglas County was in session at Lecompton. This jury Judge S. D. Lecompte, chief justice of the territory, instructed at large in reference to the extraordinary conditions and responsibilities under which they met. An exposition of the nature of treason figured in the address, the tenor of which, the judge writes, December 31st, 1884, " has been most grossly misrepresented."

" I have been charged with resorting to a constructive treason as within the scope of legitimate prosecution. I made no such flagrant departure from recognized American authorities — I did not adopt as legitimate or tenable the monstrous proposition of stretching by construction the language of the Constitution to create a crime not within its clear and unavoidable import. I remember as if it were but yesterday that I distinctly and explicitly repudiated the doctrine of constructive treason. I remember, too, that I explained the phraseology of the Constitution on this point in the spirit, if not in the words, of Wharton. Passing to the state of public affairs I took up the question whether treason could be committed against the United States by levying war upon the territorial government. I then held and still hold such hostility to be treason against the federal government. What constitutes hostility in this penal sense I also expounded with careful avoidance of adding a word beyond established doctrine. In my opinion the jury that dealt with these questions was not inferior to any of its successors in patriotism, fairness, or intelligence. That, in the madness of partisan strife, under the provocations of unprincipled leaders, when the laws of the territory were denounced as 'bogus,' their authority defied, and an opposing legislature, without semblance of authority, set up, when insurgent military forces were organizing, equipping, drilling — that, I say in such untoward circumstances, the judiciary should have felt called upon to instruct the grand jury upon the subject of treason, that the grand jury should have made presentments, and the district attorney preferred indictments, can hardly be a cause for wonder."

On the list of traitors were Robinson, Reeder, Lane, and several other men prominent in free-state circles. A companion indictment for "usurpation of office" was also issued against Robinson.

In the reorganized campaign the first attack fell

upon Reeder, who was summoned May 6th before the grand jury of Douglas County, while in attendance upon the investigating committee at Tecumseh. He declined to obey the subpœna on the ground that it was of more importance that he should attend the sessions of the committee than of the grand jury. Thursday, May 8th, the committee returned to Lawrence. There Deputy Marshal Fain appeared with an attachment against Reeder for " contempt of court." Reeder refused to be captured, and told the marshal that if he touched him it would be at his peril — a show of spirit that pleased the spectators, who came crowding into the room. But the situation soon grew intolerable, and there was safety only in flight. Reeder succeeded in reaching Kansas City, where he lay concealed some days at the American House, a hotel kept by the Eldridge brothers. The well-known free-state character of the hotel gave it about town a bad name, which was now blackened especially by rumors that abolitionists were skulking there — rumors that subjected it to constant mob-surveillance. On one occasion, suspicious border-ruffians resorted to a formal search of the premises, and it was only by the cleverest ingenuity and presence of mind on the part of the household that they failed to unearth the fugitive. While concealed in the hotel, Reeder concluded that the time had fully come to make his will, into which he incorporated a brief but vigorous description of the men who were frothing about his hiding-place, "I, Andrew H. Reeder : . . . in danger of being murdered by a set of wild ruffians and outlaws, who are outside of all restraints of order, decency, and all social obligations, and who are below the savage in all the virtues of civilization . . . in view of my death, which may happen to-day or to-morrow, make this last will and testament."

Reeder escaped in disguise. Donning a suit of blue jean, with a battered straw hat on his head, a clay pipe in his mouth, and an axe in his hand — presenting the appearance of a seedy journeyman wood-chopper — he walked out of the hotel undetected, was rowed down the Missouri to an out-of-the-way landing, where a friendly river captain, who was in the secret, stopped for him. "Get aboard, you old scallawag," shouted the captain with simulated gruffness as the steamer touched the landing. "I won't wait two minutes for you!"

The Lecompton authorities intended to act with no less vigor in Robinson's case. The general plan of operations came to his ears through some defection among the grand jury. What course ought to be pursued in the crisis was the subject of anxious discussion. An all night consultation took place in Topeka, at which John Sherman, W. A. Howard, Charles Robinson, and W. Y. Roberts, together with Mrs. Sherman and

Mrs. Robinson, were present, to settle upon a line of policy. Should the territorial laws, which denounced penalties of imprisonment against the utterance of anti-slavery sentiments, be enforced, a wholesale locking up of free-state men would follow. The conclusions reached at the conference had a belligerent look. For the first and last time, representatives of the state government seriously entertained purposes of resisting the territorial authorities. The plans as outlined contemplated further appeals to the North in hope of stirring it to active measures of sympathy, urged free-state men, obnoxious to the authorities, to avoid arrest as far as possible, and recommended the calling of an extra session of the state legislature for the purpose of putting the militia on a war-footing, in order to be prepared for emergencies. A halt must be called somewhere. If pro-slavery men were determined to force a collision, no better spot offered for a hostile stand than the state government. It was agreed that Governor Robinson should proceed eastward without delay to avoid the grand jury, as that body had as yet taken no action in his case; that he should confer with anti-slavery friends, and put the testimony thus far taken before the investigating committee beyond the reach of pro-slavery men, who would have been glad to get possession of it.

The plan miscarried. Governor Robinson got no farther eastward than Lexington, Missouri, where he was seized and detained. Mrs. Robinson, who was allowed to proceed, delivered the papers of the congressional committee to Governor Chase, of Ohio, and prosecuted the political functions of the embassy by visiting New England and by attending the republican state convention of Illinois.

The arrest at Lexington was entirely arbitrary. Robinson remained there under surveillance nearly a week before the necessary legal papers could be obtained from Kansas. When they arrived he was handed over to Federal Colonel Preston, who set out with him for Lecompton. The route lay through Lawrence. "If the people of Lawrence," said Preston, "attempt a rescue, of which I hear rumors, the escort will shoot you on the spot." This communication was not kindly received. "Well," the Colonel replied, "such are my orders." Governor Shannon, apprehending trouble, stopped the party at Franklin, and ordered it back to Kansas City. From that point the party proceeded up the river to Leavenworth, which was reached Saturday, May 24th. The prisoner experienced no special ill-usage in Leavenworth until Monday, the 26th, when there was a tremendous ferment. During the day newspaper extras arrived containing reports of free-state outrages on the Pottawatomie — reports that pro-slavery settlers in that region had been dragged from their cabins at dead of night and butchered. The news quickly called together an excited, angry, desperate crowd. A proposition to retaliate by mobbing the free-state governor roused general and boisterous enthusiasm. Thomas H. Gladstone, correspondent of the London "Times," and author of "Kansas; or, Squatter Life and Border Warfare in the Far West," mingled among the rioters and caught some of their talk: "Let *us* get hold of him; if we don't sarve him out powerful quick. The hangin' bone villain, he may say his prayers mighty smart now. I'll be dog-gauned if we don't string him up afore the day's out. Hangin's a nation sight too good for him, the mean cuss. He ought to have been shot through the head right away — that's how I'd sarve him." A Missourian — an old California acquaintance whose life Robinson had saved years before by timely medical service in a cholera panic — called toward evening. He seemed very much affected, and did not speak for some minutes. "You once did me a good turn," he finally managed to say, "and I've been trying to repay it all day. The boys have decided to kill you. I've done everything in my power to quiet them, but it's no use. I thought I'd come and tell you about it." Only by the greatest exertion did the authorities succeed in defeating the plans of the lynchers. The chief justice of the territory, whose discourse on treason before a grand jury initiated the whole movement, a major-general of militia, and a

United States marshal stood guard over the prisoner during the night and saw him on the way to Lecompton early in the morning before the town was astir.

The grand jury of Douglas County wrought great havoc among free-state leaders — Reeder fleeing in the disguise of a wood-chopper, Robinson a prisoner, Lane out of the territory, and other men, to whom the public confidence had been given, soon to be successfully hunted down. But this triumphant grand jury had not yet run its course. It found bills of indictment against two newspapers of Lawrence — the "Herald of Freedom" and the "Kansas Free State" — whose inflammatory and seditious language overpassed the limits of sufferance, and against the principal hotel of that town, which some extraordinary obliquity of vision transformed into a military fortress, "regularly parapeted and port-holed for the use of cannon and small arms."

Well aware that the business in hand could not be accomplished unless aided by a military force, Marshal Donaldson issued a proclamation calling upon law-abiding citizens to rally at Lecompton for his assistance. It was time to cease dawdling. Lawrence, that "foul blot on the soil of Kansas," must be humiliated; her newspaper press, wagging its tongue most vilely, silenced; her battlemented stone hotel, headquarters of abolitionism and property of the infamous Emigrant Aid Company, demolished, and any skulking and uncaged remnant of traitors that were harbored in the town seized or scared out of the territory. Marshal Donaldson's proclamation, circulated for the most part in three or four pro-slavery towns of the territory, and in the border counties across the river, precipitated a large armed multitude toward the rendezvous at Lecompton — wild, hectic, mischief-meaning gangs, men cultivating the proprieties more or less in Missouri, but relapsing into a state of semi-barbarism when they touched the soil of Kansas. Governor Shannon was not at ease over the matter. "Had the marshal called on me for a posse," he wrote President Pierce, "I should have felt bound to furnish him one composed entirely of United States troops." President Pierce also was in a disquieted frame of mind. "My knowledge of facts is imperfect," he wrote Shannon May 23d, "but with the force of Colonel Sumner at hand I perceive no occasion for the posse, armed or unarmed, which the marshal is said to have assembled at Lecompton."

Lawrence took apprehensive note of the hostile preparations and resorted, as during earlier troubles, to a committee of safety. Great confusion prevailed. None of the old leaders were on the ground, and new ones had not yet won their spurs. After many conferences and discussions the committee decided to temporize, to expostulate, to manœuvre — in a word, to do anything except fight. This unwarlike diplomacy, though not particularly soul-inspiring, was doubtless politic. When Donaldson's proclamation reached Lawrence, the citizens held a public meeting and pronounced the charges of insubordination and disloyalty contained in it unqualifiedly false. They sent messages, expostulations, appeals to Lecompton in swift, nervous succession. Nothing of overture and concession did they leave untried. "We only await an opportunity," pleaded these unappreciated and despondent patriots, "to test our fidelity to the laws of the country, the Constitution, and the Union." Deprecatory and exculpating talk fell unheeded. No humilities of concession could divert the invaders from their prey.

Discomforts and perils thickened. May 19th a detachment of the marshal's posse shot a young man — mainly for the sensation and satisfaction of killing an abolitionist. Three adventurous fellows, presumably intoxicated, on hearing the news, snatched their weapons, dashed out of Lawrence to hunt the scoundrels, and began a fusillade upon the first travelers they encountered without any nice preliminary investigations. The expedition turned out unfortunately for the assailants. Another abolitionist was converted into "wolf-meat."

Tuesday, May 20th, was a day of quiet. Little of the stir and confusion that naturally belong to military operations appeared. Citizens of Lawrence began to take heart, and to conjecture that the peril might have been exaggerated. But Wednesday morning they were undeceived. At an early hour a troop of horsemen quietly took possession of the bluffs west of town. Reinforcements gradually swelled the numbers during the morning until they reached several hundreds. It was a representative gathering — including the principal pro-slavery leaders, with Atchison at their head, the recent recruits from South Carolina and other states, the usual delegations of Missourians, and a sprinkling of actual residents in the territory.

The town lay in Sabbatic repose at the foot of the bluff. When it was definitely settled that there should be no resistance, most of the arms-bearing population whisked away like sea-birds blown landward by a tempest. The committee of safety instructed citizens who remained in town to ignore with lofty unconcern the whole noxious brood of marshals, sheriffs, and posses, and to go about their affairs as usual. Fearing that the unnatural quietude might hide some ambush, Atchison dispatched runners from the bluff to reconnoitre. They reported that the cowardly Yankees would not fight — a disposition that radically simplified the business of writ-service.

At eleven o'clock Deputy Marshal Fain, attended by an escort of six coatless men with revolvers belted about them, walked down into the village and arrested three men whose names were on the treason-list. Never were fewer obstacles thrown in the path of an officer. The alleged traitors, if they did not actually present themselves for arrest, conformed to the meekest and most inoffensive models of behavior. What is more, the committee of safety handed the deputy marshal a note addressed to Donaldson, in which they virtually abandoned everything for which free-state men contended, and whipped over upon out and out law and order ground. But this last and unreserved concession availed as little as those which preceded it.

After Deputy Marshal Fain's peaceable and easy success in making arrests, pro-slavery leaders — Atchison, Jones, Donaldson, General Richardson, of the territorial militia, Colonel Titus, of Florida, Major Jackson, of Georgia, and others — ventured from the bluffs and rode about town on a tour of observation. S. W. Eldridge, proprietor of the hotel, so ill-reputed in pro-slavery quarters, politely asked the strolling gentry to dine, and they cheerfully accepted the invitation. But even a good dinner, and that without charge, carried no more influence as a town-saver than the surrendering protocols.

The afternoon presented a more exciting scene. With the successful bagging of traitors, the primal and technical duties of the escort were concluded. But the nuisances were not yet abated. Marshal

Donaldson and his advisers, though some of them belonged to the legal fraternity, reposed an astonishing confidence in the virtues and prerogatives of the famous grand jury of Douglas County. Scorning such intermediate steps as citations, hearings, opportunities for explanation or defense, and the like, they wrecked a hotel and threw two printing-presses into the river, upon the authority of a bare grand jury presentation. "That presentment," said Judge Lecompte in a letter, August 1st, 1856, to Hon. J. A. Stewart, of Maryland, "still lies in court. No time for action on it existed — none has been had — no order passed — nothing done, and nothing ever dreamed of being done, because nothing could rightly be done but upon the finding of a petit jury."

But let the posse give attention. A crier is riding about among the men shouting — "I am authorized to say that the marshal has no further use for you; thanks you for the manner in which you have discharged your duties; asks you to make out a statement of the number of days of service with affidavit and you shall be paid. Now, gentlemen, I summons you as the posse of Sheriff Jones. He is a law and order man, and acts under the same authority as the marshal."

Jones, scarcely recovered from his wound, was received with applause. The situation pleased him well, much better than it did Atchison, who thundered indeed, during the months of preparation, against the Yankees with full throated oratory — outdone in verbal savageness only by the junior editor of the "Squatter Sovereign," a modern Herod, who swore that he was prepared " to kill a baby if he knew it would grow up an abolitionist." But now, in the presence of opportunities for transmuting words into deeds, Atchison urged moderation. "I made several speeches, at least half a dozen," he said, in an account of the affair October, 1884, "riding horseback, to the different companies. I spoke in the interest of peace — exerting myself to check, not to incite, outrage. It was not my wish that the hotel should be destroyed. I urged Jones to spare it. I told him that it would satisfy the ends of justice if he should throw a cannon-ball through it and there let the matter rest. But Jones was bent on mischief, and I could do nothing with him." The "Squatter Sovereign" of June 24th, 1856, denounces current free-state versions of Atchison's talk as false, and gives what it alleges to be a trustworthy text. " He exhorted the men above everything to remember that they were marching to enforce, not to violate, laws; to suppress, and not to spread, outrage and violence." Nor was Atchison alone in deprecating excesses. On the day after the destruction of the town, nine citizens of Lawrence met in Lane's cabin and drew up a memorial to President Pierce, denouncing the territorial officials as a set of men who "attempt the administration of law on principles of perjury and brigandage, . . . utterly ignoring the oaths they have taken, . . . at will despoiling men of their property and lives." These nine sharp-tongued citizens wish to put on record the fact that many "captains of the invading companies exerted themselves to the utmost for the protection of life and property. Some of them . . . endeavored to dissuade Samuel J. Jones from [his fell designs]. . . . Colonel Zadock Jackson, of Georgia, did not scruple to denounce either in his own camp or in Lawrence the outrages. . . . Colonel Buford, of Alabama, also disclaimed having come to Kansas to destroy property." But the immitigable Jones successfully faced down all pacific talk.

It was three o'clock in the afternoon when the great posse marched down from its camp, dragging along five pieces of artillery, and began slowly to feel its way up Massachusetts Street — a main thoroughfare of the town. The caution and deliberation of the movement indicated fear that a hidden enemy might suddenly dash out from the cabins, or deliver an unexpected volley from behind the still extant earth-works built during the Wakarusa war. Banners this host bore with various devices — "South Carolina," "Southern rights," "Superiority of the white race," "Kansas the outpost." One flag was alternately striped in black and white; another had the national stripes with a tiger in place of the union. But no ambushing enemy sprang upon the wary warriors. When the last rifle-pits were reached, and all visions of peril vanished like smoke-wreaths into the air, a yell of triumph burst from the ranks. It was now straightforward, innoxious, larkish business. The posse made short work of the printing-offices — breaking up presses, rioting calamitously among files, type, stock, exchanges; hurling the ruins into the street, or dumping them into the river. Here assuredly was a legible lesson which impudent newspapers that railed against territorial laws and spoke disrespectfully of slavery might profitably lay to heart.

The stone hotel required more elaborate and painstaking attention. Jones rode up in front of it, called for S. C. Pomeroy, a representative of the Emigrant Aid Company, and as "deputy marshal of the United States and sheriff of Douglas County" demanded possession of all Sharpe's rifles and all artillery in town. Pomeroy, after an expeditious and fugitive consultation with the committee of safety, replied that the rifles were private property, and therefore beyond his control, but that a cannon had been secreted thereabouts which would be turned over to him. The concession was enhanced by the fact of Pomeroy's consenting to act as guide to the surreptitious arsenal. Such service ought to have put him on good terms with the champions of law and order, but the ingrates, so far from appreciating his exertions, had the heartlessness to discuss, though probably with no very serious intent, the question of hanging him.

Jones directed the hotel to be emptied of furniture, but his order was only partially carried out. The five pieces of artillery bristled in a row just across the street, and opened fire upon the nuisance that had sinned so grievously and unforgivably against the public safety. "I counted thirty shots," said an on-looker. The cannonade inflicted trifling damage in the porous concrete walls, and a swifter method of destruction was sought out. If the building could not readily be battered down, certainly it could be blown to pieces. A keg of gunpowder was carried into the parlor and a slow-match of bepowdered lard prepared. Furiously did the train hiss and sizzle and splutter, emitting great volumes of smoke, and promising a hideous climax of devastation; but the explosion, which reminded the spectator, who counted the artillery discharges, of "a blast down in a well," accomplished little beyond breaking a few panes of glass. In the discomfiture of more pretentious appliances of destruction, an elemental and primitive leveler remained, to which there was successful resort — the torch. The sons of law and order victoriously fired the hotel, but not until after a careful examination of the liquor cellar. Researches in that quarter may have been in some degree responsible for the turbulence with which the nuisance-abating concluded. Stores were pillaged, houses rummaged, and Governor Robinson's residence was burnt to the ground. Nothing escaped the curious and inquisitive marauders — neither trunks, drawers, cupboards, nor clothes-presses. More than one seedy wardrobe was refitted out of the spoils. Gladstone encountered some of the ruffians at Kansas City on their return, and remarked a "grotesque intermixture in their dress, having crossed their native red shirt with a satin vest or narrow dress-coat pillaged from some Lawrence Yankee, or having girded themselves with the cords and tassels which the day before had ornamented the curtains of the free-state hotel."

While these calamities were overtaking the territory a startling pro-slavery *denouement* occurred in Washington. Charles Sumner began his speech on "The Crime against Kansas" May 19th, which he concluded on the afternoon of the 20th, when the posse of Marshal Donaldson was tightening its coils about Lawrence. The speech, a brilliant, indignant, unmeasured, exasperating philippic against the course of the slave-power in Kansas, raised a violent and angry excitement. General Cass pronounced it "the most un-American and unpatriotic speech that ever grated on the ears" of Congress. "He has not hesitated to charge more than three fourths of the Senate with fraud, with swindling, with crime, with infamy, at least a hundred times over in his speech," roared Douglas; "is it his object to provoke some one of us to kick him as we would a dog in the street, that he may get sympathy upon the just chastisement?" Mason, of Virginia, lamented that public interests and usage forced association in the Senate Chamber with "one utterly incapable of knowing what truth is " — with "one whom to see elsewhere is to shun and despise."

Preston S. Brooks, representative from South Carolina, reduced to practice Douglas's suggestion. After the adjournment of the Senate, May 22d, while Sumner remained writing at his desk, Brooks approached, muttered out charges of libeling South Carolina and her sons, and followed them up by repeated blows on the head with a cane. The senator fell insensible to the floor. This affair was a fit companion piece to the destruction of Lawrence.

When one more blow should be delivered — the dispersal of the free-state legislature, which was to meet at Topeka on the 4th of July — would not the pro-slavery triumph be complete? On whom should be conferred the honor of administering a *coup de grâce* to abolitionism in Kansas was a matter of debate. The patriots who distinguished themselves in May were anxious to take the field again in July. A hum of preparation ran along the border. Buford and the Southern colonels put their men into training, but the authorities in Washington began audibly to demur. The suspicions and fears of President Pierce ripened into convictions; he did not wish to have any more armed mobs convoked to enforce the laws. It was settled that federal troops should furnish whatever assistance territorial officers might need in their dealings with the pin-feather state government. These functionaries concurred in advising a semi-heroic treatment as the mildest recommendable course. Governor Shannon, temporarily out of the territory, wrote Colonel Sumner to disperse the legislature, should it assemble — "peaceably if you can, forcibly if you must." Sumner, though friendly to free-state interests, disapproved the Topeka movement. "I am decidedly of opinion," he wrote Acting-governor Woodson June 28th, "that that body of men ought not to be permitted to assemble. It is not too much to say that the peace of the country depends upon it." June 30th Woodson wrote Sumner in an apprehensive strain. "There is now no ground to doubt," he said, "that the bogus legislature will attempt to convene on the 4th proximo at Topeka, and the most extensive preparations are being made for the occasion. The country in the vicinity of Topeka is represented to be filled with strangers, who are making their way toward that point from all directions. Last evening I received information . . . that General Lane was on his way to Topeka with a very large force, and was then somewhere between that place and the Nebraska line. . . . It is deemed important that you should be at Topeka in person. . . . Judge Cato will be on the ground, and I have addressed a letter to the United States district attorney, Colonel Isaacs, requesting him to come over at once and attend in person to getting out the necessary legal processes." Colonel Sumner left Leavenworth for Topeka July 1st, where he concentrated five companies of dragoons with two pieces of artillery. "I shall act very warily," he wrote the adjutant general, " and shall require the civil authorities to take the lead in the matter throughout."

The bustle of hostile preparations in federal camps and in Missouri, as well as among territorial officials, had a discouraging and unbracing influence upon members of the state legislature. Unless a tonic of some kind could be administered, many of them might fail to appear in Topeka on the 4th of July, and the whole anti-slavery movement come to an inglorious collapse. To keep up courage, to secure a general interchange and discussion of opinion, a curious double-headed conference began in Topeka on the 3d — an extra and informal session of the legislature and a numerously attended mass-convention. Both legislature and convention wrestled with the same perplexing question — What ought to be done in the present emergency? No formal and accredited policy emerged from the babel of discordant sentiments. Some members of these bodies urged that the state legislature should meet and proceed with business until dispersed by the federal authorities; others denounced further resistance to the territorial laws as a blunder, and counseled immediate submission. Governor Robinson and the free-state prisoners confined at Lecompton addressed a letter to the legislature, deprecating the adoption of any timorous, faint-hearted policy. That in the disjointed condition of affairs there might be some recognized authority, the mass-convention appointed a "Kansas Central State Committee," thirteen in number, and authorized it " to assume the management and control of the free-state party of Kansas." The general committee chose an executive committee of five: J. P. Root, president; H. Miles Moore, secretary; James Blood, William Hutchinson, and S. E. Martin.

Colonel Sumner, on reaching Topeka, opened communications at once with free-state men. He sent for Captain Samuel Walker — a personal friend and a member of the legislature. "I hear Lane is on the other side of the river," said Sumner, "and means to fight. How is that?" "There is n't a word of truth in the story. Lane is not in the territory. He is somewhere in the East making speeches." Marshal Donaldson, who was present, listened to the conversation with interest. "If I should get up before those legislative fellows," he inquired, "to read a proclamation, would n't some devil shoot at me?" "Nobody," said Walker, "will lift a finger against you."

The convention sent a committee to confer with Colonel Sumner. He was very anxious that the legislature should not meet at all, as he wished to escape the odium of coercive measures. That point the committee refused to yield. An understanding, however, was reached that the legislature should assemble and begin to organize, but quietly disperse at the command of the federal authorities.

The 4th of July found Topeka thronged with men, women, and children. Two free-state military companies were also in town. A nervous, wistful, depressed sentiment prevailed, as people at large were not in the secret of the cut-and-dried programme. The mass-convention, thinking its mission not yet fully accomplished, fearing that at the last moment a panic might seize upon the legislature and prevent it from assembling, resumed its sessions in the morning and fell lustily to work.

During the forenoon Marshal Donaldson, accompanied by Judge Rush Elmore, associate justice of the territory, sallied forth with a batch of official documents: President Pierce's proclamation of February 11th, which commanded "all persons engaged in unlawful combinations against the constituted authority of the territory of Kansas . . . to disperse;" Governor Shannon's proclamation of June 4th; a proclamation fresh from Acting-governor Woodson's own hand, forbidding "persons claiming legislative powers and authorities," on the point of assembling in Topeka, to organize "under the penalties attached to all willful violators of the laws of the land;" and finally a proclamation from Colonel Sumner, who announced that he should "sustain the executive of the territory."

Mistaking the mass-convention, gasconading in the streets, for the legislature, Marshal Donaldson informed the presiding officer that he had communications for the assembly. The marshal declined to risk so doubtful an experiment as reading aloud in public, and asked Judge Elmore to take his place. Donaldson retired with confusion of face when he discovered that he had pitched his bombshells into the wrong camp.

As the hour of twelve, when the legislature was to meet, approached, the dragoons, encamped on the outskirts of the town, formed in order of battle, dashed toward Constitutional Hall and surrounded it, while the two pieces of artillery, with gunners at their posts and slow-matches burning, commanded the principal street.

It lacked a few minutes of noon when Colonel Sumner entered the House of Representatives.

Roll-call soon began, but no quorum was present; or, rather, a majority of the members, not understanding that the perils which seemed so formidable were of a pasteboard sort, did not answer to their names. After some activity on the part of the sergeant-at-arms there was a second reading of the membership list. Only seventeen responded. Colonel Sumner then rose and commanded the legislature to disperse — a duty which at the beginning and at the close of his brief speech he declared to be the most painful of his whole life.

This 4th of July demonstration was accorded a cold reception in Washington. Jefferson Davis, secretary of war, was disturbed by the affair. "I looked upon them [the members of the state legislature]," said he, "as men assembled without authority, men who could pass no law that should ever be put in execution, and that the crime would be in attempting to put the law in execution, and in the mean time they might be considered as a mere town meeting." Colonel Sumner did not escape official displeasure for his part in the transaction. In defense he fell back upon verbal requisitions of Acting-governor Woodson, who "was personally present in my camp desiring the interposition of the troops."

Missouri leaders, not sharing in the apprehensions of reaction that troubled the administration, now sunned themselves in the glow of victories apparently decisive. "It was everywhere anticipated," in the words of an address issued January, 1857, by the National Democracy of Kansas, "that these events would put an end to violence and restore the country to law and order and quiet." But these anticipations turned out to be delusive. Heavy blows had indeed been struck, but they were ill-advised, misdirected blows, and recoiled disastrously upon those who delivered them.

CHAPTER VIII.

DUTCH HENRY'S CROSSING, BLACK JACK, AND OSAWATOMIE.

JOHN BROWN is a parenthesis in the history of Kansas. The immense vibration of his career upon the nation had its source in the Virginia campaign and its ill-fated but heroic sequel, rather than in contributions to the territorial struggle. His course there — at war with the policy which finally defeated the slave power and saved Kansas from its clutch, pitched to the strain of revolution, tending to inaugurate a conflict of arms on the border — would never have given wing to his renown.

Born in Torrington, Connecticut, May 9th, 1800, and descended from substantial Puritan ancestors, John Brown had a youth and boyhood full of hardships and privations. He pursued different vocations — was successively tanner, wool-merchant, and farmer — but won no great success in any of these callings. Other interests absorbed him.

> "From childhood I have been possessed
> By a fire — by a true fire, or faint or fierce."

That fire was a consuming sentiment of anti-slavery passion.

John Brown reached Kansas in the autumn of 1855. He came in response to appeals for arms from his sons, five of whom preceded him to the territory and settled at Osawatomie. He found them in circumstances sufficiently uncomfortable: "no houses to shelter one of them; no hay or corn-fodder of any account secured; shivering over their little fires, all exposed to the dreadfully cutting winds morning and evening and stormy days."

It was not the purpose to make a home for himself in Kansas, nor to aid his sons in their wilderness-struggle, that brought John Brown to the territory, but the conviction that opportunity, long deferred, had at last offered for a blow at the slave system.

> "'T is time
> New hopes should animate the world, new light
> Should dawn from new revealings to a race
> Weighed down so long."

Such were the inspirations that dictated an immediate and personal response to the western signal of distress. Whatever else may be laid to his charge — whatever rashness, unwisdom, equivocation, bloodiness — no faintest trace of self-seeking stains his Kansas life. In behalf of the cause which fascinated and ruled him he was prepared to sacrifice its enemies, and if the offering proved inadequate to sacrifice himself. He belonged to that Hebraic, Old Testament, iron type of humanity in which the sentiment of justice — narrowed to warfare upon a single evil, pursuing it with concentrated and infinite hostility as if it epitomized all the sinning of the universe — assumed an exaggerated importance. It was a type of humanity to which the lives of individual men, weighed against the interests of the inexorable cause, seem light and trivial as the dust of a butterfly's wing. John Brown would have been at home among the armies of Israel that gave the guilty cities of Canaan to the sword, or among the veterans of Cromwell who ravaged Ireland in the name of the Lord. When the "Souldier's Pocket Bible" — a collection of texts which lent inspiration to Cromwell's veterans, and shows the "qualifications of his inner man that is a fit Souldier to fight in the Lord's Battels both before he fight, in the fight, and after the fight" — was once put into his hands he sat down and read it, apparently with the most intense and absorbing interest. There he read, "Scriptures . . . fitly applied to the Souldiers several occasions" — read that the soldier must be valiant for God's cause, must put his confidence in God's wisdom and strength, must pray before he goes to fight, must love his enemies as they are his enemies, and hate them as they are God's enemies, and must consider that God hath ever been accustomed to give the victory to a few!

That such a man, an astray and out-of-season Puritan, persuaded that God had called him, as prophets and priests were called in ancient times, to the work of fighting slavery, his policy one seamless garment of force — that such a man should stand almost alone in Kansas, should fail to rally any large following, should touch the general councils and activities spasmodically, incidentally, was inevitable. The policy of free-state leaders, in general harmony with the advice of outside friends, shunned violence of every sort. It especially avoided collision with the federal authorities. This wise policy experienced comparatively few lapses, though at times the temptation to abandon it was very strong. John Brown distrusted peaceful methods. He was quite as ready to fight as "the adventurous young men from South Carolina." In his opinion all marauding rascals from Missouri and elsewhere should be asked to show their passports. For the disorders of the territory (mere local eruptions of a chronic, deadly national malady, the cure of which rather than the salvation of Kansas haunted him) he had one sovereign remedy — violence. Gerrit Smith, in a speech before the Kansas Convention at Buffalo, July 9th and 10th, 1856, gave expression to sentiments of which John Brown was a strenuous, uncompromising exponent on the border. " You are here," he said, " looking to ballots when you should be looking to bayonets;

counting up voters when you should be mustering armed, and none but armed, emigrants. . . . They [members of the convention] are here to save Kansas. . . . But I am here to promote the killing of American slavery."

News of the attack upon Lawrence May 21st reached Osawatomie by courier during the day. Two rifle companies, recently organized for the defense of the neighborhood, and numbering fifty or sixty men, hastily mustered under command of John Brown, Jr., and began a forced night march toward Lawrence. John Brown accompanied the expedition. On the morning of the 22d they halted and went into camp near Palmyra, where they were joined by Captain S. T. Shore with a number of armed men, who informed them of the destruction of Lawrence. Here they remained until the 23d, when they moved on to Palmyra. Two days later Lieutenant J. R. Church with thirteen men reached their camp.

"I came upon a body of men from Osawatomie and the surrounding country," the lieutenant reported, "who, as well as I could judge, numbered some seventy or eighty, although they pretended to have about a hundred and thirty. This body was commanded by a Captain Brown. . . . They had been at Palmyra two days, and had frightened off a number of pro-slavery settlers, and forced off, as far as I could learn, two families. I immediately stated to Captain Brown that the assembly of large parties of armed men, on either side, was illegal, and called upon him to disperse. After considerable talk he consented to disband his party and return home."

Two days before this interview with Lieutenant Church, disquieting rumors reached camp from Dutch Henry's Crossing. H. H. Williams arrived from this neighborhood- and reported that pro-slavery men, in the absence of the rifle companies, were attempting a line of policy which Captain John Brown, Jr., prosecuted successfully at Palmyra — the expulsion of obnoxious people. Border-ruffian notifications to leave the country breezed with particular violence about a timid, nervous old shop-keeper, by the name of Morse, who supplied the riflemen with ammunition.

Though a company of Buford's men had pitched camp not far away, to which John Brown once paid a visit of espial in the mask of a federal surveyor; though the Rev. Martin White, a devout, biblical, rabid, shot-gun pro-slavery divine, resided in the neighborhood, yet no serious disturbances had hitherto broken out in the vicinity of Osawatomie, or Dutch Henry's Crossing — nothing worse than gusty, sulphurous, foul-mouthed talk, in which both parties were remarkably proficient.

Williams's narrative caused the sudden organization of a secret foray into the troubled district. Williams represents John Brown, who had joined the group of listeners gathered about him, as saying at the close of his story, "It is time to stop that sort of thing. It has gone on long enough. I'll attend to those fellows." An hour or two later Williams visited a shed near the camp, under which stood a grindstone. A squad of men were there sharpening their cutlasses. "What's up?" asked Williams. "We are going down upon the Pottawatomie to take care of the ruffians who are making trouble there," somebody replied. "We are going down," added John Brown, who was watching operations with interest, "to make an example. Won't you go?" Williams declined.

The expedition was a meagre affair numerically. Seven or eight men comprised the entire muster-roll. They were all members of John Brown's household with two exceptions — James Townsley and Theodore Weiner. Early in the afternoon of May 23d the raiders — bestowed in Townsley's farm-wagon, except Weiner, who rode a pony — left camp, amid a round of cheers, for Dutch Henry's Crossing. Toward sundown, and not far from his destination, Brown met James Blood, of Lawrence, with whom he became acquainted during the Wakarusa war. Brown talked for a few minutes. His habitual reserve relented into a nervous impetuosity of speech. The sack of Lawrence and denunciation of the peace-policy as cowardly, ignoble, ruinous were chief matters in his discourse. "We are on a secret mission — don't speak of meeting us," said the old man as the little company moved on.

At night-fall Brown encamped in a gulched, wooded, ledgy tract about a mile north of Pottawatomie Creek, his point of destination. Townsley states, in his confessions, that it was not until the party had reached this lair that Brown fully disclosed to him the mission of the expedition. Up to this time he had enveloped it in vague and general phrases which might mean much or little. Now he threw aside disguise, and announced his purpose to sweep off all pro-slavery men up and down the Pottawatomie. In this work of death Townsley, familiar with the region and its population, should act as guide. Townsley demurred. This was an unexpected hitch which gave twenty-four hours more of life to five unsuspecting pro-slavery squatters on the Pottawatomie. During the interval of delay, according to Townsley's report, Brown's tongue was again loosed, and he talked at large. He said they must fall upon the enemy with such remorseless and destructive surprise as would overwhelm them with terror. Border ruffians in the service of slavery were worthy of no more consideration than wolves that prey upon the farmer's sheepfold. Finally, he took refuge in the stronghold of predestination: "I have no choice. It has been decreed by Almighty God, ordained from eternity, that I should make an example of these men." Townsley, whose theological education had evidently been neglected, interrupted the discourse at one point: "If God is such a powerful *man* as you say, why does n't he attend to the business himself?"

Saturday night, May 24th, the blow was struck, the example made. Brown and his men stole out of ambush and executed pro-slavery squatters whose names were pricked. A compromise was effected by abridging the death-list. This concession appears to have allayed Townsley's scruples. At the first cabin where the raiders halted and knocked there was no response. "It seemed to be empty," said Townsley, "though I thought I heard somebody cock a rifle inside." Three other cabins were visited, out of which five men were dragged to sudden death in the name of "the Northern army"—James P. Doyle and his sons William and Drury, Allan Wilkinson, and William Sherman. They were all mortally hacked and slashed with cutlasses, except the elder Doyle. Through his forehead, burned and blackened by the proximity of the pistol, there was a bullet-hole.

It was a misfortune that Howard and Sherman, Republican members of the congressional investigating committee, should have declined to explore this ghastly affair, which has given rise to so much controversy. That refusal enabled the pro-slavery leaders to charge them with fear of facing the record of anti-slavery men in the territory. "It [the Pottawatomie massacre] revealed on the part of their friends such a picture of savage ferocity that the committee for once blushed and stultified themselves rather than receive the testimony as competent" — the testimony of Wilkinson's widow "lately tendered at Westport." There was, however, an *ex parte* investigation conducted by Mr. Oliver. When the widows, children, and neighbors of the slaughtered men gave evidence, he said in a speech in the House of Representatives — witnesses " whose tears in testifying were streaming down their cheeks," "who gave the greatest assurance that the words spoken came truthfully from the heart, because chastened by the hand of affliction and sorrow " — "my blood ran cold at the recital." Among those who have denounced the raid none have surpassed Andrew Johnson in bitter, unsparing, execrative words.

"Innocent, unoffending men," he said in the Senate of the United States, "were taken out [of their cabins], and in the midnight hour, and in the forest, and on the roadside fell victims to the insatiable thirst of John Brown for blood. Then it was . . . that hell entered into his heart — not the iron into his soul. Then it was that he shrank from the dimensions of a human being into those of a reptile. Then it was, if not before, that he changed his character to a demon who had lost all the virtues of a man!"

In appraising the motives which underlay the slaughter at Dutch Henry's Crossing, we are shut up more or less completely to conjecture. John Brown's statements were sufficiently evasive to deceive members of his own family and personal friends, who long denied that he led the foray, or that he was implicated in it otherwise than by shouldering responsibility after the event. Measured upon the scale of the times, the five squatters, upon whom he laid a tiger's paw, were not exceptionally bad men. Doyle and Wilkinson were of Northern extraction, and do not appear to have reached any evil eminence that shot above ordinary altitudes of border partisanship. William Sherman may have been more noisy and less respectable, but the evidence fails to show that he had done anything worthy of assassination. That intelligence of alarming pro-slavery outbreaks on the Pottawatomie could not have been brought to camp by Williams, nor by anybody else, is evidenced by the fact that the rifle companies, organized and equipped for the defense of that particular locality, so far from speeding homeward lingered at Palmyra for two days after John Brown's departure — lingered until they were dispersed by Lieutenant Church. Another circumstance is of the same import. May 27th squatters upon Pottawatomie Creek, "without distinction of party," held an indignation meeting and denounced the killing as " an outrage of the darkest and foulest nature," perpetrated by " midnight assassins unknown, who have taken five of our citizens at the hour of midnight from their homes and families, and murdered and mangled them in the most awful manner." They pledged themselves "to aid and assist in bringing these desperadoes to justice." Members of the rifle companies who saw Townsley drive away from camp on Middle Creek with his farm-wagon full of armed men, escorted by Weiner, and who, doubtless, joined in the parting round of cheers, had a hand in this meeting for public and indignant protest. As an index of sentiment in the community, which the massacre purported to shield, it is decisive. If perils had brooded over it which invited and vindicated extreme measures of defensive violence, a unanimous repudiating mass-meeting would have been impossible. "It will take a great deal to justify night attacks and shooting men after drum-head courts-martial," said Thomas Hughes in a lecture at the Working Men's College, London, on "The Struggle for Kansas."

Unquestionably rumors from the Pottawatomie wrought upon Brown, but yet more potent were the disheartening tidings from Lawrence. He thought the cause of freedom had been piloted through bad seamanship of peace-policies into dangerous shallows. That was the burden of his talk in the accidental interview with James Blood, where motives of family or local defense appeared faintly, if at all. Habitually verging toward infatuation on the subject of slavery, belonging to the class of men who talk on great themes — themes which move them like the sound of a trumpet —

"in a tone perfectly level and without emphasis and without any exhibition of feeling," he was presumably pushed by the exigencies of the crisis into a condition of actual mania. The occasion called, in his overwrought judgment, for an unforgetable example, at once a protest against popular theories of non-resistance and a bloody lesson to enemies. Should the outrage lead to civil war, should it embroil the country in a conflict of arms, that would only hasten the day of proclaiming liberty to the captive.

"Why move thy feet so slow to what is best?"

The impersonal, missionary motive — remembering those in bonds as bound with them — flames like sunshine on spear-points where everything else is hideous and ghastly. To the long list of violences committed under worthy but misguided inspirations must be added the massacre at Dutch Henry's Crossing. Every great cause has effected complete conquest of impressible and unbalanced disciples, thrown over them spells of victorious fascination, harnessed them to its service with absolute capitulation of self, blinded them hopelessly to interests and methods other than their own, and reduced to a minimum in their estimate the sanctities and rights of those who ran counter to their fanaticism.

Naturally the killing made a commotion among pro-slavery squatters and territorial officials in the vicinity of Dutch Henry's Crossing. "All is excitement here," was the burden of letter-writers who sent off appeals to Governor Shannon from Paola, a neighboring town, on the morning of the 26th; "court cannot go on. . . . Families are leaving for Missouri. . . . We can perhaps muster to-day, including the Alabamians, who are now encamped on Bull Creek, about one hundred and fifty men." "These murders, it is supposed," wrote General W. A. Heiskell, of the territorial militia, "were committed by abolitionists of Osawatomie and Pottawatomie creeks on their return from Lawrence. How long shall these things continue? How long shall our citizens, unarmed and defenseless, be exposed to worse than savage cruelty? . . . We have here but few men, and they wholly unarmed. We shall gather together for our own defense as many men as we can; we hope you will send us as many arms as possible; and if, under the circumstances, you can do so, send as many men as you think may be necessary. General Barber is here. He has sent to Fort Scott for aid. We must organize such force as we can, but for God's sake send arms. . . . We hope to be able to identify some of the murderers, as Mr. [James] Harris, who was in their hands, was released, and will probably know some of them." Harris happened to be at the house of William Sherman on the night of May 24th, when, as he stated, October 23d, 1857, in his deposition before the Strickler Commission, which was appointed by the territorial legislature to audit claims for losses during the troubles, "an armed body of men, in command of the notorious Captain John Brown, . . . by force and arms and with threats and menaces of violence and bodily harm, took and carried away from your petitioner one horse, saddle, bridle, and gun ; . . . your petitioner further showeth that, being repeatedly threatened by said Captain Brown and followers, and living in great fear of my life, I was forced by their menaces and threats to abandon the territory." Minerva Selby was also at Sherman's on the fatal evening. She testified that she saw Harris there with his horse, but went away before the arrival of Brown's party. "Harris with his family came to my house. He said that he had been robbed at Sherman's the preceding night by Brown's men ; . . . that Sherman had been murdered the same night by Brown and his men ; . . . that . . . he was threatened frequently, and was obliged to leave his home — the safety of himself and family required it." The Rev. Martin White testified in a similar strain : "I am acquainted with . . . Mr. Harris. Saw him a short time after William Sherman had been murdered. Know that the petitioner was greatly alarmed; seemed to apprehend danger from the murderers of Sherman, as the petitioner was at the premises of Sherman when the act was committed. The petitioner expressed his fears of being killed to prevent his divulging the murder. Believe he was in danger of being murdered. The safety of himself and family required him to leave his home." Judge Cato wrote from Paola May 27th: "I shall do everything in my power to have the matter investigated, and there seems to be a disposition on the part of the free-state men in Franklin [county] to aid in having the laws enforced. As soon as proper evidence can be procured, warrants will be issued for the arrest of the parties suspected. . . . These murders were most foully committed in the night-time, by a gang of some twelve or fifteen persons, calling on and dragging from their houses defenseless and unsuspecting citizens, and murdering, and, after murdering, mutilating their bodies in a very shocking manner." Governor Shannon promptly dispatched a military force to the Pottawatomie. "The respectability of the parties and the cruelties attending these murders," he wrote President Pierce May 31st, "have produced an extraordinary state of excitement in that portion of the territory which has heretofore remained comparatively quiet."

Extra-judicial agencies for redressing the Pottawatomie outrages began to move at once. Newspaper extras, with sensational details of the affair, set a Leavenworth mob upon Governor Robinson. Captain H. C. Pate, Kansas correspondent of "The Missouri Republican," who led "the

Westport Sharpshooters "— a company recruited largely among the rowdies of Westport, Missouri, to assist in abating nuisances at Lawrence May 21st — was still in the neighborhood of Franklin when the Pottawatomie massacre occurred. On receiving intelligence of it, he hastily broke camp for Osawatomie, to wreak vengeance upon the perpetrators. He scoured the country in no gentle fashion, but missed the main object of his mission. Saturday, May 31st, Pate went into camp at Black Jack, three quarters of a mile west of the village, on the edge of the prairie. A line of wagons drawn up in front of the bivouac formed a straggling, intermittent breastwork, while the rear was protected by a wooded, water-rutted ravine.

There was no lack of predatory energy in the border-ruffian camp. A squad of Pate's men looted Palmyra, a settlement of four or five families, Saturday evening. They returned with some plunder and two prisoners.

The easy success at Palmyra stimulated further depredations. Sunday, six of the band at Black Jack rode over to Prairie City, — a neighboring hamlet — in search of fun and booty. They anticipated nothing more serious than a profitable frolic. But some circuit preacher had an appointment at Prairie City for that Lord's Day. To this service came people of the vicinity in considerable numbers. Apprehensive that the order of service might suddenly change from spiritual to carnal, they brought along their guns. In the midst of worship there was an alarm — "The Missourians are coming!" Never did religious exercises conclude more abruptly. Six horsemen, charging into town with rifles across their saddles, instantly absorbed the attention of the congregation. The troopers, surprised at the number of people in the miniature village, halted before they reached the cabin which served for a church. Two raiders, desperate characters if the recollection of their captors may be credited — one of them with blackened face and sporting chicken's feathers in his hat — were bagged. The remainder, though exposed to a random musketry, escaped.

These marauding operations stimulated the local campaign against Pate. Old John Brown, hearing of his anxiety to meet him, started after the Missourian with twenty-eight men; ten belonging to his own company, and the remainder to Captain S. T. Shore's. "We did not meet them on that day" (Sunday), said John Brown in an account of the battle of Black Jack first printed in Sanborn's "Life and Letters." ... "We were out all night, but could find nothing of them until about six o'clock, when we prepared to attack them at once. ... We got to within about a mile of their camp before being discovered by their scouts, and then moved at a brisk pace; Captain Shore and men forming our left, and my company the right.

When within about sixty rods of the enemy, Captain Shore's men halted by mistake in a very exposed situation and continued the fire, both his men and the enemy being armed with Sharpe's rifles. My company had no long shooters. We (my company) did not fire a gun until we gained the rear of a bank, about fifteen or twenty rods to the right of the enemy, where we commenced and soon compelled them to hide in a ravine."

There was a desultory fire for two or three hours, during which Pate's situation grew more and more critical. Half of his men had skulked away, and the assailants were slowly but surely closing in upon the remainder. Free-state reinforcements might appear at any moment. Pate finally sent out a flag of truce. Brown declined to negotiate with subordinates, and the commander of "the Westport Sharpshooters" appeared forthwith. "I approached," he said, "and made known the fact that I was acting under the order of the United States marshal, and was only in search of persons for whom writs of arrest had been issued." But talk of that sort had no more effect upon Brown than the iris above a cataract on the waters plunging below it. He would hear of nothing except unconditional surrender. Trivialities like flags of truce and writs of territorial marshals he unceremoniously brushed aside. Fifteen minutes were modestly asked to consider the proposition for capitulation. "Brown refused," said Pate in "The

Missouri Republican," "and I was taken prisoner under a flag of truce. . . . I had no alternative but to submit or to run and be shot. . . . I went to take Old Brown, and Old Brown took me."

Brown captured twenty-three men — some of them residents of the neighborhood — and commissary supplies of considerable amount, all of which were conveyed to his camp on Middle Creek. He narrowly escaped failure in the expedition, as only a single round of ammunition remained when the flag of truce appeared. Just after the fight had closed free-state reinforcements arrived from neighboring towns.

The capture of Pate was not the only exploit of Brown's company in the vicinity of Black Jack. At St. Bernard, five miles from camp, a successful pro-slavery trader had a miscellaneous store filled with dry goods, clothing, groceries, drugs, firearms, hardware, boots and shoes. A necessitous company of guerrillas could scarcely be expected to neglect so favorable an opportunity to supply their wants at the expense of a Southerner. Certainly the company encamped on Middle Creek did nothing of the kind. About nightfall June 3d — such is the drift of testimony before the Strickler Commission — " part of a company commanded by one John Brown," "armed with Sharpe's rifles, pistols, bowie-knives, and other deadly weapons, came upon the premises and

attacked and rushed into the said store" — a
sudden condition of affairs so warlike that the
employees "were deterred, threatened, and overpowered by the desperadoes, . . . who demanded
a surrender of the goods and chattels, . . . threatening immediate death and destruction should the
slightest resistance be offered." Finding the prize
richer than had been anticipated and their appliances of transportation inadequate, the gang returned in the morning and resumed operations.
They evidently left nothing to be desired in point
of thoroughness. A young woman, into whose
private apartments the rascals forcibly intruded,
and at whom they "presented several guns,"
though perhaps unfavorably circumstanced for dispassionate criticism, gave her impressions concerning their personal appearance. "They were desperate and vicious looking men," she said, . . .
"more like barbarians than civilized beings."

Black Jack was not the only disordering consequence swiftly following the 24th of May. The
Missouri border rushed to arms. Whitfield, territorial delegate to Congress, put himself in the
lead. Westport, Lexington, and Independence
raised companies for the army of invasion, which
gathered with celerity, was well equipped, and on
the 3d of June reached Bull Creek, twelve miles
east of Palmyra. It was planned that a junction
should be formed with Pate, and then the consolidated force would scourge every abolitionist from

the country. This pretty campaign the disaster at Black Jack somewhat disconcerted.

Free-state men also were astir. Their military companies, snuffing mischief in the air, concentrated near Palmyra — detachments of Captain Samuel Walker's "Bloomington Rifles," of Captain Joseph Cracklin's "Lawrence Stubbs," of Captain J. B. Abbott's "Blue Mound Infantry," of Captain McWhinney's "Wakarusa Boys," and of Captain S. T. Shore's "Prairie City Company" — amounting altogether to about one hundred and fifteen men. Brown lurked in the woods of Middle Creek, fully occupied with the care of his prisoners. June 5th Kansans and Missourians were facing each other with arms in their hands, and apparently on the eve of collision.

Governor Shannon became alarmed, and roused himself into a vigorous activity. He published a proclamation June 4th commanding all armed and illegal organizations to disperse. Citizens "without regard to party names or distinctions" were assured of protection, and invaders warned to retire. The proclamation, though a little tardy, had the right ring. Colonel Sumner thought that if it "had been issued six months earlier and rigidly maintained these difficulties would have been avoided."

Fifty federal dragoons, with Colonel Sumner at their head, hurriedly left Lecompton June 5th to part the belligerents concentrating near Palmyra.

"Any delay . . . will lead to fearful consequences," the governor urged. Deputy Marshal Fain, supplied, it was supposed, with a liberal assortment of warrants, accompanied the expedition. The colonel found a larger disturbance brewing at Palmyra than his imperfect knowledge had led him to suspect. The tone of his official report indicates that in his view the main business of the expedition was "to disperse a band of free-soilers, who were encamped near Prairie City; this band had had a fight with the pro-slavery party, and had taken twenty-six prisoners." During the day Sumner reached the vicinity of Old John Brown's lair, from which his approach could be distinctly seen across the prairie. Unmistakably he intended to visit the camp, and after a hurried consultation it was thought prudent to send out a messenger with proposals for an interview. "What's going on down there?" Sumner asked, pointing toward the free-soil bivouac. "Captain John Brown has Pate and his men prisoners. He sent me to meet you and to inquire where an interview can be held." "Tell him he can see me right here." The messenger returned and made his report. "We must see Colonel Sumner apart from his men," suggested Captain Shore. Brown concurred, and the runner, though with some reluctance, set out again. "Well, what is it now?" the colonel asked with evident impatience. The request of Brown and Shore was stated. "Tell them," he growled, "that I make no terms with lawless men — tell them that. Dragoons, form a company — march." The runner flew back to camp at a break-neck pace, and the horsemen followed on behind. Brown and Shore sallied forth to meet the not very welcome visitors. After some parleying Brown led the dragoons into camp. Colonel Sumner stated that his orders were to release Pate, and to aid the officers in serving writs. Marshal Fain fumbled among his papers, but finally said he could find none for the apprehension of anybody in the camp. It is reported that Sumner afterwards took Brown aside and told him that a warrant for his arrest had been issued, but that the marshal had inadvertently mislaid it.

A good deal of stir and bustle ensued in setting the prisoners at liberty, and in restoring to them as far as possible their effects. The mere humdrum formality of regaining his freedom — the bare, unadorned act of escaping from Old Brown's lair with a whole skin — did not quite fill out Pate's idea of what belonged to the proprieties of the occasion. One thing was yet lacking — a speech from himself, extenuating any infelicities, and illuminating any obscurities that might vex his recent record. Mounting upon a log he began a speech, upon which, before it had fairly got under way, came sudden extinction —

"As when a lamp is blown out by a gust of wind in a casement."

"I don't want to hear a word out of you, sir," thundered Sumner — " not a word, sir. You have no business here. The governor told me so!"

While breaking up Brown's camp Sumner learned, with evident astonishment, " that two or three hundred of the pro-slavery party from Missouri and elsewhere were approaching," to whom he gave attention. " I found them halted," he reports, "at two miles distance (about two hundred and fifty strong), and to my great surprise I found Colonel Whitfield, the member of Congress, and General Coffee, of the militia, at their head. . . . I then requested General Coffee to assemble his people, and I read to them the president's dispatch and the governor's proclamation." Whitfield and Coffee made fair promises, and "moved off," though Sumner did not feel assured they were not bent on mischief-making somewhere. He remained in the disquieted district until the 22d of June, when he considered the work of pacification accomplished. Only a few freebooters kept the field. " These fellows," he reported, "belong to both parties, and are taking advantage of the present political excitement to commit their own rascally acts."

The Missourians retired sullenly across the border. Their leisurely and circuitous path was marked by the customary excesses, including the dead bodies of two or three free-soilers. For a portion, at all events, of Whitfield's expedition the line of return dipped southward through the odious village of Osawatomie. So far the victims of Dutch Henry's Crossing had been feebly and imperfectly avenged. To smite the town with which John Brown was most intimately associated, in default of larger game, would yield a qualified and secondary satisfaction. "The abolition hole" — containing some thirty buildings and a population of two hundred souls — was surprised and pillaged. The raiders expected to fire the town, but as federal troops were near, and free-state rangers might be in close pursuit, nothing worse than plundering happened. A final reckoning with Osawatomie was deferred. The calamitous consequences of the night raid upon the Pottawatomie had not yet spent their fury.

CHAPTER IX.

PER ASPERA.

THE calamities of free-state men in Kansas were stepping-stones to final success. They moved Northern sentiment profoundly. Speakers fresh from the border addressed great public gatherings and inflamed the excitement by the adventurous, romantic, far-away interest that attached to them, by unmeasured denunciations of the slave power, by sensational narratives of the hardships, robberies, and murders that had befallen anti-slavery settlers in the territory. Pulpit, press, and convention caught up and reverberated their impassioned message. The legislatures of several Northern States passed resolutions recognizing the services and sufferings of Kansas pioneers in the cause of liberty. "We have heard," said the legislature of Massachusetts, "the call for aid and sympathy which has come up . . . from the settlers of Kansas with the deepest solicitude; . . . their sufferings have touched our hearts; and the manly defense of their rights has won our admiration."

In the autumn of 1856 two books appeared

which stimulated and perpetuated public interest: "Kansas, Its Exterior and Interior Life," by Mrs. Sara T. L. Robinson — a brave, graphic, realistic, clear-eyed narrative of border experiences, exhibiting their social, domestic, every-day phases as well as their turbulent, political constituents, and running through nine editions; "The Conquest of Kansas," by W. A. Phillips — a breezy, readable book, not without sense of humor, but marred by inaccuracies and exaggerations.

A fierce agitation flamed and roared like a prairie fire from Boston to the Northwest. But the movement did not spend itself in flame and smoke. Societies of semi-military cast, no less willing to furnish guns than groceries, sprang up as if by magic, and overshadowed the earlier, more pacific organizations. A national society, with auxiliaries in almost every free state except Massachusetts, which had a flourishing "State Kansas Committee" of its own, got afoot and harvested not less than two hundred thousand dollars for Kansas purposes. The Massachusetts committee secured funds to the amount of eighty thousand dollars in addition to large supplies. Eager, coöperative activities woke on every side. "I know people," said Emerson in a speech at Cambridge, "who are making haste to reduce their expenses and pay their debts, not with a view to new accumulations, but in preparation to save and earn for the benefit of Kansas emigrants."

> "Thou hast great allies;
> Thy friends are exultations, agonies,
> And love and Man's unconquerable mind."

The volume of anti-slavery migration toward the territory swelled like mountain streams after heavy showers. A constant movement thitherward had been in progress through the spring and early summer. Among the companies who arrived during that period were the widely-heralded "rifle Christians" from New Haven, Connecticut — seventy-nine resolute men, under the conduct of C. B. Lines, armed with bibles and Sharpe's carbines. "We gratefully accept the bibles," said the leader of the colony, "as the only sure foundation on which to erect free institutions. . . . We . . . accept the weapons also, and, like our fathers, we go with the bible to indicate the peaceful nature of our mission and the harmless character of our company, and a weapon to teach those who may be disposed to molest us (if any such there be) that while we determine to do that which is right we will not submit tamely to that which is wrong." "We will not forget you," said Henry Ward Beecher, prominent in securing for the colony an outfitting of guns. "Every morning breeze shall catch the blessings of our prayers and roll them westward to your prairie home."

Pro-slavery leaders on the border viewed with alarm these unwonted exhibitions of Northern energy and anger. Rumors of impending invasions — of populous, grimy, fanatic abolitionist hordes, with hate in their hearts and arms in their hands, hurrying toward the frontier — flew thick and fast. Steps must be taken at once to meet the new and multiplying perils. Unless the great inflowing current of Northern life could be checked, all hope of Southern supremacy in Kansas must be at once and forever abandoned.

Atchison and his associates attacked the problem before them with no half-way policy. They resolved to police the great national highway of the Missouri River against all traffic inimical to the interests of slavery. Steamers were overhauled, free-state consignments of merchandise seized, Kansasward travelers unable to give satisfactory accounts of themselves arrested and sent down the river. A. A. Lawrence and Dr. Samuel Cabot, of Boston, shipped for the territory four thousand dollars' worth of Sharpe's rifles, which happened to be *in transitu* when the embargo began to stiffen. These guns the volunteer river commissioners seized. The Boston gentlemen were naturally anxious to recover the arms, but felt a little awkward and embarrassed in making the effort. "If we were not officers of the Emigrant Aid Company," Lawrence wrote, "(which takes no part in such matters . . .) we could get them by suit; but whether we can do it by proxy remains to be seen."

The first considerable party — seventy-five in number — to which the revised code of inter-state traffic was applied came from Chicago. They were recruited at an immense mass-meeting in that city May 31st, which Lane, who was a stump orator of remarkable power, addressed with great effect. The Chicago immigrants met with no special annoyance until they reached Lexington, where they were subjected to a preliminary investigation and lost their Sharpe's rifles. They then proceeded to Leavenworth, where a second examination took place, which resulted in the capture of "about two bushels of revolvers, pistols, and bowie-knives." Finally, they were sent back down the river, put ashore near Alton, Illinois, in a drenching rain-storm, and left to shift for themselves.

Overland immigrants fared no better when they touched the soil of Missouri, but encountered the same belligerent policy that threw its obstructions across the river. This policy, it should be remarked, commanded general though not universal credit among the valiant friends of law and order. It was too flat and insipid for some of the newspaper editors. "We are of the opinion," said "The Squatter Sovereign," "[that] if the citizens of Leavenworth . . . would hang one or two boat-loads of abolitionists it would do more towards establishing peace in Kansas than all the speeches that have been delivered in Congress during the present session. Let the experiment be tried!"

The Missourians did not succeed in their efforts at obstruction. They could no more balk the great Northern movement toward Kansas than they could check the Missouri with the palm of the hand. Perplexity, agitation, experiment, shifting of routes, they compassed, and that was all. Various plans for breaking the embargo on the Missouri River were rife in Eastern anti-slavery circles, such as the purchase of an armed vessel to cruise upon its forbidden waters; the assembling of friendly legislatures with a vague, undefined purpose of state interference; a protest of state executives against violations of constitutional rights of travel prevalent in Missouri, which Mr. Thaddeus Hyatt volunteered to carry to every Northern governor for his signature.

None of these projects ever reached the stage of practical experiment. The crisis was hardly serious enough to call for heroic remedies. Missouri did not command all accessible routes to Kansas. It were easy to flank the blockade by opening communications through Iowa and Nebraska. This measure was successfully accomplished through the energy of the "Kansas State Central Committee," appointed by the Topeka mass-convention. Toward the close of July the Chicago emigrants, together with fresh companies from Massachusetts, Ohio, Illinois, Indiana, and

Wisconsin — reaching an aggregate of three hundred and ninety-six persons — were encamped near Nebraska City *en route* for Kansas. This company had been loudly noised abroad as Lane's Northern army. Governor Shannon, in no little alarm, urged General P. F. Smith, who succeeded Colonel Sumner in command of the department, "to take the field with the whole disposable force in the territory," to keep this ill-reputed horde at bay, which he declined to do on the ground that the governor's information was untrustworthy. July 29th Dr. S. G. Howe and Thaddeus Hyatt, representatives of the National Kansas Committee, sent out to investigate matters, reached the Nebraska camp. They found many of the immigrants in a forlorn condition — ragged, almost penniless, poorly supplied with even the scanty furniture of a camper's outfit. Leadership had fallen into Lane's hands, and the whole expedition became accredited to him, though he was neither directly nor indirectly concerned in raising more than a fourth part of it. The committee demanded that his connection with it should be completely severed on penalty of withholding further supplies. Considerations which led to this summary step were the fact that papers had been made out for Lane's arrest — a circumstance which might lead to complications; that in an emergency his discretion and self-command could not be trusted. These considerations, the committee reported, "conspired to create a well-grounded apprehension in our minds that by some hasty and ill-timed splurge he would defeat the object of the expedition if suffered to remain even in otherwise desirable proximity." Lane took the decision much to heart. "If the people of Kansas don't want me," he said, "I'll cut my throat to-day." But he sullenly yielded, set off toward the territory with Old John Brown, Captain Samuel Walker, and three or four others, outrode his escort, and reached Lawrence alone August 11th, disguised as Captain Jo Cook. He tarried long enough in Topeka to write the free-state prisoners at Lecompton a note, offering to attack the federal soldiers who guarded them if they could not otherwise escape. The so-called Northern army pursued its way leisurely into the territory and founded along the line of march two towns — Plymouth and Holton. Members of the expedition, who did not tarry for these enterprises, reached Topeka on the 13th of August.

Other overland parties followed. Late in September James Redpath, with one hundred and thirty men, appeared on the northern boundary. A martial, non-agricultural reputation preceded this company. Colonel J. E. Johnston with four companies of dragoons marched toward the Nebraska line to insure it a fitting reception, but after applying suitable tests he pronounced the travelers to be "real immigrants."

The Redpath scare had no sooner abated than another still more violent succeeded. Reports reached Lecompton that six or seven hundred men, with three pieces of artillery, were on the point of crossing the Nebraska line. Colonel P. St. George Cooke hurried forward reinforcements, increasing the number of federal troops along the frontier to five hundred strong. One heavy disappointment befell the colonel during the northward expedition. "I just missed the arrest of the notorious Osawatomie outlaw, Brown," he reported October 7th. "The night before, having ascertained that after dark he had stopped for the night at a house six miles from the camp, I sent a party, who found at twelve o'clock he had gone." Colonel Cooke was more successful in catching the latest overland immigrants, who were brought to a halt near the Nebraska line on the morning of October 10th. The excess of men in the company excited suspicion, as the two hundred and twenty-three persons reported by the officer of the day included only "five women of marriageable age." "I do not see many spinning-wheels sticking out of the wagons," said Colonel Cooke as he walked about them. Indeed, they contained "no visible furniture, agricultural implements, or mechanical tools," but abounded in "all the requisite articles for camping and campaigning purposes." Marshal Preston, in spite of much protesting, searched the wagons and unearthed a remarkable assortment of farming implements — Hall's muskets, Sharpe's carbines, revolvers, sabres, bayonets, fixed ammunition, kegs of powder, and dragoon saddles. "It was raining on the day of arrest," reported Marshal Preston, "which subjected us all to a drenching. It was to be regretted, but could not be prevented." The grumbling expedition was escorted to Topeka, where the conductors of it, S. W. Eldridge, S. C. Pomeroy, and others, laid their grievances before the governor, resented the meddlesome interference of "one Preston, deputy United States marshal," and disavowed with much posturing of injured innocence every warlike purpose. These flower-soft, unmilitary gentlemen forgot to inform the governor, to whom the intelligence would have been of interest, that the bulk of their formidable military munitions had been obtained from the Iowa state arsenal; that the authorities allowed Robert Morrow to help himself to whatever it contained on the not very onerous condition that he would manage the operation discreetly; that Morrow seized at night three wagonloads of guns and ammunition, and added them to the resources of immigrants who were lustily protesting, "Our mission to this territory is entirely peaceful." They escaped with no severer penalties than a lecture on the rules and maxims of behavior appropriate for new-come Kansans.

When they began to comprehend in some measure the extent and intensity of anti-slavery sentiment moving among the Northern States ; when they saw great tides of hostile immigration pouring around their ineffectual barriers into Kansas — a spectacle tending to cloud the hopes of the most confident and optimistic — pro-slavery leaders began to question the wisdom of that insolent and contemptuous confidence which had thus far ruled their councils. They revised their tactics so far as even to catch a lesson from their enemies, and attempted, though with the awkwardness of novices and of pupils to some other manner born, the effective guise of martyrs. Atchison, B. F. Stringfellow, Buford, and others published an address, June 21st, setting forth pathetically and voluminously the calamities that were upon them : —

" Kansas they [the abolitionists] justly regard as the mere outpost in the war now being waged between the antagonistic civilizations of the North and South, and, winning this great outpost and standpoint, they rightly think their march will be open to an easy conquest of the whole field. Hence the extraordinary means the abolition party has adopted to flood Kansas with the most fanatical and lawless portion of Northern society, and hence the large sums of money . . . expended to surround . . . Missourians with obnoxious and dangerous neighbors. On the other hand, the pro-slavery element of the law and order party in Kansas, looking to the Bible finds slavery ordained of God. . . . Slavery is the African's normal and proper state.

... We believe it a trust and guardianship given as of God for the good of both races. ... This is ... a great social and political question of races, ... a question whether we shall sink to the level of the freed African and take him to the embrace of social and political equality and fraternity; for such is the natural end of abolition progress. ... That man or state is deceived that fondly trusts these fanatics may stop at Kansas. ... The most convincing proof ... of this was recently given before the congressional investigating committee. Judge Matthew Walker ... testified ... that before the abolitionists selected Lawrence as their centre of operations their leader, Governor Robinson, attempted to get a foothold for them in the Wyandotte reserve. ... Robinson, finding it necessary to communicate their plans and objects, divulged to Walker (whom he then supposed to be a sympathizer) that the abolitionists were determined on winning Kansas at any cost; that then, having Missouri surrounded on three sides, they would begin their assaults on her, and as fast as one state gave way attack another, until the whole South was abolitionized. ... We are confident that ... the abolition party was truly represented by Robinson, who has always been their chief man and acknowledged leader in Kansas. ... It was proved before the investigating committee that the abolition party had traveling agents in the territory whose duty it was to gather up, exaggerate, and report for publication rumors to the prejudice of the law and order party. ... In the present imperiled state of your civilization, if we do not maintain this outpost we cannot long maintain the citadel. Then rally to the rescue."

The " Appeal " was printed in " De Bow's Review " for August, 1856, and is much soberer, less confident in tone, than an article which appeared two months earlier in the same magazine under the title " Kansas a Slave State."

" Slaves will now yield a greater profit in Kansas," said the writer, " either to hire out or cultivate the soil, than any other place. . . . Those who have brought their slaves here are reaping a rich reward, . . . and feel as secure in their property here as in Kentucky or Missouri. . . . Why it is that more of our friends in the old states have not brought their slaves with them we are at a loss to divine, unless the falsehoods and threats of the abolitionists have frightened them. . . . Should Kansas be made a slave state? We say that location, climate, soil, productions, value of slave labor the good of the master and slave — all conspire and cry aloud that it should be. . . . The squatters, too, have already said three successive times, at the polls, that Kansas should be a slave state. But if all this is not enough, then we say, without fear of successful contradiction, that Kansas must be a slave state or the Union will be dissolved. . . . If Kansas is not made a slave state, it requires no sage to foretell that . . . there will never be another slave state. . . . Can Kansas be made a slave state? Thus far the pro-slavery party has triumphed in Kansas in spite of the abolitionists and their Emigrant Aid Societies. . . . We have peaceably whipped them at the polls and forced them to beg for quarter in the field, and proven to the world that truth and justice are on our side. . . . The stake is surely worth a struggle; and if not won by the South, God alone can foresee the evils that are to follow. . . . Will the South come to the rescue and make Kansas a slave state? We are sure she will. We know her people, and when once aroused . . . they will fly to the rescue of their friends in Kansas, where all the combined forces of abolitionism will quail and skulk back to the dark sinks and hiding-places from which they came by the assistance of the aid societies. Such creatures cannot stand before the forces of honest freemen. . . . Kansas should, can, and will be a slave state."

These papers and others which were issued sent a spasm of excitement through the South, but received no such response of partisan immigration as streamed into Kansas from the North.

With the sack of Lawrence, the dispersion of the Topeka legislature, and the flight or capture of prominent free-state leaders, the territory plunged into chaos. So far from befriending anti-slavery interests, the Pottawatomie massacre at once fomented and embittered the struggle. A period of lawlessness and marauding now set in that left stains on both parties as inevitably as the snail slimes its track. Which faction surpassed the other in misdeeds it would be hard to say. Free-state men seized the opportunity to rid the territory of obnoxious persons. The experiences of Rev. Martin White, for instance, were far from griefless. His troubles dated back to a public meeting at Osawatomie April 16th, 1856, which passed resolutions against the payment of taxes levied by the territorial legislature.

In the course of the discussion he crossed swords with Old John Brown. White was a furious, unmeasured partisan, and made himself so unpopular that on the night of August 13th free-state men assailed his cabin. "I was frequently menaced and threatened with certain and immediate destruction," he testified before the Strickler Commission October 23d, 1857, "and was once attacked in my dwelling by a body of armed men, who were repulsed and driven away after a contest of half an hour" — retiring with a booty of seven horses. "A body of armed men commanded by [J. C.] Holmes came to my premises," said one of White's sons. . . . "They took what they wanted, and inquired how many men were at my father's, saying that when they got old Martin White and killed him they would have all the pro-slavery men in the neighborhood." Such was the temper exhibited by "the outlaws and followers of Lane and Brown" that on the 14th of August the Rev. Martin White fled precipitately to Missouri. "In consequence of their manifest determination to take my life," he said, "I was forced to beat a hasty retreat from the territory."

The pro-slavery party had one great advantage: the most practicable avenues of communication and traffic were in their possession. They infested the country adjacent to Lawrence and Topeka, so that these towns might be loosely considered in a state of siege. No doubt scarcity of provisions in some degree stimulated the marauding habit, but it had little need of artificial cultivation.

Topeka felt the pressure of the blockade much less than Lawrence, yet it was the centre of a prosperous series of maraudings upon the surrounding country. So great was the enterprise and success in what one of the victims called "the roguing business" that few pro-slavery men of the neighborhood escaped spoliation. Free-state depredators, in larger or smaller gangs, scoured the region, filling the air with profanity, intimidating pro-slavery settlers, shooting at those who were not sufficiently docile, and plundering right and left. A curious observer has chronicled the contents of a single foray-wagon: green corn in the ear, surmounted by a cooking-stove, a crib-cradle, a dining-table, clothing, bedding, and a great variety of miscellaneous articles. Tecumseh in particular, a town just east of Topeka, was visited by "robberies, plunderings, and pilferings." A witness, who testified before the Strickler Commission, happened to be in Topeka at the height of the freebooting season, and "saw a company of men and teams leave town and go in the direction of Tecumseh" for the indefinite purpose of obtaining provisions. Just after the raiding of that village, again in Topeka, "I saw quite a large amount of goods, of various kinds, being divided out among the crowd present. . . . I was invited among others to come up and take part, and finally did select a broom and meal sieve, thinking that should I ever find the proper owners . . . I would pay them." This conscientious mortal actually carried out his purpose, and paid the Tecumseh shop-keeper — an event without parallel in the territorial annals.

The pro-slavery beleaguerment of Lawrence assumed a more serious aspect. In the vicinity several block-houses, well situated as points of rendezvous for operations against the town, had been fortified and garrisoned. There was one of these semi-forts at Franklin; another on Washington Creek, called Fort Saunders; another near Lecompton, known as Fort Titus. These "nests of land-pirates" succeeded in cutting off supplies to such an extent that food became scarce at Lawrence. "The boys lived for days on ground oats," said Captain J. B. Abbott, of the Blue Mound Infantry — "on oatmeal unbolted and unsifted. It was like eating hay." S. W. Eldridge gave the result of special inquiries in the matter of food-supplies before the second Board of Commissioners, appointed by the territorial legislature in 1859 to reopen the matter of claims for losses in the border troubles.

"On the 14th of August, 1856," he said, "or thereabouts, I was delegated to ascertain the quantity of supplies in the town. . . . The soldiers and citizens . . . assembled in Lawrence were reduced to the lowest point of sustenance: many of them for weeks together had nothing to subsist on but green corn, squashes, watermelons, and other vegetables; hundreds had no flour, meal, or meat of any kind for days and days together. Sickness prevailed among those subjected to such a diet. In Lawrence a large proportion of all here assembled were reduced to straits, and as a matter of necessity and self-preservation . . . the surrounding country as well as the city itself had to furnish such means of sustenance as the wants of the hungry and the necessities of the sick demanded. On the day mentioned I went to every store in town and every supposed depot to ascertain what amount of flour or meal was on hand, exclusive of such limited supplies as might be in dwelling-houses for temporary family use; after a thorough search and examination made for the purpose of ascertaining the condition of the town and to calculate how long it could sustain the existing pressure, I found there were but fourteen sacks of flour— I repeat it, only fourteen sacks of flour in town that could have been bought for public or private use; could find no meal, bacon, or beef of any consequence; stocks were exhausted."

Offensive operations were first directed against Franklin. On the night of June 4th a handful of men from Lawrence crept into that village with the stealth of Indians, began a brisk rifle-practice in the darkness, which accomplished nothing beyond killing one of the defenders and wounding several. With the approach of day the raiders beat a successful retreat. But there was a second, a more elaborate and effectual attack. Eighty-one men, accompanied by Lane, fresh from Nebraska, to a point sufficiently near Franklin for agreeable spectatorship, sallied forth, August 13th, after dark, to the attack. The block-house was flanked on either side by a log-cabin; one serving as a post-office, the other as a hotel. Under cover of night the slender army of investment got into position, and summoned the entire compound structure to surrender. The proposition was indignantly declined. Thereupon followed three hours of musketry — to no purpose beyond the hurting of a few men. Tiring of the waste of ammunition, the assailants hit upon the expedient of igniting a load of hay and wheeling it against the house of the Franklin postmaster, " with whom," as pro-slavery writers put it, " a party of Southern men were boarding." The fiery battering-ram succeeded far better than Sharpe's rifles. " When the flames burst forth," an eyewitness relates, " the poltroons cried lustily for quarter." Loopholes became silent, and on an entrance being effected a brass field-piece and a few muskets were found, but no " boarders." Some of the assailants thought that a postmaster who kept the sort of "boarders" found in Franklin should be made an example of. "Oh, don't shoot my husband — don't shoot him," pleaded his wife. "He deserves to die; he's a great villain," somebody blurted out.

"I know it," was the quick retort, "and that's just the reason why I don't want him shot."

Two days afterwards there was a reconnaissance upon Fort Saunders, the intrenched "den of thieves" on Washington Creek. The murder of Major D. S. Hoyt by members of the gang was the immediate occasion of the expedition. Four hundred men, with the cannon captured at Franklin, marched against the post, but the garrison fled on their approach. The block-house stood near a wooded gulch. Finding it deserted, Lane, who was nominally in command, shouted, "The devils are in the ravine — charge." Into the ravine some of the troopers dashed, but found nobody there.

After this easy success the expedition went into camp on Rock Creek. For reasons which he did not take the trouble to explain, Lane, with half a dozen companions, set out at once for Nebraska, though less than a week had elapsed since his arrival from the North. On his departure the command devolved upon Captain Samuel Walker. There was considerable discussion as to what more, if anything, should be done. Captain Walker advised the expedition to disband. A part of the men followed his suggestion and started for Lawrence, while he himself went to the cabin of a friend some miles in the direction of Lecompton. In the evening rumors came to the men who remained on Rock Creek — in the mood of further campaigning — that free-state prisoners at Lecompton were in peril of the gibbet. They resolved to attempt a rescue, and sent a runner to notify the men who were returning to Lawrence. Nothing of importance occurred until the expedition reached a point within six or eight miles of Lecompton, when the advanced guard encountered Colonel Titus and his band, who were given to the habit of night-raids. A skirmish took place, which frustrated the plan for surprising Lecompton. Captain Walker, who had been summoned, persuaded the expedition out of attempting anything more, and went to his own cabin, which was in the neighborhood, for what little of the night remained. The Topeka, Lecompton, and Lawrence stage line passed his door. In the morning the coach stopped, and the driver, taking Walker aside, said, " I've got Titus' wife and two children in the stage. If you want to get the d—d scoundrel, now is your time." Colonel Titus, who had distinguished himself by great activity in harrying free-state people, was probably the most obnoxious border ruffian in the territory. Walker was personally anxious to catch him, and the halted expedition quickly broke camp. Fifty horsemen dashed on in three divisions to surround the stout log-cabin which went by the name of Fort Titus, and cut off communications with Lecompton, while the infantry made what speed they might. Federal troops were plainly in sight, but Major John Sedgwick privately hinted to Walker a few days before that if he wished to nab Titus, and would make quick work of it, his dragoons might not be able to reach the block-house in time to interfere. Walker's horsemen got in position and opened fire with Sharpe's carbines. Titus replied spiritedly, killed one of the assailants, and wounded others. Rifle-balls buried themselves harmlessly in the walls of the cabin, but the arrival of footmen with a six-pound gun put a new face upon affairs. The cannonade was plainly audible in the federal camp scarcely a mile distant. Mrs. Robinson says in her "Kansas" that a stray shot whizzed past the tent where the free-state prisoners were confined. After a brief bombardment a white flag appeared, and the whole garrison of seventeen men capitulated. Colonel Titus presented a sorry sight as he emerged from his battered domicile — coatless, covered with blood, wounded in the hand, face, and shoulder. The assailants fully purposed to kill Titus if they caught him — to such an intensity had the bitterness against him mounted.

"But the cuss," said Captain Walker to the writer, "got me in the right place when he surrendered. He saw the devil was to pay, and made a personal appeal to me. 'You have children,' he pleaded, 'and so have I. For God's sake save my life.' Somehow I could n't resist. We had n't been on good terms at all. Not long before the rascal had sent handbills all about offering a reward of five hundred dollars for my head 'off or on my shoulders.' I noticed one of them plastered upon the side of his cabin while he was talking to me. The boys swore they would kill him. One of them was so obstreperous that I had to knock him down before he would be quiet. At last I got mad and said, 'There Titus sits. If any one of you is brute enough to shoot him, shoot.' Not a man raised his gun."

Two inmates of Fort Titus were killed, and two wounded. Among the free-state men the casualties were one killed and six wounded. Titus was taken to Lawrence, where a fresh rage to dispatch him broke out, but wiser counsels prevailed, and the mob was baffled.

Sunday, August 17th, Governor Shannon, accompanied by Major Sedgwick and Dr. Aristides Rodrigue, postmaster at Lecompton, rode to Lawrence in the interest of peace-making. Then occurred an unwonted spectacle. After negotiations consuming almost the entire day a treaty of peace was consummated, involving an exchange of prisoners and other acts customary only among recognized belligerents standing upon an equal footing; the high contracting parties being on the one hand the federal government in the person of Governor Shannon, and on the other a minority of the sub-committee chosen out of the larger committee appointed at the miscellaneous Topeka convention July 4th — Colonel James Blood and William Hutchinson, correspondent of the "New York Times." In this transaction free-state audacity reached the high-water mark of the Wakarusa war treaty. The United States stipulated to return the cannon captured by Sheriff Jones at Lawrence May 21st, to liberate five or six men arrested for participation in the attack on Franklin, while the minority of the sub-committee agreed to release Titus and his men.

When the treaty had been arranged, Governor Shannon attempted to address a street-mob, composed of recent immigrants from Chicago and elsewhere rather than of residents of Lawrence. There was still another outbreak of furor for shooting Titus. Major Sedgwick, who was not given to alarms nor exaggerations, described the excitement as " almost uncontrollable." When Governor Shannon began to speak a tremendous yell went up from the spectators, and revolvers were pulled out to shoot him. Walker leaped upon a horse, and, drawing his pistols, dashed into the street, shouting, " The first man who insults the governor does it over my dead body! He shan't be insulted. Boys, I'm with you, but he shan't be insulted!" Instant silence followed. Finally some one said, " We'll hear him as Shannon, but not as governor!" The speech then went on.

When Governor Shannon returned to Lecompton he assuredly had occasion for writing the nervous letter which he sent off at once to the department commander: "This place is in a most dangerous and critical situation. . . . We are threatened with utter extermination by a large body of free-state men. . . . I have just returned from Lawrence, where I have been this day with the view of procuring the release of nineteen prisoners that were taken. I saw in that place at least eight hundred men who manifested a fixed purpose to destroy this town. . . . The women and children have been mostly sent across the river, and there is a general panic among the people."

With the treaty at Lawrence, Governor Shannon's official career substantially closed. "I am unwilling to perform the duties of governor of this territory any longer," he wrote President Pierce August 18th. "You will therefore consider my official connection with this territory at an end." He gave mortal offense to the pro-slavery leaders in the latter days of his administration by declining to be a mere sounding-board for their policies. Like Reeder he left the territory in fear for his life. His success had scarcely been greater than that of his predecessor. "Govern the Kansas of 1855 and '56," he once exclaimed in later years, when he had become a resident of Lawrence and territorial unpopularity had modulated into universal respect, — "you might as well have attempted to govern the devil in hell!"

It must not be supposed that pro-slavery people were idle during this interval of freshened free-state activity. Though scarcely taking the lead, they accomplished considerable marauding, which, as usual, consisted in highway robbery and the pillage of cabins interspaced with an occasional murder. In the practical conduct of such matters there is wearisome sameness of method and detail, like

> " A belt of mirrors round a taper's flame."

At Leavenworth there belched forth a perfect chaos of pro-slavery outrages, which held on into the early days of September — a Missouri ruffian making and winning a bet of six dollars against a pair of boots that he would scalp an abolitionist within two hours; William Phillips, the lawyer who fared roughly at the hands of a mob some months before, assassinated,

> " With twenty trenched gashes on his head,
> The least a death to nature,"

one hundred and fifty men, women, and children driven upon river-steamers, leaving all their effects behind as spoils for Captain Emory's eight hundred pro-slavery regulators, who swore they would expel every abolitionist from the region.

But the larger Missouri activities awoke once more. August 16th, the day when Fort Titus was destroyed, Atchison and the pro-slavery junta, in an address to the public, announced the opening of civil war, and urged all friends of law and order " who are not prepared to see their friends butchered, to be themselves driven from their homes, to rally instantly to the rescue." The border roused by this call, which pro-slavery newspapers caught up with various and inflammatory exaggerations, again flew to arms. But the swelling hordes of armed men paused on the Missouri side of the line. Governor Shannon, who had not forgotten his experiences with the militia in the Wakarusa war, declined to give them any legal pretext for crossing it. On the 21st of August Secretary Woodson succeeded him as acting governor, and the halted but now jubilant Missourians prepared to advance. For a third time their ideal executive was in power. "If Mr. Atchison and his party had had the direction of affairs," reported General P. F. Smith, who succeeded Colonel Sumner in command of the department, "they could not have ordered them more to suit his purpose." Woodson bestirred himself to issue a proclamation, which appeared on the 25th, declaring the territory "in a state of open insurrection and rebellion," and calling upon all patriotic citizens to rally for the defense of law and for the punishment of traitors. The pamphleteering cabal of Missouri managers reinforced Woodson's proclamation by a new manifesto. Now an irreparable blow can be delivered. The noble Woodson occupies the executive chair, and there is a clear field. What the character and policy of the next governor may be is a matter of uncertainty. He may prove "a second edition of corruption or imbecility." Such was the energy and dispatch with which preparations were pushed, that Atchison moved into Kansas August 29th and encamped on Bull Creek, fifteen miles north of Osawatomie.

To Dutch Henry's Crossing must be charged much of the havoc and anarchy in which the Kansas of 1856 weltered. That affair was a festering, rankling, envenomed memory among pro-slavery men. It set afoot retaliatory violences, which for a while were successfully matched, and more than matched, by their opponents, but finally issued in a total military collapse of the free-state cause. Now Osawatomie, "the headquarters of Old Brown," lay within easy reach of Atchison's camp. General John W. Reid, with two hundred and fifty men, took in hand the business of destroying it. He approached the town about dawn, August 30th, under pilotage of the Rev. Martin White, whose experiences two weeks before had not served to promote the passive virtues. On the outskirts of the village, the expedition met Frederick Brown, a son of John Brown, whom the divine shot dead — " the ball passing clean through the body."

The entire force available for the defense of Osawatomie was only forty-one men, seventeen belonging to John Brown's band, and the remaining twenty-four divided between the companies of Dr. W. W. Updegraff and Captain Cline. These twoscore men, equal to nothing more than a resolute-show of fight, took post near the town and the line of Reid's approach, among trees and underbrush that skirted the Marais des Cygnes. When the enemy came within range, they opened fire and caused some temporary confusion. The Missourians unlimbered a field-piece and belched grape-shot at the thicket, which crashed harmlessly above the heads of the concealed riflemen. Tiring of the inconsequent bombardment, they charged and brought the skirmish to an abrupt conclusion. Only one practicable course then remained for the handful of men in the thicket, and that was to get out of the way with all possible dispatch. This they did without standing upon the order of their going, and scattered here and there after an every-man-for-himself fashion. Six free-state men were killed, including assassinations before and after the fight, and three wounded. Reid's loss was probably not more than five killed — in his own account of the affair the number is put at two — and a few wounded. Only four cabins escaped the torch, so completely did the raiders accomplish their mission.

There was a retaliatory stir among the free-state clans. Lane, after two weeks' absence in Nebraska or elsewhere, suddenly reappeared. He gathered up the available fighting material about Lawrence and Topeka, amounting to three hundred men, and marched against the camp on Bull Creek. Nothing came of the expedition. The hostile parties approached, surveyed each other, exchanged a few scattering shots, and retired — Atchison toward Missouri, and Lane toward Lawrence.

A strong counter-irritant activity burst forth from Lecompton while Lane was campaigning against Bull Creek. In two days seven cabins belonging to free-state men of the neighborhood were given to the flames. Sheriffs drove a lively traffic in arrests and confiscations. Acting-governor Woodson, eager to make the most of his brief sunshine, ordered Colonel Cooke " to invest the town of Topeka, and disarm all the insurrectionists or aggressive invaders against the organized government of the territory, to be found at or near that point, retaining them as prisoners, subject to the order of the marshal of the territory. All their breastworks, forts, or fortifications should be leveled to the ground." Though the sins of Topeka were just then at their worst, as the maraudings heretofore mentioned were in progress, yet Colonel Cooke flatly declined to execute the order, and was fully sustained by General Smith in his disobedience.

Pro-slavery enterprise at Lecompton led to a formidable expedition against that town. The attacking force was divided into two columns. One column of a hundred and fifty men, led by Colonel J. A Harvey, marched up the north bank of the Kansas River September 4th, and reached its assigned position opposite Lecompton in the evening, to cut off retreat in that direction. Harvey waited anxiously but vainly through a cold, rainy night, listening for the guns of the other column which was to assail the town. Then he concluded the expedition had been abandoned, and returned to Lawrence.

But the main body — three hundred men with two pieces of artillery, commanded by Lane in person, and assigned to the southern route — delayed moving twenty-four hours, and did not reach Lecompton until the afternoon of September 5th. The advent of the belated column threw that town into a spasm of terror. Acting-governor Woodson, territorial officials, and private citizens all appealed to Colonel Cooke for protection. The federal troops encountered the advanced guard of Lane's column, under command of Captain Samuel Walker, about a mile from the village. "What have you come for?" Colonel Cooke demanded. Walker replied that they " came to release prisoners " — men seized for offenses at Franklin and elsewhere — " and to have their rights." Collecting the officers — twenty or thirty responded to his request for audience — Colonel Cooke addressed them at some length on the condition of affairs. He deprecated the demonstration against Lecompton, since the Missourians were dispersing, the prisoners about to be set at liberty, and things generally going in their favor. The conference issued peacefully, and the expedition returned to Lawrence without firing a shot. Lane took no part in the negotiations. When federal dragoons appeared he seized a musket, and stepped into the ranks as a common soldier. Rumors of his presence reached Sheriff Jones, who clamored for his arrest. Woodson proposed to write out a requisition, but on second thought it was concluded to let him alone. Colonel Cooke in his official account lapsed into a forgivable rhetoric of congratulation. " Lecompton and its defenders," he said, " were outnumbered, and evidently in the power of a determined attack. Americans thus stood face to face in hostile array and most earnest of purpose. As I marched back over these beautiful hills, all crowned with moving troops and armed men, . . . I rejoiced that I had stayed the madness of the hour, and prevented, on almost any terms, the fratricidal onslaught of countrymen and fellow-citizens."

Woodson's lease of power ran only three weeks, but in that brief period he drew over the territory the sorrowfulest night that had settled upon it. Free state men, who appealed to him, received very cavalier treatment. Even that distinguished minority of a sub-committee, which captured Governor Shannon, could not tame him. " Your troubles," Woodson wrote September 7th, in reply to a remonstrant communication, are " the natural and inevitable result of the present lawless and revolutionary position in which you have, of your own accord, placed yourselves." The minority of a sub-committee retorted with spirit: "You have left us no alternative but to perish or fight. . . . You have called into the field under the name of militia a set of thieves, robbers, house-burners, and murderers to prey upon the people you have sworn to protect. This is the position you occupy before the country and a just God, and on you, not on us, must rest the responsibility."

The only cheerful event that illuminates Woodson's inhospitable three weeks' incumbency, and for that no credit accrues to him, was the release on bail, September 10th, of Governor Robinson, after an imprisonment of four months. This consummation was reached principally through the unremitting efforts of A. A. Lawrence, who had connections of family affiliation as well as of personal friendship with President Pierce. "Having been the means of sending Dr. Robinson to Kansas," Lawrence wrote August 13th, 1856, "I feel bound to take every measure to secure his release. . . . Mr. Pomeroy, of Kansas, is now in Washington, and has taken from me a letter to Mr. Pierce, with whom he has had several interviews; but in regard to the prisoners he has accomplished nothing." Pomeroy, in his report of negotiations, represents the president as discoursing copiously "about 'disobedience to law, and punishment as the necessary consequence.' I told him there was no treason . . . in Kansas. He was very severe on the 'unauthorized' free-state movement in Kansas. Both of us got hot and showed some passion. I content myself by feeling that I did not show more than he did. . . . On the whole, the interview about the prisoners was very unsatisfactory." The untoward state of negotiations reported by Pomeroy only stimulated Lawrence to more vigorous mediatory efforts, which shortly brought about a hopeful change in the aspect of affairs. "Some action was to have been taken yesterday at their [the cabinet's] meeting," he writes early in September, "and a favorable result may be looked for at once. It is said that a letter was received from a lady — the wife of one of the prisoners, and probably Mrs. Robinson — which put the case in a favorable light, and being read aloud by Mrs. Pierce to her husband it took hold of the feelings of both." These expectations were not disappointed. "I have given such orders concerning Dr. Robinson as will please you," President Pierce informed the Boston friends, and the "Bastile-on-the-prairies" was broken up. Mr. Lawrence's knowledge of the letter, a not inconsiderable factor in effecting the modification of federal policy toward Kansas, which now took place, and in hastening the arrival of Woodson's successor in the territory, was not so slender as his language might seem to imply. He drafted the letter himself, and sent it to Mrs. Robinson, who copied and forwarded it to Mrs. Pierce.

The administration, after much careful search, pitched upon John W. Geary, of Pennsylvania, for the vacant gubernatorial post in Kansas, and he reached Lecompton September 10th, just as the storm raised by Woodson was culminating. He owed his selection to a reputation for great executive ability. The administration perceived that, for political reasons, the disorders in Kansas must be composed, and he was expected to accomplish that feat.

Governor Geary stepped into the border tumult with the assertive bearing of a Titan. Superb and not wholly misplaced was his self-confidence. That he did not idealize the situation is clear, as he took pains to say that it could not be worse. Not only did he fully anticipate success, but the very desperation of affairs fascinated him. November 28th, after more than ten weeks in the territory, he could write to Lawrence, "I am perfectly enthusiastic in my mission."

The policies and measures with which Governor Geary began did him no discredit. "When I arrived here," he confided to a friend, "I perceived at once that, in order to do any good, I must rise superior to all partisan considerations, and be in simple truth the governor of the entire people." He concluded to disband the militia called into the field by Woodson, and all unauthorized bodies of armed men. If there should be need for soldiers, he would enroll actual residents of the territory and muster them into the federal service. Then, in reference to the laws, they must be obeyed until expunged from the statute-book.

The proclamation which was issued ordering the militia to 'disband produced less effect than could have been wished. Lane, it is true, turned his face once more toward the familiar regions of Nebraska without waiting for its appearance. Free-state organizations were inclined to disperse, but hesitated, feeling anxious about the movements of the other side. The governor told them under his breath that they might be leisurely in their obedience.

The Missourians had been busy, since the reconnaissance upon Bull Creek and the destruction of Osawatomie, in fitting out a military force, the most formidable in numbers and equipment that invaded the territory during the border struggle. If Woodson's administration could have been stretched into a few days more of life, the complete conquest of Lawrence and of Kansas would have been assured. Neither inaugurals, nor proclamations, nor explicit orders from Lecompton brought to a halt the pro-slavery leaders. They pushed on to Franklin. Their approach spread so much consternation throughout the region that the governor, accompanied by Colonel Cooke with four hundred dragoons, set out from Lecompton for Lawrence at two o'clock on the morning of September 13th, where he found two or three hundred men, poorly armed and completely disorganized, awaiting attack. The resuscitated fortifications did not find favor with the military folk. "The town has some ridiculous attempts at defenses," said Colonel Cooke, "with two main streets barricaded with earth-works, which I could ride over. . . . Few of the people had arms in their hands." Governor Robinson wrote Mr. Lawrence on the 16th, "I found our people in a bad fix when I came out of confinement. We have no provisions, and not ten rounds of ammunition to a man." The scare was premature, as the Missourians drew off under cover of darkness without pressing an attack. Governor Geary made a reassuring speech, and returned to Lecompton.

But the blow was delayed, not averted. About noon on the 14th couriers, riding at a tearing pace, began to arrive in Lawrence with intelligence that the enemy was advancing in force. The town presented a scene of gloomy, almost helpless confusion. Captain J. B. Abbott was nominally in command, though Governor Robinson, Colonel Blood, Captain Walker, and Captain Cracklin acted with more or less independence of headquarters. Here and there Old John Brown urged his favorite maxim, — "Keep cool and fire low." During the afternoon a troop of the enemy's horse pushed their reconnaissance within range of the few Sharpe's rifles which the free-state men had. A volley checked their advance and sent them back toward Franklin. The Missourians missed their opportunity if they really wished to destroy the town. Lawrence, with its rickety fortifications and its handful of demoralized, poorly armed defenders, was utterly at their mercy. "So far as its inhabitants were concerned," said Governor Geary, "the place was almost in a defenseless condition, and the sacking and taking of it under the circumstances would have reflected no honor upon the attacking party."

At sundown dispatches, apprising the governor of the situation at Lawrence, reached Lecompton. He immediately sent Colonel Johnston with cavalry and artillery to the scene of disturbance, and proceeded thither in person next morning at an early hour. When he arrived the advanced guard of the Missourians was in sight and marching toward the town. Governor Geary and Colonel Cooke hastened to intercept it, and were escorted to headquarters at Franklin. "Here about twenty-five hundred men," said Colonel Cooke, "armed and organized, were drawn up, horse and foot, and a strong six-pound battery."

The governor summoned to a conference the principal leaders — Atchison, Whitfield, Reid, Titus, Jones, and others — and made a speech flavored to the latitude. "Though held in a board house," he said, characteristically magnifying the occasion, "the present is the most important council since the days of the Revolution, as its issues involve the fate of the Union then formed." The governor assured the Missourians that as Democrats they could not afford to destroy Lawrence, and that he could take care of the abolitionists without their help. "He promised us all we wanted," said Atchison, and the council broke up generally satisfied with the governor's plans and purposes. The largest and best appointed force Missouri ever sent into the territory dissolved, and Lawrence was saved, solely by Geary's energy and decision.

The governor pushed the work of pacification effectively. One hundred free-state men — fighting material that should have remained at Lawrence in the lowering aspect of affairs — made an expedition against Hickory Point, Jefferson County. Lane, in his progress toward Nebraska, stopped to chastise a pro-slavery band, which took refuge in log-cabins at that place and bade him defiance. He sent a courier to Lawrence for help, who arrived September 13th, and Colonel J. A. Harvey immediately responded with one hundred or more men. Abandoning his campaign before their arrival, Lane expected to meet and turn back these reinforcements, it is said; but they missed him, pushed on to Hickory Point, which they reached the next forenoon, and fought a miniature battle in which one pro-slavery man was killed. Then followed a treaty. Both parties agreed to retire, and celebrated the conclusion of peace by passing round a demijohn of whiskey. "The drinking was not general on either side," says Captain F. B. Swift. "There was no carousal or jollification, but the consequences were serious. We had been without sleep for thirty-six hours, and without food for twenty-four hours, and without drinkable water all through that hot afternoon's skirmish, so that the whiskey proved too much for those who drank, and it became necessary to go into camp a few miles from the scene of the fight instead of pushing on to Lawrence." Here they were surprised and captured by federal Captain T. J. Wood, taken to Lecompton, and arraigned before Judge Cato, whom Governor Geary found at Franklin serving in the Missouri army. Judge Cato refused bail, and committed eighty-seven prisoners on charges of murder in the first degree. A doleful experience of captivity succeeded. Trials began in October, and resulted variously, the verdicts ranging from acquittal to five years in the penitentiary.

Nor did Governor Geary overlook the judiciary in his efforts for reform. He addressed communications to the judges, calling them to account for the inefficiency of the courts — courts whose restraining and punitive authority over the calamitous course of territorial affairs had been as slight and inappreciable as the sway of drift logs over the Gulf Stream. Criminal offenses of every grade shot up luxuriantly and overshadowed the territory with their noxious umbrage — thefts, arsons, manslaughters, murders — yet the paltry account of criminal convictions footed up two sentences for horse-stealing, three or four for assumption of office, and twice that number for unlicensed selling of liquor. Chief Justice Lecompte replied at length. He claimed that partisan bias had never tarnished his judicial record, and insisted, with some show of reason, that the unhappy, inhospitable times were answerable for the paralysis of the judiciary.

Temporarily Governor Geary succeeded. The territory gradually settled into something like repose. Marauders of every sort, free-state and pro-slavery, who had so successfully established a reign of terror, abandoned the field. After a pleasant tour of observation, which occupied twenty days, finding "the benign influences of peace" everywhere prevalent, the governor appointed Thursday, November 20th, "as a day of general praise and thanksgiving to Almighty God." Department commander Smith shared in his hopefulness. "I consider tranquillity and order," he reported November 11th, "entirely restored in Kansas."

An astute, unpublic movement was also afoot to put the peace on permanent foundations by a transfusion of the territorial government into the Topeka state government. "What if by means of certain influences," Governor Robinson wrote Mr. Lawrence December 21st, "the Topeka constitution should be admitted, the state governor should resign, the territorial governor be unanimously elected, and we should have a peaceable free state? Of course the Senate will need to compromise the matter with the House by providing for submitting the constitution once more to the people. This with an election law by Congress and Governor Geary to execute it would be no very serious objection." The short cut into the Union offered many advantages over competing methods. It involved the resignation of Robinson, the election of Geary in his place, and a little favorable congressional action. Geary advocated the scheme enthusiastically. In his anxiety to elude observation, and not seem to be on too friendly terms with prominent free-state men, he made an appointment to meet Robinson in the attic of a log-cabin at Lecompton, a low, dingy store-room, in which it was impossible to stand upright except directly under the roof-tree. "I am sure my friend Buchanan," said Geary, "will be glad to get out of the scrape in this way." The date of an adjourned meeting of the Topeka legislature was January 6th, 1857. Robinson, who went to Washington to engineer the consolidation project, left behind his resignation as governor. On the first day of the session no quorum appeared. The second brought larger numbers and organization. But at the close of business the federal marshal, who was lying in wait, arrested a dozen members, and the legislature took a recess until the 9th of June. Robinson's mission to Washington did not prosper. The administration was unfriendly, and nothing could be done. In truth, Geary, fast falling under suspicion at Washington, had seen his brightest Kansas days. The confusion and alarm of a reawakened anarchy followed hard upon the pæans of his public thanksgiving.

The territorial legislature began its second session at Lecompton January 12th, 1857, and gave Governor Geary plenty of wormwood to bite upon. Substantially the council of the first legislature reappeared, but a new and undissenting pro-slavery House of Representatives had been elected. Gihon, in his rather intemperate and heavily-colored book, " Governor Geary's Administration in Kansas," describes the legislature as chiefly a vulgar, illiterate, hiccoughing rout — blindly, madly, set on planting slavery securely in the territory. His picture, however, after all abatements and concessions are granted, still retains large elements of historic fidelity. At every turn this brass-throated legislature confronted the governor and his fair-play policy. Not satisfied with the din stirred up in Kansas, pro-slavery leaders sent on men to plot and vociferate in Washington. Locally affairs came to a crisis in the death of a young man by the name of Sherrard — well-born, with generous traits of character, but under the influence of drink or bad advice a desperado. Sherrard failed to secure an office for which he was an applicant, and charged his disappointment to the governor, whom he endeavored to draw into an altercation as an excuse for shooting him. He equipped himself for the encounter with two heavy revolvers and a bowie-knife. Meeting Geary as he left the legislative hall, he began to assail him with abusive words. Geary did not notice the insult. His coolness and self-command probably saved his life. This ineffectual essay at assassination received, perhaps, some inspiration from members of the legislature. In the House of Representatives the Rev. Martin White presented laudatory resolutions, but that body shrank from so formal an encomium.

Governor Geary became alarmed. He applied to the federal commander at Leavenworth for additional troops, and was rebuffed with the announcement that they were otherwise occupied. By this denial of protection, the fact that the administration had abandoned him passed from hint and conjecture into declaration. Free-state men rallied in support of the deserted governor. There began a series of indorsing, panegyric mass-meetings, which reached a tragic conclusion at Lecompton February 18th. Here the usual resolutions friendly to the governor were introduced, which threw Sherrard, who took pains to be present, into a paroxysm of rage. Leaping upon a pile of boards, he delivered a brief but clear and pithy address : "Any man who will indorse these resolutions is a liar, a scoundrel, and a coward." One man in the crowd did indorse them, and said so rather loudly and defiantly. This exhibition of frankness was resented by an appeal to pistols. The fight spluttered and fusilladed for a time without much execution ; then concluded abruptly with the death of the desperado. "I saw Sherrard leap into the air as a bullet struck him in the forehead," said a quiet, pacific spectator. "I don't think anything ever happened in the territory that pleased me so much as the shooting of that man." The fatal pistol shot also dispersed numerous pro-slavery roughs in attendance, and spoiled a pretty programme of mischief which they had sketched.

Governor Geary's extraordinary hopefulness and self-confidence temporarily gave way. The enthusiasm for his mission, which blazed and crackled so brilliantly three months before, now burned feebly and intermittently like a twinkling flame among dying embers. "My only consolation now is," he wrote A. A. Lawrence February 25th, "that my labors are properly appreciated by, and that I have the sympathy of, very many of the best citizens of the Union. . . . How much longer I shall be required to sacrifice pecuniary interests, comfort, and health in what appears almost a thankless work remains to be determined."

The sacrifice continued only a few days, when the governor abandoned the territory very hastily and informally. The end had been predicted from the beginning. "What you say suits us first-rate," said Captain Samuel Walker, an old acquaintance, as he was eloquently expounding his purposes to a little knot of listeners in his office at Lecompton soon after his arrival; "but mark my word, you'll take the underground railroad out of Kansas in six months." "I'll show you," Geary retorted, with the emphasis of a smart blow on the table at which he sat, "and all the d—d rascals that I am governor of Kansas. The administration is behind me." The prophecy was literally fulfilled. About midnight March 10th a heavy knock at his cabin door roused Captain Walker. Great was his surprise to find that the belated visitor was Governor Geary, with two revolvers buckled about his waist, on his way out of the territory. Though agitated and shaken by the perils hounding his trail, his self-assertion was not wholly extinguished. "I'm going to Washington," he informed his host, "and I'll straighten things out."

But Geary found the authorities at Washington deaf to his talk. Nothing remained for him but to print a leave-taking address and make his exit, after a stirring, egotistic, even-handed, almost brilliant six months in Kansas.

CHAPTER X.

THE LECOMPTON STRUGGLE.

The presidential election of 1856, which resulted in a Democratic victory, turned chiefly upon questions brought to the surface by the contest in Kansas. Into all the national conventions — American, Whig, Republican, and Democratic — the territory thrust its disturbing presence. The struggle was remarkable in many respects. Never before did a presidential election turn so largely upon questions of statesmanship, of ethics and the higher law. A variety of influences contributed to this temporary lustration of national politics, but they all radiated from the slavery problem, the compromise of 1850, the tempest in Kansas, and the phenomenal currency of "Uncle Tom's Cabin."

The Democratic campaign dealt heavily in threat and menace. Southern orators and newspapers drew lamentable pictures of the woes that would succeed a Republican triumph. Such an untoward event, they did not scruple to announce, would certainly justify, if it did not absolutely necessitate, a destruction of the Union. James

Buchanan's election as president postponed the date of secession.

Two days after the inauguration of Mr. Buchanan, Chief Justice Taney, of the Supreme Court, delivered the famous Dred Scott decision, the purport of which was that slavery should have the freedom of the public domain — that nobody should meddle with it before the adoption of a state constitution.

President Buchanan, alarmed by the disastrous effect of the Kansas disturbances, immediately cast about for some cloud-compelling successor to Governor Geary. Robert J. Walker, a Pennsylvanian, though long resident in Mississippi — an active, shrewd, tonguey, intellectual, withered little man, experienced and not unsuccessful in public vocations — was selected as the best protagonist within call to invade the perilous nether world of Kansas.

Walker's appointment indicated a change in federal tactics and policy. It was now conceded that Kansas could not with any likelihood be made a slave state, but it was hoped that by a skillful disintegration of existing parties, and the formation of an administration party out of their ruins, it might be made a Democratic state. To this task Walker brought a veteran political astuteness, from which much was expected. That the work of any constitutional convention which might convene should be fully and unqualifiedly submitted to the people for ratification or rejection was a prominent feature of the revised programme, and one to which President Buchanan gave assent.

Meanwhile the new territorial secretary, Frederic P. Stanton — an able, scholarly lawyer who had served ten years in Congress as representative from Tennessee — proceeded to Kansas in advance of the governor. He immediately issued an address in which the policy of the new administration was briefly set forth. The address did not have an enthusiastic reception. Pro-slavery adherents viewed with apprehension the fact that the secretary seemed to have a mind of his own, while the other side preferred to withhold their approval until the new régime should have passed successfully a period of probation.

A pro-slavery constitutional convention had long been preparing. The movement began in the first territorial legislature, which submitted the question of its expediency to the people in October, 1856. At the polls there was a favorable verdict. The next legislature passed a bill authorizing the election of delegates June 15th, 1857. Governor Geary vetoed the measure, because it failed to provide that the people should pass upon the proposed constitution at the polls, and because he regarded it impolitic "for a few thousand people, scarcely sufficient to make a good county," to set up an establishment of their own; but his effort to check the legislature was like trying to drain an Irish bog with a sponge. The census, prefatory to this election, turned out to be a very imperfect affair. Apportionment of delegates depended on population, but nobody could vote whose name did not appear in the registry lists. In sixteen only out of the thirty-four organized counties was there any registration, and the census tables showed still larger gaps. For this condition of things the pro-slavery party was not wholly responsible. Free-state men perplexed the enumeration by embarrassments of omission and commission, and were not ill pleased at the starved and skeleton returns. Unfortunately, Secretary Stanton, fresh upon the ground and not fully cognizant of the situation, apportioned delegates for the convention on the basis of the defective census. Here was another firebrand flung upon free-state straw. The territory was again in a flame. After much talk and some fruitless negotiation, the anti-slavery party concluded to let the election go by default. "Men who could expend thousands, and travel many a weary mile to fill Kansas with rifles," said Representative Hughes, of Indiana, "could not walk across the street to vote." The election passed off tamely. Less than one fourth of the nine thousand two hundred and fifty-one registered voters took part in it. The material and animus of the convention were completely satisfactory to the pro-slavery party.

Governor Walker reached Lecompton May 26th, and gave his inaugural to the public the next day. It was a diffuse, reverberating, able exposition of the new policy which had been agreed upon in Washington. Shortly after he made a tour of observation and of exposition. By conferences with the people, public and private, he hoped to convince them that his purposes were pacific and honorable, and that their interests lay in discarding every form of controversy except "the peaceful but decisive struggle of the ballot-box." He was in Topeka June 6th, and made a cogent, unequivocal, manly address. In three days a session of the state legislature, adjourned from the disconsolate January meeting, would begin. Should the state legislature enact a code of laws and attempt to put it in force, as some free-state men still urged, there could be, in the opinion of Governor Walker, only one issue — "absolute, clear, direct, and positive collision between that legislature and the government of the United States." In the most explicit and reduplicative language he declared that henceforth the people of Kansas were to manage their own concerns. If the forthcoming convention, auditors asked, should decline to submit the new constitution to the people, what then? "I will join you, fellow citizens," the governor replied, "in opposition to their course. And I doubt not that one much higher than I, the chief magistrate of the Union, will join you."

Walker tarried in Topeka to watch the legislature. This session, like that of July 4th, 1856, was yoked with a mass convention which began at an early hour June 9th, and did not dissolve until eight o'clock at night. The convention undertook the same functions of coaching and surveillance as its prototype. It wrestled with the perennial question whether the Topeka government should be placed squarely on its feet, or merely take such measures as would keep a breath of life in the organization without clashing with the territorial authorities. Though the discussions frothed and declaimed, the conclusions were of a mild, do-nothing order. Walker with all his astuteness did not wholly fathom the tremendous oratory of the convention. It was craftily handled so as to impress him with the conviction that unless the anti-slavery folk should receive fair treatment, unless constitutional conventions should remand their instruments to the polls for final adjudication, revolutionary convulsions would certainly break out. The convention accomplished its mission. Walker wrote his superiors in Washington that had it not been for his intervention "the more violent course would have prevailed, and the territory immediately involved in a general and sanguinary civil war."

When the legislature assembled no quorum appeared. This fact was carefully hidden from the impressionable Walker. Governor Robinson, finding the shrewd scheme of merging the territorial in the state government impracticable, recalled his resignation at the instance of the legislature, and read a message before that unpopulous body, which once more adjourned after transacting a little harmless amateur business.

In addition to the constitutional convention an event of no secondary importance would take place in the autumn. That event was the election of a new territorial legislature, preparations for which filled the summer with tumult. The law and order gentry, who now called themselves "National Democrats," gathered at Lecompton early in July, to make nominations and lay plans for the campaign. Forty-three delegates were in attendance, who put forth a series of moderate resolutions compared with the highly seasoned viands which the border palate heretofore demanded. Some fire-eater presented a resolution in convention, asking Congress to receive the territory into the Union under the forthcoming constitution, whether the people would be allowed to vote upon it or not; but the resolution was effectually disposed of by a vote of forty-two in opposition to one in the affirmative. Governor Walker, who seldom declined invitations to make a speech, delivered an address that was favorably received.

In free-state quarters the question now began to be agitated, whether the policy of non-participation in territorial elections did not need revising. Governor Walker's vehement pledges of fair play produced an impression. The mischief of a vicious census could not be completely undone, yet with a square-dealing executive success was possible in the face of it. Henry Wilson, of Massachusetts, visited the territory for the purpose of urging upon free-state men the imperative necessity of their making an effort to capture the legislature, and offered to raise funds among Eastern friends to meet the campaign expenses. In these views he was heartily supported by Governor Robinson, who had always been ready to meet the pro-slavery party at the polls whenever an honest count of ballots could be assured.

A series of conventions now began which rivaled in noise and frequency the series of 1855. Nearly two hundred delegates, representing the whole territory, assembled at Topeka July 15th. Though the special business of this gathering was to nominate certain state government officers, that did not preclude general discussions and the adoption of resolutions which freely abused the "bogus" legislature, authorized Lane to put the militia on a war-footing, and called another convention at Grasshopper Falls to settle the question of voting or not voting.

August 26th the free-state people met at Grasshopper Falls. There the unanimity which prevailed at Topeka two months before gave way. A minority of indignant, impracticable radicals, like Redpath and Conway, denounced the proposition to contest the election for members of the territorial legislature as "a back-down in principle and unpromising in practical results." The ignominies of stultification they set forth in dark, repulsive colors, but to no purpose, as the convention went unanimously and demonstratively against them. It was the judgment of the convention that the free-state party should make an attempt to get possession of the legislature. On the point of consistency, little can be said in defense of this conclusion. But the convention agreed with Governor Robinson that "men who are too conscientious and too honorable to change their tactics with a change of circumstances are too conscientious for politics."

The convention did not regard its work complete without the preparation of an address to the people. It confided this duty to a committee of fourteen, which, in spite of its own bulk that ought to have been reassuring, surveyed the future with the bilious eyes of a Jeremiah. "We frankly avow ourselves," said the committee, "not sanguine of success." Voters disfranchised in many counties; threats of invasion from Missouri; distrust of Governor Walker; "a hellish system of districting and apportionment;" election judges mostly "border ruffians of the deepest dye"—such were some of the calamities that oppressed the fourteen and saddened their vision.

Prophets of evil misread the signs of the times. The 5th of October, on which members of the territorial legislature were elected, proved to be a red-letter day for freedom in Kansas. Probably the fact that federal troops were sent into no less than fourteen precincts, with orders to prevent all illegal voting, discouraged invasions from Missouri. The election was unprolific in tumults. Even the redoubtable town of Kickapoo did not get beyond a rather prosy brawl. At two points extensive frauds were attempted. McGee County was then an Indian reservation, and therefore not open to settlement. It contained a very sparse white population. At the June election only fourteen votes were cast. Yet in October twelve hundred and sixty-six pro-slavery ballots purported to have been polled there. The town of Oxford, Johnson County, made a still more flagrant showing. This paltry hamlet "of six houses, including stores," reported sixteen hundred and twenty-eight votes.

The Oxford and McGee returns brought on a crisis. If they should be counted, the legislature would remain pro-slavery; if they should be rejected, it would pass into control of the opposition. A little inspection showed them to be clumsily executed forgeries. October 19th Walker and Stanton issued a proclamation throwing out the Oxford returns on the ground of technical informalities, and in three days those from McGee fared in the same way.

This action made a tempest among the National Democrats. On the 23d they held an indignation meeting at Lecompton, and gave vent to their sentiments in seventeen furious but idle resolutions. Then Judge Cato came to the rescue with a mandamus, ordering the governor and secretary to issue certificates of election to the pro-slavery candidates from Douglas and Johnson counties; but the judge had no better success than the mass-meeting. Other resources failing, Sheriff Jones, who was one of the excluded candidates, attempted to get his credentials by violence. Striding into Stanton's office with a companion, he demanded that the papers should be at once filled out; but he found the secretary could not be intimidated. This gross outrage stirred up excitement. On the evening of the succeeding day a company of mounted free-state men called upon Stanton, and assured him that if it would be a convenience to have Jones put out of the way, and if the authorities would wink at the affair, he should be strung up before morning. Their services were politely declined. Jones and his confederates escaped with a light and whimsical penalty. The affair threw the excitable governor into a great rage. He was sick at the time, and could do nothing. On recovering, he made a demonstration upon what he called the enemy. Arming himself with a small "pepper-box" pistol, he began a tour of objurgation. "Come along," he said to Stanton, "let us go to see the Bengal tigers." And this puny incarnation of a tremendous choler — lapse of time inflaming rather than cooling his passion — visited the dens and drinking saloons of Lecompton, and denounced their inmates with a savage energy that Timon of Athens could not have outdone. The governor returned from his circumnavigation of invective, happy in the thought that for once the "Bengal tigers" had heard themselves described in faithful and unmistakable English.

The proclamations of October 19th and 22d dashed all schemes of building a victorious administration party out of existing political organizations. The animosities, to which they imparted large and tempestuous vitality, defeated the latest, craftiest strategy of the administration. These consequences, which wrote failure in large letters across their personal and special mission to Kansas, were not hidden from Walker and Stanton. They issued the crucial proclamations, which conceded to the free-state party nine of the thirteen councilmen and twenty-four of the thirty-nine representatives, with the keenest appreciation of all they implied — issued them in honorable fulfillment of public pledges that the polls should be protected.

The pro-slavery party made one more desperate effort to stay their foundering fortunes. Only in the direction of the constitutional convention, of which they had absolute control, were there signs of promise. That body, representing a small minority of actual voters in the territory, gathered at Lecompton September 7th. Forty-four members in a total of sixty responded to their names. John Calhoun, surveyor general of the territory, was elected president, with the usual complement of subordinate officials, including a chaplain. Some members of the convention regarded the employment of a man to pray foolish, but a majority believed it "would have a good effect on the country," however bootless it might be locally. The convention remained in session four days, which were principally devoted to organization, and then adjourned until October 19th. The special motive for delay was the approaching election for members of the legislature, the issue of which would, in large measure, mould its policy.

Lecompton was in an uproar October 19th. Thither on that day flocked hundreds of free-state men, inspired by the thought that "nothing is so difficult for a scoundrel to do as to meet the clear, honest gaze of the man whom he is trying to wrong." So they thronged Lecompton to look into the eyes of members of the convention. What they might have done in addition to this personal scrutiny, had not the appearance of the Walker-Stanton proclamation sweetened their temper, is not entirely certain.

The demonstration impressed the convention deeply. For three days in succession no quorum appeared; but on the fourth day a sufficient number of absentees for the transaction of business was secured. The convention found itself tangled in the meshes of a very perplexing task. It had essayed to saddle a pro-slavery constitution upon a community overwhelmingly anti-slavery. The constitution which it made was well enough, except in the matter of slavery, in regard to which it took extreme ground. "The right of property," it announced, "is before and higher than any constitutional sanction, and the right of the owner of a slave to such slave and its increase is the same and as inviolable as the right of any property whatever." This doctrine, as Mr. Douglas said, would deprive the State of all authority to abolish or prohibit slavery.

But it was plain as a pike-staff that the people would make short work of the new constitution if they should be allowed to vote upon it. In this unhappy situation, it only remained to devise some make-shift in the place of unqualified submission, or abandon the fight. A part of the convention, under the lead of Judge Rush Elmore, advocated full submission, let the result be what it might, but were voted down. Then came a compromise. The entire constitution should not go before the people, but only the slavery article. Ballots might be cast indorsed "Constitution with slavery" or "Constitution with no slavery." Should the first proposition carry, slavery with restricted emancipation possibilities would be definitely planted in the State. If the second proposition prevailed, then "slavery shall no longer exist in the State of Kansas, except that the right of property in slaves now in this territory shall in no manner be interfered with." Free-state men commonly interpreted this qualification of the no-slavery alternative as utterly foreclosing all hope of success on their part. A no-slavery victory must not disturb the slavery which had already secured a foothold in the commonwealth. The alternative presented " was like submitting to the ancient test of witchcraft, where if the accused, upon being thrown into deep water, floated he was adjudged guilty, taken out, and hanged; but if he sunk and was drowned he was adjudged not guilty — the choice between the verdicts being quite immaterial." When legitimately interpreted, however, the proviso would probably yield no such sense as free-state exegesis found in it. This point was pretty conclusively established by Senator Bayard, who contended that the right of property vested in existing slaves, and not in their unborn children. That construction, he maintained, was forced by the general intent and scope of the declaration, " Slavery shall no longer exist in the State of Kansas."

The compromise divided the convention, in

which there was a strong faction that protested against every sort of submission. "This is a grand humbug," said a furious Riley County delegate, echoing free-state expositions of the no-slavery alternative. "It is not fair. . . . I tell you this scheme of swindling submission will be the blackest page in your history, and we will never hear the end of it. We won't make much capital out of it, I tell you. Those Black Republicans will get to the bottom of it so quick that you'll never cease to hear from this dodge. . . . I'm opposed to submission. I tell you these Republicans will vote down both of them. . . . The only consistent, honest, straightforward way is to make our constitution and send it on to Congress. I believe Congress will admit us. If it will not, then let our defeat lie at its door. This humbugging, dodging way I do not believe in. I want to be open and above board." Another Riley County implacable declaimed in the same strain. He said the compromise carried "falsehood on its face in letters of brass. . . . It is a lie, cheat, and swindle. I'm a pro-slavery man. I want to make Kansas a slave state. . . . The trick was concocted by free-state Democrats. If they pass this majority report they will make Kansas not only a free but a Republican state. . . . The South has reached a crisis in her fortunes and must have Kansas. . . . Make Kansas a slave state and the abolition element will flee out of it."

The compromise was carried after a stubborn fight, and the convention dissolved November 7th. John Calhoun issued proclamations designating December 21st as the day for voting on the slavery article, and January 4th, 1858, for election of officers under the new constitution. The convention, contemptuously ignoring Governor Walker, authorized its president to take such measures as might be necessary to carry its purposes into effect.

The sequel at Lecompton again stirred the embers. Free-state men had taken comparatively little interest in the convention during its earlier stages, as they intended to dispatch at the polls any constitution that might be put together. Now, to their astonishment, they found that only a fragment of it would be submitted, and to that fragment they applied the fallacious witch-test construction. The enemy were manœuvring to turn their flank and convert the October victory into a barren triumph. Mass-meetings gathered here and there in which the "robber" convention was cursed in copious Thersitean dialect. Radicals demanded that now, after so many empty threats, the state government should be made something more than a name. Among these anti-Lecompton gatherings, the largest and most important met at Lawrence on the 2d of December. The one hundred and thirty delegates in attendance included nearly all the prominent free-state leaders.

Governor Robinson presided. Impassioned harangues evoked a vast amount of enthusiasm. Resolutions were adopted alive with hostility to the new constitution: "Appealing to the God of Justice and Humanity, we do solemnly enter into league and covenant with each other that we will *never*, under any circumstances, permit the said constitution, so framed and not submitted, to be the organic law for the State of Kansas, but do pledge our lives, our fortunes, and our sacred honor in ceaseless hostility to the same."

Amidst the general confusion and casting about somebody bethought himself of the recently captured and fumigated legislature as a possible source of deliverance, and suggested that it should be called together. What it could accomplish was uncertain, but it would not, at all events, fail to make itself useful. Governor Walker had set out in chagrin for Washington — his astute schemes overset, execrated by pro-slavery men, deserted by the administration. His departure shifted all executive responsibility upon Secretary Stanton, who was sorely beset on all sides to convene the legislature. That step he finally took, though foreseeing that it would be followed by his dismissal from office, of which he received formal notification December 16th.

The territorial legislature, "dipped into the turbid waters of Black Republicanism" and made clean, assembled at Lecompton December 7th.

There was a roistering free-state jubilee that day in the old pro-slavery stronghold. From all parts of the territory came throngs of people to participate in the festivities, which comprised speeches, resolutions, groans for the "Lecompton swindle," and cheers for the Topeka constitution. So powerful were outside attractions that they thinned the legislature out of a quorum. It could do nothing until the hurrahing pother subsided and the rout dispersed. As a defense against pro-slavery movements, the legislature very sensibly ordered an unreserved submission of the constitution to the people on the 4th of January. A third ballot was added to those already authorized, indorsed "Against the constitution formed at Lecompton."

The Lawrence mass-meeting of December 2d pronounced the elections which the Lecompton convention ordered to be unworthy of free-state countenance. In regard to the election of December 21st, when only pro-slavery voters went to the polls, the wisdom of its sentence was unquestioned. But the January matter was not so clear. An impression got abroad that the mass-meeting had blundered; that it would be prudent — an anchor cast to the windward — to furnish the Lecompton constitution with an equipment of free-state officials as a precaution against possible contingencies. Therefore the convention was reassembled on the 23d of December to review in part its proceedings. At this later session two parties appeared. One faction defended and the other combated the proposition to put a state ticket in the field. To take possession of a possible state government, not for purposes of establishing but of destroying it, it was urged, was a simple dictate of prudence. The radicals rang changes upon the inconsistency of such a course for free-state men, after calling the "Eumenides and all the heavenly brood" to witness that they would never recognize the "Lecompton swindle" in any shape, and they carried the day.

The defeated party immediately resolved itself into "a bolter's convention," named a full ticket of state officers, and elected them. Against the Lecompton constitution, for which anti-slavery officers were provided, ten thousand two hundred and twenty-six votes were polled. That vote, though it did not escape irregularities of form, showed incontrovertibly the drift of public sentiment in the territory.

In the mean time a new acting-governor had appeared in the territory — General John W. Denver, a Virginian and a lawyer, well reputed for successful service in the Mexican war and in California. At the time of his appointment he held the office of Indian Commissioner, was visiting Kansas, and domiciled with Secretary Stanton. "I had been repeatedly solicited," said Denver, "to take the position, but I did not want it. I used to live on the border before Kansas was thrown open to settlement. I chummed with Senator Atchison at Platte City, and knew personally all the leading men of western Missouri. I was afraid, if I accepted the post, that they might ask of me what I should not wish to do." The more conservative free-state sentiment Denver conciliated at the beginning of his term of office, by announcing that he should carry out in good faith the policy of his predecessor.

The elections appointed by the Lecompton constitutional convention had a long appendix of investigations, which made havoc with the original returns. A legislative committee examined them, and reported that the alleged vote December 21st, of six thousand two hundred and twenty-six for the constitution with slavery, contained twenty-seven hundred and twenty fraudulent ballots, which were cast mostly at Kickapoo, Delaware Crossing, and Oxford. In the contest for state officers, January 4th, the number of fraudulent ballots fell off to twenty-four hundred and fifty-eight in a pro-slavery vote for governor of six thousand five hundred and forty-five.

A curious history attaches to these election returns. The legislative investigating committee were anxious to secure them. John Calhoun, surveyor general and president of the constitutional convention, taking alarm at the situation, prudently left the territory. The coveted ballots were supposed to be in the hands of L. A. McLean, his chief clerk, who appeared before the committee and testified that he had forwarded them to Calhoun. February 1st a messenger reached the cabin of Captain Samuel Walker, then sheriff of Douglas County, bringing information from General William Brindle that the returns were secreted under a wood-pile near McLean's office. Arming himself with a warrant which instructed him to "diligently search for the said goods and chattels," Walker appeared in Lecompton the next morning and apprised McLean of his business. "You are welcome to search," he responded. "I have sent the returns to Calhoun. They are not here." "I think you are mistaken," said the sheriff. "I know where they are." "Where?" "Under the wood-pile." "I forbid you to search," McLean rejoined, and began some warlike demonstrations, which were speedily quelled. Walker dug up the returns, concealed in a candle-box, and carried them to Lawrence. Naturally the investigating committee decided to recall Chief Clerk McLean, who consulted Sheriff Jones as to whether he should obey the subpœna. "I told him to come down and face the music; he said he was going to Missouri; I saw him start toward the river . . .; I think he got a mule from some one on the road."

President Buchanan, retreating from his pledges to Governor Walker in obedience to Southern dictation, transmitted, February 2d, the Lecompton constitution to Congress, accompanied by a special message, in which he urged that Kansas should be speedily admitted to the Union, though the instrument had not been fully submitted to the people. Of the actual condition of Kansas he was not ignorant. Soon after his arrival in the territory Governor Denver forwarded to Washington by special messenger a long communication fully setting forth the state of affairs, and urgently counseling the president not to present the Lecompton constitution to Congress at all, but to advocate the passage of an enabling act and let the people make a fresh start. Mr. Buchanan was impressed by the letter. He said "that he was very sorry that he had not had the information sooner, because he had prepared his message in relation to the Lecompton constitution, and had shown it to several senators, and could not withdraw it."

When the Lecompton constitution reached Washington, the general reputation of Kansas in pro-slavery circles was greatly depressed. "The whole history of Kansas is a disgusting one from beginning to end," said Senator Hammond, of South Carolina. "I have avoided reading it as much as I could." Senator Biggs, of North Carolina, confessed to "misgivings whether the people of Kansas are of that character from which we may hope for an enlightened self-government." Representative Anderson, of Missouri, fell little behind the North Carolinian in unfriendliness of opinion: " No part of our Union has ever before been settled by such an ungovernable, reckless people." Mr. Atkins, representative from Tennessee, described free-state immigrants as "struggling hordes of hired mercenaries, carrying murder, rapine, and conflagration in their train." But Senator Alfred Iverson topped all competitors in screechy, fishwife violence of phrase; " Why, sir, if you could rake the infernal regions from the centre to the circumference and from the surface to the bottom, you could not fish up such a mass of infamous corruption as exists in some portions of Kansas!" An estimate of the Kansas migration, wholly antipodal and dissenting, may be found in the "Christian Examiner" for July, 1855. " It was reserved," says the writer, " to the present age, and to the present period, to afford the sublime spectacle of an extensive migration in vindication of a principle. . . . Neither pressure from without, nor the beckonings of ambition, nor the monitions of avarice, control the great Kansas migration. . . . In the unselfishness of the object lies its claim . . . to the highest place in the history of migrations!"

Arguments in defense of the Lecompton measure — the debate filled more than nine hundred pages of the " Congressional Globe " — made the most of technicalities. Samuel A. Smith, representative from Tennessee, stood almost alone in advocacy of its claims to popular approval. " The whole people of Kansas," he said, " are in favor of the admission of the State under the Lecompton constitution," except "Lane with his marauders, his murderers, and his house-burners " — an insignificant gang that did not "number more than eight hundred." Foolish talk of this sort found little favor. For the constitution there was a single tenable line of defense — that it was the work of a legitimate convention which had observed all indispensable formalities. The successive stages of its history were elaborately rehearsed. The constitution dates back to the first territorial legislature which submitted to the people the question of calling a constitutional convention. Fifteen months afterwards — a period ample for mature consideration — they respond favorably at the polls. After a lapse of three months the question reaches the second territorial legislature, which "bows to the will of the people and provides for the election of delegates." Then between the legislative sanction and the election of delegates four months intervene. Before the delegates meet and enter upon their duties a further delay of three months occurs. They submit a single but vital article of the constitution to the people for acceptance or rejection, December 21st, and they ratify it almost unanimously. "When we view these proceedings of the people of Kansas," said Senator Polk, of Missouri, "in forming for themselves a state constitution, in the successive stages of their development, not from the low arena of partisan strife and passion, but from the elevated standpoint of a patriot, ... what a majestic spectacle is presented — the people marching forward in stately pace to the accomplishment of their purposes with a movement as grand as the lapse of the tide or the travel of a planet!"

Though there could be no real question that the Lecompton constitution was not " the act and deed" of the people of Kansas; though Douglas and other Northern Democrats fought it, yet it passed the Senate March 23d by a vote of thirty-three to twenty-five. In the House the Lecompton constitution failed. There a substitute was carried, known as the " Crittenden-Montgomery bill," which referred it back to the people. Should they ratify it, then Kansas would be proclaimed a state within the Union without further ado. If they voted it down, they were to call a new convention and make a constitution that pleased them better. The sharp-eyed " Democratic Review " did not fail to call attention to the fact that in espousing the Crittenden-Montgomery bill Republican congressmen accepted the doctrine of popular sovereignty. It was the same doctrine which they stigmatized in 1854–56 " as an outrage upon public honor, ... as a departure from justice and from the original policy of the national government."

The Senate rejected the substitute, and there was resort to a committee of conference: J. S. Green, R. M. T. Hunter, and W. H. Seward representing the Senate; W. H. English, A. H. Stephens, and W. A. Howard the House. This committee — Seward and Howard dissenting — elaborated a novel measure called the "English bill." An ordinance accompanied the Lecompton constitution which asked the cession of land-grants which were much larger than any other state had ever received on its entrance into the Union. In these land-grants the committee suggested a change. They proposed to reduce the twenty-three million acres of land claimed to about one sixth of that amount. The fate of the constitution they linked with that of the land-grants. To accept the modified ordinance was accounted by some curious doctrine of imputation as approval of the constitution, and at once clothed Kansas with the functions of a state. Rejection of it, on the other hand, involved not only rejection of the constitution, but continuance of territorial conditions until a population of ninety-four thousand should be reached. The majority report, which stoutly denied that any such thing as submission of the Lecompton constitution to the people lurked in this unhackneyed device, was a very excellent piece of quibbling. The constitution we accept, its validity we acknowledge; it was urged, but we do not like the ordinance. We are willing to waive the population rule, provided the vexatious business can be concluded. If Kansas should reject our overture, it may remain a territory until better manners are learned and a larger and more stable population is obtained.

Though objections were plenty — charges of unwarrantable discrimination, of intervention with inducements to control results, of violence to the principle of popular sovereignty — yet the English bill gave the people of Kansas opportunity to put their heel on the odious Lecompton instrument, and that consideration carried it through Congress. The vote of the Senate stood, ayes, thirty-one; nays, twenty-two — of the House, ayes, one hundred and twelve; nays, one hundred and three. Pro-slavery partisans espoused it; not all of them heartily. "I confess my opinion was," said Senator Hammond, of South Carolina, in a speech October 29th, 1858, at Barnwell Court House, "that the South herself should kick that [Lecompton] constitution out of Congress. But the South thought otherwise." In Kansas the question came to a decision August 2d. Thirteen thousand and eighty-eight votes were cast — eleven thousand three hundred of them against the English proposition.

CHAPTER XI.

JAYHAWKING.

GEOGRAPHICALLY the capital events of Kansas history in the territorial days covered a narrow space. With Lawrence for a centre, the revolution of a radius thirty miles in length would include them all. Yet the Southeast, embracing Bourbon, Linn, and Miami counties, though contributing little to the ultimate results of the struggle, is not destitute of picturesque and sanguinary exhibitions of border lawlessness.

At the outset, and for a considerable period, proslavery settlers had a comparatively clear field in the Southeast, as it lay off the line of Northern immigration. "It has occurred to our friends," a correspondent of the Kansas Association of South Carolina wrote from Platte City, Missouri, "that it would be better, as a matter of policy, and as being more Southern — more agreeable to the Southern emigrants — that a good portion of them would settle south of the Kansas River. By this means we will secure the southern half of the territory before it is filled by abolitionists; the northern half will be saved by Missourians. . . . I would suggest that you should seek, as far as possible, to induce all who have a small number of slaves to come out. To such, this is a peculiarly desirable country, and they need have no fear of slaves escaping." Fort Scott — a federal military post from 1842 to 1854 — was the principal town of the Southeast, and began to have some reputation as a border-ruffian stronghold in 1856. The arrival of armed "settlers" from the South laid the foundation of that reputation which was largely increased afterwards by accessions from Lecompton.

As abolitionists were not plenty in the Southeast, the Southerners at first found their opportunities for usefulness rather limited. But in August, 1856, the monotony was broken by news of General Reid's intended attack upon Osawatomie. Ambitious to share in the glory of destroying that town, a hundred and fifty men collected at Fort Scott and marched northward. When encamped in Liberty township, eight or ten miles south of Osawatomie, they were surprised by a hundred free-state guerrillas just as they thought of dining. So rude and uncivil an invitation to fight could not be accepted, and the company fled in the greatest confusion, "leaving," as an eye-witness says, "their baggage and most of their horses, boots, coats, vests, hats, and a dinner ready cooked," not to mention a black flag on which was inscribed in red letters "Victory or Death." The fugitives mostly fled toward Fort Scott, where they arrived in the middle of the night, fully persuaded that the abolitionists were at their heels. The town was roused. Panic-stricken men and women, believing it would be given over to fire and sword, wildly escaped anywhere chance or instinct might lead. Quite a large company took refuge in a cabin at considerable distance from the village. Soon rumors came that the work of slaughter and pillage had actually begun, and a scene of indescribable confusion followed. Englishmen, harried by Northern pirates, found consolation in the petition, "Good Lord, deliver us from the Danes;" and why should not the aid of Heaven be invoked against Northern abolitionists? A season of prayer was suggested, and the ensuing devotions had no lack of fervor or unanimity. The alarm proved groundless. When day dawned the town was found to be safe, and no abolitionists could be seen.

During the autumn of 1856 Indian Agent G. W. Clarke, with a picked-up gang of Missourians, overran portions of Linn and Miami counties into which considerable Northern population had sifted. He threw down fences, destroyed crops, seized horses and cattle, burnt a few cabins, and occasionally drove an obnoxious settler out of the country. "Clarke's company," said one of the victims, "took everything they wanted, and I think they took what they did not want, to keep their hands in — had ribbons on their hats, side combs in their hair, and other things they did not need." An old soldier gave his impressions of the raid before the Strickler Commission: "I was in the Black Hawk war, and have fought in the wars of the United States, and have received two land-warrants from Washington City for my services, but I never saw anything so bad and mean in my life as I saw under General Clarke."

Free-state men in the Southeast, comparatively isolated, having little communication with Lawrence, and consequently almost wholly without check, developed a successful if not very praiseworthy system of retaliation. Confederated at first for defense against pro-slavery outrages, but ultimately falling more or less completely into the vocation of robbers and assassins, they have received the name — whatever its origin may be — of jayhawkers.[1]

[1] In Bartlett's *Dictionary of Americanisms* jayhawker is said to be a corruption of "Gay Yorker," a phrase applied to an eminent exemplar of the business, Colonel Jennison. A more plausible derivation traces the word to a dare-devil Irishman, by the name of Pat Devlin. One morning in the summer of 1856, a neighbor is said to have met him returning from a foraging expedition, laden with spoils. "Where have you been, Pat?" "Jayhawking," was the reply. "Jayhawking? What's that?" "Well," continued the philological bush-ranger, "in the old country we have a bird called the jayhawk, which kind o' worries its prey. It seemed to me as I was riding home that this was what I had been doing." As the evidence now stands, whatever linguistic honors accrue from the word "jayhawking" belong to Pat.

JAYHAWKING.   241

The best known leader in the jayhawking episode is James Montgomery. Born in Ohio, a resident of Kentucky and Missouri for seventeen years, he reached Linn County in August, 1854, and thenceforth was a prominent figure in the affairs of the Southeast. He was courageous, an effective talker — a qualification that served him to good purpose — not devoid of craft and stratagem, but without large mental or executive force.

Montgomery's tactics after Clarke's raid were characteristic. To obtain a list of the men concerned in it he visited Missouri in the disguise of a teacher searching for a school, which he succeeded in obtaining and actually taught for two weeks — long enough to get the information he wished. That secured, the school suddenly closed, and the school-master soon reappeared transformed into a guerrilla chief. Twenty of the ex-raiders were captured and pretty thoroughly spoiled of money, weapons, and horses.

Though months of disorder followed, yet, with the exception of the Marais des Cygnes massacre, Clarke's raid was the last considerable dash from Missouri into the territory until the outbreak of the war for the Union. In these aggressions jayhawkers seem to have taken the lead, and they established a freebooting reputation that fairly intimidated pro-slavery adherents. The accounts of marauding incursions from Missouri, which appeared in contemporary prints, were mostly canards circulated by jayhawkers as an excuse for their own depredations. They occasionally dispatched a messenger to Lawrence with a budget of exaggerated or manufactured pro-slavery outrages, to keep alive their reputation as struggling, self-denying, afflicted patriots.

Disturbances continued intermittently until December, 1857, when claim difficulties of more than ordinary consequence occurred. A delegation representing the jayhawking interest had been in Lawrence to enlist Lane in their cause, but he was absorbed with agitations against the Lecompton constitution, and could give them no personal assistance. However, a small company from the vicinity of Lawrence, led by Captain J. B. Abbott, returned with the messengers, for the purpose of investigating affairs and of lending any assistance to free-state men that might be possible or advisable. Soon after their arrival in the vicinity of Fort Scott some land dispute came to a crisis. A Missourian was charged with "jumping" the claim of a free-state settler. Whether that was actually the case, or whether an enterprising jayhawker wished to drive him out of the territory as a step preparatory to seizing his property, is not wholly clear. At all events, the Missourian was arrested and arraigned before an impromptu squatters' court, the officers of which were mostly drawn from the Lawrence party. None of the usual judicial appurtenances — judge, counsel, sheriff, jury — were omitted.

Intelligence of the proceedings of this unconventional court came to the ears of Federal Marshal Little at Fort Scott, and he sallied forth with a small armed escort on a reconnaissance. The court, hearing of his approach, suddenly abandoned its judicial functions and prepared to fight. When the marshal appeared and asked for explanations he was assured, with all the gravity of truth-telling, that the legislature then in session had repealed the entire code framed at Shawnee Mission, that a provisional committee had been appointed to conduct the government of the territory until a new code could be framed, and that there was, consequently, nothing for him to enforce.

The court successfully threw dust in the marshal's eyes, and he returned to Fort Scott. Soon discovering that he had been duped, Little gathered a second and larger expedition, and set out again, determined effectually to disbar the insolent attorneys. On his return there was a suitable preamble of parley. "Gentlemen," he said in a very black mood, "you will understand that you are dealing with the United States, and not with border ruffians. You will learn that there is a difference between them. I order you to surrender and prepare to accompany me to Fort Scott." The court scouted the idea. Half an hour was allowed for reflection, with an intimation from Little that if the period of grace brought forth no works meet for repentance he should "blow them all to hell." At the expiration of thirty minutes — no signs of surrender appearing — the marshal ordered a charge upon the recent judiciary, members of which were partly intrenched in a log-cabin, and partly posted behind neighboring trees. A dozen Sharpe's rifles responded to the charge, and that spoiled all the fun in a twinkling. Numerous loungers and roughs, who accompanied the expedition as a fine lark, disliked the appearance of things, and the road toward Fort Scott smoked with the precipitation of their return. Rumors of the encounter blew about the territory with various exaggerations. Reinforcements hurried down from Lawrence. Marshal Little's force was considerably increased, but belligerents finally drew off, and there was no more fighting.

In the spring of 1858 Captain Charles A. Hamilton surpassed all preceding guerrilla exploits by a deed "which the ibis and crocodile trembled at." Hamilton was a Georgian, of excellent family and reared in wealth. Restless and fond of adventure, his ear was caught by the Kansas crusade proclaimed in Georgia in 1856. He settled in Linn County and built a substantial loghouse, which served as political headquarters for the vicinity. But Hamilton hardly maintained himself against the superior prowess of the jayhawkers, and with the decline of the pro-slavery cause in the territory soured into desperation. He resolved that the victors should pay heavily for their success, and compiled a list of obnoxious men in his neighborhood whom he planned to seize and execute. This death catalogue in some way fell into Montgomery's hands, who immediately took measures to kill the compiler. He caught him in his log-house, to which he laid siege, but was driven off by federal troops before he could effect his purpose.

Then a lull followed, the opinion became general that Hamilton would not push his schemes of assassination, precautions were relaxed, and vigilance grew weary; but it was a fatal calm, —

"Like the dread stillness of condensing storms."

Hamilton suddenly appeared in the neighborhood of Trading Post May 19th, 1858, with a gang of Missourians, and began to scour the region for his enemies, political and personal. He was particularly anxious to capture a certain resolute, saucy, belligerent blacksmith — Captain Eli Snyder — with whom he had an altercation not long before. Snyder, armed with a shot-gun "loaded with sixteen buckshot," encountered Hamilton and one or two companions near Trading Post. A spirited colloquy followed. "Where are you going?" Hamilton demanded. "You are going to Trading Post." "If you know better than I do why do you ask?" "If you don't look out,

I'll blow you through," growled the Georgian. Snyder leveled his shot-gun — "If you don't leave I'll tumble you from your horse." The interview concluded abruptly. "I afterwards mentioned the affair to Old John Brown," said Snyder, "and he remarked — 'If you had killed Hamilton what a mangling up it would have saved! The Dutch Henry business was at the right time!'"

Hamilton, with a small detachment of his gang, gave personal attention to the capture of Blacksmith Snyder whom he found at work in his shop. One of the visitors entered and made the colorless announcement — "A man wants to see you." Snyder appeared — "Good morning, Mr. Hamilton." "I've got you," hissed the cut-throat. "Yes — what do you want?" retorted the blacksmith, striking one of the horses which were crowding around him a smart blow that threw all the pistols out of range, and enabled him to regain the shop, and secure his gun. Though severely wounded, Snyder managed to reach his cabin a few rods distant. His young son covered his retreat with a double-barreled shot-gun. "Burn the devils," he shouted, as the boy opened fire; "cut away at them with the other barrel." The party retired in discomfiture.

Elsewhere the desperadoes met with better success. Out of a considerable number of prisoners eleven were selected, marched off to a neighboring gulch, and drawn up in line before their captors.

"Gentlemen," said one of the eleven, among whom there was no flinching or parleying, "if you are going to shoot, take good aim." "Ready," Hamilton shouted, but before he could speak the word "Fire," a repenting ruffian turned away, and said, with an oath — "I'll have nothing to do with such a piece of business as this." Hamilton discharged his own pistol, and a general volley followed. The entire line of prisoners went down — five of them killed outright, five wounded, and one unharmed.

The shocking affair produced a tremendous excitement far and wide. There was a hot, clattering, idle pursuit of the assassins. Justice overtook but one of them, and that after a delay of five years.

The authorities at Lecompton did not lay the responsibility for a state of things that culminated in the Marais des Cygnes assassinations wholly or chiefly at the door of pro-slavery men. At all events, soon after receiving intelligence of them, Governor Denver placed warrants in the hands of Deputy Marshal, Captain Samuel Walker for the arrest of Montgomery. When Walker reached Raysville, ten or fifteen miles northwest of Fort Scott, he found a large convention in session. "What are you after?" asked an acquaintance under his breath. "I've come down to take Montgomery." "You can't do it. That thing's out of the question." The marshal concluded that it would be wise to keep his writs out of sight.

"I don't know Montgomery," he said, "and I don't wish to have him pointed out. If he is, I shall have to make an effort to take him."

The speaking, inflamed by the recent massacre, proceeded with furious energy. Nothing less than the extinction of Fort Scott — an infamous nest of border ruffianism which was at that moment sheltering some of the Marais des Cygnes murderers — would pacify the convention. The authorities sent down sheriffs to arrest free-state men, but they shunned that vile robbers' den. The sneer brought Walker to his feet. He volunteered to serve any warrants in Fort Scott with which he might be furnished, and the proposal touched a popular chord. An unexpected difficulty threatened to frustrate the whole enterprise. Nobody could be found authorized to issue the necessary papers. "Get a common justice's writ," said Walker, "and I'll go, though as a federal officer I have no business to serve it."

Walker, escorted by Montgomery *incognito*, reached Fort Scott on the 30th, and proceeded at once to the house of G. W. Clarke, who, as leader of the Linn County raid in 1856 as well as for other reasons, had incurred great unpopularity in free-state quarters. The marshal vainly pounded upon the door with his fist, and then tried the butt of his pistol without eliciting any response. But the town was astir. The street swarmed with Clarke's friends armed to the teeth, while

Montgomery and his band were fully prepared for anything that might happen. Walker, having procured some heavy iron implement from a government wagon standing near, was about to renew his attack on the door when Clarke thrust his head from a window, and offered to surrender. In a few moments the door swung open, and he appeared curiously accoutred. His wife clung to one arm, and his daughter to the other, while in his hands there was an old-fashioned cavalry carbine. Very properly Clarke wished to examine the marshal's papers, which that gentleman declined to exhibit, since legally they were of no more account than a handful of pages plucked from the life of Jack the Giant Killer. "I'll give you two minutes to surrender," thundered the marshal, drawing his pistol. "I heard the click of rifles about me," Walker relates, "as I covered Clarke with my revolver. There was a silence like death. Nobody said a word. Major Williams held his watch to count the time. I saw nothing except the ruffian before me. I was told that pro-slavery rifles were pointed at me while my escort aimed at Clarke. It was a mighty solemn state of affairs. The two minutes, I think, must have almost expired when Clarke, white as a sheet, handed me his carbine." Walker afterwards arrested Montgomery himself, but all the prisoners managed to escape, and he returned to Lecompton empty-handed.

The escort retired in a soured, disappointed frame of mind. A dramatic tableau which dissolved and left no rack of vengeance behind — whatever may be said of it from a scenical point of view — failed to satisfy the matter-of-fact jayhawkers. They projected a second expedition, hoping to retrieve thereby the inconsequence of the first. On the night of June 6th, Montgomery made a descent upon the town. Quietly securing the sentinels before they could raise an alarm, he applied the torch to some of the public buildings and retreated to a neighboring ravine. An alarm was shortly raised, and citizens hurriedly collected to extinguish the conflagration, when the marauders skulking in the ravine opened fire. Never was a crowd taken more completely by surprise or dispersed more precipitately, though replying to the attack, when some covert had been reached, with an irregular, spluttering fusillade. The attempted incendiarism did not prosper. It accomplished nothing beyond a little blackening and charring. A lively scare, houses fire-stained and bullet-marked, an interesting exhibition of helter-skeltering — such is the summary of results.

Finally, Governor Denver, accompanied by Governor Robinson, made a tour through the Southeast, with a view to composing, by personal intervention, the difficulties which had so long distracted it. They visited different points and were kindly received. On the 14th of June the trip reached a sort of climax at Fort Scott, where there was a large mass-meeting and full service of speeches. Governor Denver made a conciliatory address. "I shall treat actual settlers," he said, "without regard to former differences. I do not propose to dig up or review the past. Both parties, I believe, have done wrong and are worthy of censure, but I shall let all that go. My mission is to secure peace for the future." The governor suggested the election of new county officers, the patrolling of the border by federal troops, delay in the execution of old writs until they should pass the ordeal of competent judicial tribunals, and the dispersion of all guerrilla bands. These measures received general approval, and introduced a few weeks of comparative repose.

Shortly after Governor Denver's peace-making tour Old John Brown, absent for some months, reappeared in Kansas — an untranquilizing event. Treachery on the part of a confidant led to postponement of the contemplated Virginia campaign, and his return was a feint to throw the public off the scent. During his absence in the East Brown was able, with the assistance of friends, to put his family, which remained at North Elba, New York, on a more comfortable footing than had been their fortune.

"For one thousand dollars cash," he wrote Mr. Lawrence from New Haven, Conn., March 19th, 1857, "I am offered an improved piece of land, which, . . . might enable my family, consisting of a wife and five minor children (the youngest not yet three years old), to procure a subsistence should I never return to them; my wife being a good economist and a real old-fashioned business woman. She has gone through the two past winters in our open, cold house; unfinished outside and not plastered. . . . I have never hinted to any one else that I thought of asking for any help to provide in any such way for my family. . . . If you feel at all inclined to encourage me in the measure I have proposed I shall be grateful to get a line from you. . . . Is my appeal right?"

John Brown's final visit to Kansas lasted about six months. That interval he spent mainly in the Southeast. On his way thither he stopped in Lawrence and had a talk with Governor Robinson — "You have succeeded," he said, "in what you undertook. You aimed to make of Kansas a free state, and your plans were skillfully laid for that purpose. But I had another object in view. I meant to strike a blow at slavery."

In the Southeast Brown attempted nothing of importance, except an expedition across the Missouri line in December, which resulted in the destruction of considerable property, the liberation of eleven slaves, and the death of a slave-owner. The raid caused great excitement, especially in Missouri, and resulted in legislative action, which brought the territorial jayhawking era substantially to a close. During the autumn Governor

Stewart, of Missouri, opened correspondence with Governor Denver and with President Buchanan in regard to the troubles. He informed Denver that it might be "necessary to station an armed force along the border, in Missouri, for purposes of protection." Governor Denver promised to leave nothing undone to suppress the outrages, but hoped that it might not be necessary for Missouri to put an armed force into the field. August 9th Governor Stewart wrote President Buchanan that he had ordered a body of militia into Cass and Bates counties, because they "have been subjected to the repeated depredations of one or more marauding parties from the territory of Kansas, in consequence of which there is no security for either life or property. Citizens of Missouri have been driven from their homes, their property taken or destroyed, and their farms laid waste; and without the protection of an armed force our citizens have not dared to return to their homes to reside." These measures allayed the disorders, and there was no further serious trouble until Brown's raid. January 6th, 1859, Governor Stewart sent a message to the Missouri legislature, asking that steps be taken for redressing the outrage. He also transmitted memorials from thirty-five citizens of Bates and Vernon counties to the effect that there is "a regularly organized band of thieves, robbers, and midnight assassins . . . upon the western border of our county," begging him "to take into consideration the accompanying affidavits of citizens . . . who have been robbed and outraged at their homes by a band of lawless men from the territory of Kansas, supposed to be headed by the notorious Brown and Montgomery; and also the terrible situation of the family of the late and lamented David Cruise, who has been foully murdered in the bosom of his family by these desperadoes." A bill was introduced into the state senate authorizing the employment of a military force to patrol the border, but referred to the committee on federal relations, who made a singularly dispassionate and sensible report covering the whole subject of border difficulties.

"We doubt not," said the committee, "that at least ninety-nine out of every hundred of the citizens of Kansas deplore the events under consideration. . . . The people of Kansas and Missouri are most intimately connected, not only by geographical lines, but by the tender cords of kindred. We are the same people, impelled by the same interest, and bound for the same manifest destiny. . . . Even if this difficulty be winked at by Kansas . . . we would earnestly recommend the trial of every honorable means of reconciliation before a resort to extreme measures. . . . We would act with great caution and consideration. . . . If . . . an army be stationed along the line of our frontier for the avowed purpose of protecting our border from incursions from a neighboring territory, it will do a greater injury to the cause of liberal principles and confederated government than almost any other conceivable calamity. . . . This bill . . . provides that these troops are to be raised alone from the counties on the border; taken from the midst of a people already exasperated by the murder and robbing of their kindred and neighbors. Companies formed out of such material would be hard to restrain from acts of summary punishment, should any of these desperadoes fall into their hands; and it would likewise be difficult to teach such troops the line of our jurisdiction, and in the excitement of inflicting a merited punishment on some offender it would be hard for them to comprehend the deplorable evils attending an armed invasion of a sister territory by the militia of a state." "[We] are not insensible of the obligations of the state to protect all her citizens . . . [but] we are most unwilling that the state should run wild in the remedies applied. We have evidence of the most satisfactory character that outrages almost without a parallel in America, at least, have been perpetrated upon the persons and property of unoffending citizens of Bates and Vernon counties — their houses plundered and then burned — their negroes kidnapped in droves — citizens wounded and murdered in cold blood."

The committee did not recommend the use of a military force to disperse the outlaws " that have congregated in the southern portion of the territory of Kansas for the last two years." They advise that rewards should be offered for the arrest of jayhawking leaders, and that circuit judges should hold special terms in the disturbed districts at which grievances might be investigated and redressed — rational suggestions, smoking with far less passion than might have been anticipated, which the legislature wisely adopted. Governor Stewart put a price of three thousand dollars on Old John Brown's head, but to no purpose. He successfully piloted the eleven liberated bondmen northward, and saw Kansas no more.

During the summer of 1859 better days fairly began in the lawless, turbulent, freebooting Southeast. It could not be expected that long-established guerrilla habits would instantly lose their charm and power. In spite of all repressive influences — federal, territorial, Missourian — their decline was gradual. While it may be rash to speak with confidence on a matter where so much confusion, blur, and conflict of testimony still exists, yet the conclusion seems to be forced that in comparison with the Missourians, whose sins are black enough, jayhawkers, were the superior devils. But in 1859 out of subsiding anarchy there rose a crude, rudimental order. At all events, the people so far believed in the actual establishment of peace that they devoted the 4th of July to its celebration. Ancient enemies then took vows of amity at Fort Scott, and promised to raze out of memory all belligerent records and begin anew.

CHAPTER XII.

CLOSE OF THE TERRITORIAL PERIOD.

In the town of Lawrence, on the eighth day of January, 1858, there was an unwonted spectacle. The territorial legislature had repaired thither from Lecompton and the state legislature from Topeka, that these bodies, once divided by deadly feuds, might freely and amicably confer together on matters of common interest. A revival of the transfusion project, ineffectually broached during the administration of Governor Geary, was the business which called for these unusual facilities of intercourse. The state legislature still dreamed of some cross-cutting path into the Union. It still regarded the territorial legislature, though rehabilitated and purged of the old leaven, as "an obstacle to the successful execution of the will of the people," — requested it to disperse, to vote itself out of existence, and transfer all its rights and prerogatives to the state organization.

The plan did not commend itself to the territorial body. In the uncertainties of the situation, as the issue of congressional agitations could not be forecast, it would have been palpably impolitic to abandon the only law-making assembly recognized by the federal authorities.

From this rebuff the Topeka legislature never rallied. After lingering in Lawrence for a time, with futile hopes of a more favorable response to its overtures, it adjourned until the 4th of March. The organization served a most important purpose, but its mission had been accomplished. When it reassembled there was no quorum. The few free-state men, who clung to it with misspent fidelity, printed a plaintive valedictory rehearsing the fortunes of the defunct government, lauding the admirable constancy to principle illustrated in themselves, and dispersed.

The territorial legislature was now in undisputed mastery of the situation. Yet, though revolutionized in political composition, the quality of its political morality showed little betterment. The record which it made was worse than indifferent, especially in the matter of a new capital and constitutional convention. In Lecompton, founded by the pro-slavery party, the sensitive assembly did not feel at home, and resolved to go elsewhere. A town called Minneola was projected in Franklin County. But the decisive considerations stirring in the affair were neither sentimental nor patriotic. Thirty-five of the fifty-two members of the legislature were financially interested in the venture. Under such circumstances it was to be expected that a bill transferring the capital from Lecompton to Minneola would easily survive the governor's veto. When the removal began to be agitated Minneola was a stretch of untouched prairie. Not a building of any sort existed on the proposed site of it; nothing was there except "prairie grass, bugle-brush, and weeds." In a few weeks a big, barn-like structure, designed for a capitol, and one or two other buildings were hastily and rudely flung together. The enterprise looked feasible — at least as a financial investment. But Governor Denver refused to leave Lecompton, or to allow a transfer of the records and public documents. Attorney General Black pronounced the whole scheme unconstitutional; and this adverse decision remanded the ambitious town-site of Minneola into common prairie.

Nor did the effort for a new constitution prosper. The bill authorizing a convention failed to pass the legislature until the thirty-seventh day of the session, which was limited by law to forty days. Governor Denver concluded there had been constitution-making enough for the present, and resolved to call a truce in that disquieting business. The Lecompton constitution was still vexing Congress. Irreconcilables were not wanting who clung to the Topeka movement, and Denver decided to kill the bill. This he was able to do, as the organic law permitted an absolute veto of legislation which reached him within three days of the enforced adjournment. But legislators, who originated the enterprise of removing the capital to Minneola, could not be thwarted by any such trifle as the pocketing of a bill. Just before the close of the session, Governor Denver received what purported to be the bill calling the constitutional convention, officially indorsed as having been passed over his veto. He sent for the presiding officers of the legislature, and exhibiting the spurious document asked, "Who's responsible for this?" "Lane suggested it," was the reply. "It is not the original bill," the governor continued. "That is still in my hands — has never been out of them. This bill is a forgery. Now I can make trouble for you if I choose to do it. You have certified to what is not true. The whole statement is false. But I have no wish to keep up the agitation. Two courses are open to you — either to give me a paper setting forth the fact that the original bill was never returned to the legislature with my objections, and hence never passed over my veto, or to destroy this counterfeit document here in my presence." "What shall we do with it?" the chief clerk asked. "Destroy it," the Speaker of the House promptly replied. The document was torn in pieces and thrust into the stove.

That a bill should survive such an ordeal was probably unprecedented, but this hardy bill did survive it. The legislature voted unanimously that it had passed that body in due form. March

9th there was an election of delegates to a constitutional convention, which assembled at Minneola Tuesday, the 23d. But the jobbery and other discreditable facts clouding the whole movement got noised abroad and excited great indignation. For a time the "Minneola swindle" fairly divided curses with the "Lecompton swindle." No sooner had the convention reached Minneola and effected a temporary organization, than a violent debate sprang up over the question whether it should not immediately adjourn to some other place. The discussion raged until five o'clock Wednesday morning, when the convention did adjourn to Leavenworth. There another constitution was formed, which abandoned the once popular "free white state" doctrine, and confronted the intense pro-slavery doctrines of Lecompton with an anti-slavery utterance no less unqualified.

But the Leavenworth constitution was too heavily weighted for success. When submitted to the people May 18th, only about four thousand ballots were cast, and one fourth of them in the negative. The stigma of its origin destroyed an otherwise excellent constitution.

Governor Denver, who accepted his post reluctantly and with the intention of retiring from it as soon as practicable, resigned October 10th, and was succeeded by Samuel Medary, of Ohio. Denver is the first among the territorial governors whose resignation was not practically forced.

The fourth territorial legislature convened January 3d, 1859. In comparison with preceding legislatures it presents a tame and uneventful record. The most laborious task which it attempted was the codification of the statutes. The enactments of 1855 were repealed in bulk, and as that act did not fully express public sentiment in reference to them, they were publicly burnt in the streets of Lawrence. The general laws of 1857 were repealed, and those of 1858 liberally revised. Undeterred by the experiences of former assemblies, the legislature also made provision for another constitutional convention. The question of calling this body was submitted to the people, who cast five thousand three hundred and six affirmative, and one thousand four hundred and twenty-five negative, votes. Delegates were chosen June 7th — thirty-five Republicans and seventeen Democrats.

At this election a Republican party appeared in the territory for the first time. The free-state party was an isolated, independent organization, wholly dedicated to a local mission. It avoided outside alliances lest they should distract and enfeeble its energies. Though its record is not ideal, though the odious black law sentiments enunciated at Big Springs and reaffirmed when the Topeka government was commissioned were strangely out of harmony with its general purposes, yet the party never faltered in its hostility to Southern institutions. But the question of the domestic institutions of Kansas was now settled. The organization had fulfilled its special mission, and the necessity for isolation no longer existed. A convention at Lawrence November 11th, 1857, discussed and negatived propositions to merge the free-state party in the Republican party. May 18th, 1858, the free-state combination went to pieces upon the organization of the Republican party at Osawatomie.

The Missouri faction was known by a variety of names. At first it styled itself the pro-slavery party. As the chances that Kansas would not adopt Southern institutions increased, the epithet "pro-slavery" became unpopular, and was exchanged for "law and order." But the revised title had only a brief currency, and the party finally rested its pursuit of a name in the phrase — "The National Democracy of Kansas."

These changes in the constitution and nomenclature of political organizations betokened a subsidence of party animosities. So strong was the disposition to bury the past that it ultimately took the shape of a general amnesty act, which dismissed all prosecutions growing out of "political differences of opinion," and, as a consequence, a good many people breathed freer.

The constitutional convention met at Wyandotte July 5th with a membership largely composed of new men. Few of the leaders who figured at Topeka, or Lecompton, or Leavenworth were at Wyandotte. The convention fell to work with as much freshness and zeal as if no similar body had ever broken ground in Kansas, and after a session of three or four weeks produced a fairly good instrument. In the matter of the elective franchise it retreated from the radicalism of Leavenworth, which conferred the right of suffrage upon "every male citizen of the United States," and adopted the language of Topeka, "every white male person." October 4th, 1859, the people ratified the constitution by a majority of four thousand eight hundred and ninety-one, in a total vote of fifteen thousand nine hundred and fifty-one. On the 6th of December Charles Robinson was elected governor, J. P. Root lieutenant-governor, and M. F. Conway representative to Congress.

The debate in Congress on the Wyandotte constitution lacked the bitterness and violence of earlier discussions when Kansas was the topic. Senator Wigfall revived a dialect popular in the Lecompton days. "I will not consent," he said, "that Texas shall associate herself with such a state as this [Kansas] would be. . . . The inhabitants of that so-called state are outlaws and land-pirates. The good men were abandoned by the government and were driven out. Ruffianism is all that is left, and are we to associate with it?" But outbursts of this sort were infrequent.

The opposition, led by Green, of Missouri, despairing of ultimate success, now expended its strength in retarding and deferring the entrance of the obnoxious territory into the Union. There was much criticism of the proposed boundaries, as the Missouri senator insisted that not more than two sevenths of the area included within them could be cultivated, though the western line had been moved eastward to the twenty-fifth meridian. He urged that thirty thousand square miles should be taken from Southern Nebraska and annexed to the projected state. "Without this addition . . . Kansas," he said, "must be weak, puerile, sickly, in debt, and at no time capable of sustaining herself!"

After more than four years of fruitless endeavor Kansas entered the Union. January 21st, 1861, senators of Florida, Alabama, and Mississippi announced the secession of these states and their own retirement from Congress. The election of Abraham Lincoln as president furnished a convenient pretext for revolt. "It has been a belief," said Jefferson Davis, " that we are to be deprived in the Union of the rights . . . our fathers bequeathed to us, which has brought Mississippi into her present decision. . . . When you deny them, and when you deny to us the right to withdraw from a government which, thus perverted, threatens to be the destruction of our rights, we but tread the path of our fathers when we proclaim our independence and take the hazard."

The defiant Southern valediction was barely finished when Senator Seward called up the bill for the admission of Kansas. With their depleted ranks the opposition could now offer only a feeble resistance, and it passed by a vote of thirty-six to sixteen. The House had already taken favorable action, and on the 28th of January concurred in Senate amendments. It was with memorable dramatic fitness that Kansas, the arena where the hostile civilizations met, should enter the Union just as the defeated South drew off from it.

The news reached Lawrence late at night. Territorial officials, members of the legislature, which was in session there, and people in general were roused, and there followed an impromptu jollification, to which buckets of whiskey, freely circulated, lent inspiration. The next day saw a more formal and decorous celebration. One hundred guns were fired, making noisy proclamation across the prairies that Kansas had at last become a state.

The struggle for the possession of Kansas, the loss of which to the South made secession a certainty, was essentially political and constitutional — not military. The few skirmishes that took place have a secondary if not tertiary importance. In the field of diplomacy and finesse the pro-slavery leaders were outgeneraled. Reckoning too confidently and disdainfully on numbers, on nearness to the theatre of operations and federal support, they also blundered in underrating their opponents, and in adopting consequently a policy of noise and bluff. They came thundering into the territory on the 30th of March, 1855, when quieter measures would have served their purposes far better. The dash upon the Wakarusa turned out to be a fool's errand. In the sack of Lawrence and the dispersion of the Topeka legislature, victories were won which returned to plague the victors. The career of the free-state party, under the lead of Governor Robinson, who projected and inspired the whole tactical plan of its operations, has no parallel in American history. Composed of heterogeneous, clashing, feverish elements; repudiating the territorial legislature and subsisting without legislation — an intermediate condition of virtual outlawry — from the settlement of Lawrence until 1858, the party was not only successfully held together during this chaotic period, but by a series of extraordinary expedients, by adroitly turning pro-slavery mistakes to account, and by rousing Northern sympathy through successful advertisement of its calamities, rescued Kansas from the clutch of Missouri, and then disbanded.

CHAPTER XIII.

DURING THE WAR FOR THE UNION.

The border storm blew down the loosely-rooted prosperities of the territory with sufficient havoc. For the most part the early immigrants were poor. A laudable ambition to mend their worldly fortunes blended with ethical and political convictions in their westward venture. Though the cause of liberty prospered, and slavery was driven from the debatable ground, yet, at the close of the struggle, the rudenesses, discomforts, and limitations of the frontier remained with faintly mitigated severity. Strength and enterprise that might have built comfortable homes, improved farms, and established public institutions, had been diverted to politics. The domestic experiences of the Kansas pioneers during the territorial days, subordinated in this volume to their political concerns, are full of interest. Under the most favorable circumstances, frontier life has plenty of disagreeable, slowly bettering elements. "Sleeping on the ground," wrote a pioneer in 1856, " is not confined to camping out, but is extensively practiced in all our cabins. Floors are a luxury rarely seen here [in Wabaunsee]. In our own dwelling, part of the inmates rest on the earth, while others sleep on sacking stretched between the timbers over our heads, access to which is only to be had by climbing up on the logs constituting the sides of the cabin. I noticed yesterday a member of our family making up his bed with a hoe!" Everything was on a primitive basis. Land had been preëmpted in larger or smaller amounts and a rudimentary agriculture attempted. Horses, cattle, pigs, fowls — an easy, inviting prey for raiders of every sort — gradually increased. Food was always plain, sometimes scanty, and occasionally unique. "We have a pie on the table, the first of any kind I have seen since our arrival, made of *sorrel* and sweetened with molasses." Unconventional frontier habits of dress were in vogue. Among the nearly five hundred persons who presented claims for damages before the auditing commission of 1859, very few included items of clothing. One unpractical mortal brought to the territory a large assortment of dress coats, white velvet and satin vests, trousers, calf-skin boots, and gloves. The wardrobe disappeared when the Missourians sacked Lawrence in 1856, and some of the finery which attracted Mr. Gladstone's attention on their return to Kansas City doubtless came from it. "I frequently spoke to Southmayd," said a witness before the claims commission, "about having so much good clothing in this country!" Socially there was an utter democracy — no highest, no lowest. Everybody stood on the same plane. For amusements the settlers were left entirely to their own resources. Lecturers, concert troupes, and shows never ventured so far into the wilderness. Yet there was much broad, rollicking, noisy merry-making, but it must be confessed that rum and whiskey — lighter liquors like wine and beer could not be obtained — had a good deal to do with it. In the larger towns "sprees" were by no means uncommon. Room No. 7 in the Eldridge House obtained a reputation throughout the territory as a favorite place for carousals, where the uproar frequently continued all night, as one party of roisterers succeeded another. Outside of the villages inconveniences and hardships were specially oppressive. A woman died in a country neighborhood. "The difficulty after her death was to provide a coffin. There were men who could make it, but no boards could be found. At last one person offered to use a part of the bottom of his wagon, another furnished the rest, and a box was put together." A constant back-flowing stream of disgusted settlers set eastward during the whole territorial period. Some of them gave a doleful account of the country — reported Kansas not likely to "become a free or a slave state until all the rest of the world is over-peopled, for nobody that has strength to walk, or money to pay for conveyance, will stay there long. The earth . . . is actually parched and burnt to the solidity of brick by the long droughts so that it cannot be plowed, and no vegetation appears." Schools, churches, and the various appliances of older civilization got under way and made some growth, but they were still in a primitive, inchoate condition when Kansas took her place in the Union.

The mischiefs which accompanied the strife of hostile civilizations within the territory were prolonged and aggravated by a new woe. In 1860 a great drought began. For more than a year little or no rain fell, and crops failed everywhere. Probably fifteen or twenty thousand people were thrown upon public charity. Again Kansas put out signals of distress, to which the public made a quick and generous response. Provisions, clothing, and money poured into the famished commonwealth — a magnificent largess that measurably relieved its calamities, though it did not prevent serious depopulation.

Governor Robinson took the oath of office February 9th, 1861. He found himself at a post beset by an extraordinary complication of difficulties. April 15th President Lincoln called for seventy-five thousand volunteers to put down the Southern rebellion. Kansas was in a condition the most inopportune and unpromising for a fitting response. With the subsidence of domestic troubles military organizations generally went to pieces. The exchequer of a community whose six years of territorial broil concluded with a famine could hardly be on a war footing. Yet Governor Robinson, in his message to the legislature, which met March 26th, said: "Kansas, though last and least of the states in the Union, will ever be ready to answer the call of her country." That promise was nobly kept. Governor Carney, the successor of Governor Robinson, writing President Lincoln May 13th, 1864, could say : "Kansas has furnished more men according to her population to crush this rebellion than any other state in the Union." In all the great western campaigns Kansas soldiers made an honorable record. That record belongs to national rather than state history, and no effort will be made here to disentangle and isolate it for purposes of valuation.

Governor Robinson was probably the first state executive to foreshadow the policy which the federal authorities ultimately adopted in reference to slavery "A demand is made by certain states," he said in his message, "that new concessions and guaranties be given to slavery, or the Union must be destroyed. . . . If it is true that the continued existence of slavery requires the destruction of the Union, it is time to ask if the existence of the Union does not require the destruction of slavery. If such an issue be forced on the nation it must be met, and met promptly."

The inevitable and legitimate difficulties which confronted Governor Robinson — embarrassments of poverty and of chaos — might well have staggered any man of ordinary nerve, but they were not the most formidable evils. After an exciting contest the legislature elected J. H. Lane and S. C. Pomeroy to the United States Senate. Lane celebrated his departure for Washington by laying aside the calf-skin vest and seal-skin coat, which had done service during the whole territorial era, and donning a respectable suit. On the realization of his long-cherished dream a crazy passion for power seized him — an ambition to absorb the entire civil and military functions of the state. Robinson stood squarely, if not defiantly, across his path. In the territorial struggle the natural antagonisms of these two men — antagonisms of temperament, method, and purpose — were circumscribed and held in abeyance by the compulsions of the situation —

"As the wave breaks to foam on shelves,
Then runs into a wave again."

But now disguises and restrictions were flung off. Lane, inflamed by old grudges and new provocations, by long-nursed hatreds and obstructions that crossed his plans, broke out into violent hostilities against Governor Robinson and his successor. By his overshadowing prestige at Washington he was able to wrest from them no small part of their legitimate gubernatorial functions. Lane's singular influence over Mr. Lincoln and the secretary of war, Mr. Stanton, is one of the most inexplicable and disastrous facts that concern Kansas in 1861-65. It was the source of the heaviest calamities that visited the commonwealth during that period, because it put him in a position to gratify mischievous ambitions, to pursue personal feuds, to assume duties and offices that belonged to others, to popularize the corruptest political methods, and to organize semi-predatory military expeditions. His conduct not only embarrassed the state executive and threw state affairs into confusion, but provoked sanguinary reprisals from Missouri. In 1864 Mr. Lincoln, remarking upon Lane's extraordinary career in Washington to Governor Carney, offered no better explanation of it than this: "He knocks at my door every morning. You know he is a very persistent fellow and hard to put off. I don't see you very often, and have to pay attention to him."

Lane's intrigues in Washington against the state administration prospered. Though recruiting was energetically pushed by the local authorities and three regiments were already in the field — the first and second obtaining honorable recognition for gallant conduct at the battle of Wilson's Creek, Missouri — yet in August Lane, technically a civilian, appeared in Kansas clothed with vague, but usurping military powers. He reached Leavenworth on the 15th, and announced in a public address the extinction of all his personal and political enmities — a costly sacrifice laid on the altar of his country. Two days afterwards he set out for Fort Scott, where the Kansas brigade, comprising the Third and Fourth infantry together with the Fifth and Sixth cavalry regiments, was concentrating to repel attacks upon the Southeast. He began his brief military career in this region by constructing several useless fortifications, among which the most considerable affair was Fort Lincoln, on the Little Osage River, twelve miles north of Fort Scott. September 2d there was a skirmish at Dry Wood Creek, Missouri, between a reconnoitring party and a force under the Confederate General Rains, which was not wholly favorable to the Kansans, and caused a panic at Fort Scott. Leaving a body of cavalry with orders to defend the town as long as possible, and then fire it, Lane retired to his earth-works on the Little Osage. "I am compelled to make a stand here," he reported September 2d, after getting inside Fort Lincoln, "or give up Kansas to disgrace and destruction. If you do not hear from me again, you can understand that I am surrounded by a superior force." The Confederates did not follow up their advantage, but retreated leisurely toward Independence, Missouri. Encouraged by their withdrawal, Lane took the field on the 10th "with a smart little army of about fifteen hundred men" — reached Westport, Missouri, four days later, where he reported — "Yesterday I cleaned out Butler and Parkville with my cavalry." September 22d he sacked and burned Osceola, Missouri — an enterprise in which large amounts of property and a score of inhabitants were sacrificed. He broke camp on the 27th, and in two days reached Kansas City. The brigade converted the Missouri border through which the march lay into a wilderness, and reached its destination heavily encumbered with plunder. "Everything disloyal," said Lane, ". . . . must be cleaned out," and never were orders more literally or cheerfully obeyed. Even the chaplain succumbed to the rampant spirit of thievery, and plundered Confederate altars in the interest of his unfinished church at home. Among the spoils that fell to Lane personally there was a fine carriage, which he brought to Lawrence for the use of his household.

From the first the local authorities, civil and military, had regarded the brigade with apprehension. "We are in no danger of invasion," Governor Robinson wrote General Fremont, commander of the Western Department, September 1st, "provided the government stores at Fort Scott are sent back to Leavenworth, and the Lane brigade is removed from the border. It is true small parties of secessionists are to be found in Missouri, but we have good reason to know that they do not intend to molest Kansas . . . until Jackson shall be reinstated as governor of Missouri. Indeed, a short time since, when a guerrilla party came over and stole some property from our citizens, the officers in command of the Confederates compelled a return of the property, and offered to give up the leader of the gang to our people for punishment. But what we have to fear, and do fear, is, that Lane's brigade will get up a war by going over the line, committing depredations, and then returning into our state. This course will force the secessionists to [retaliation] . . . and in this they will be joined by nearly all the Union men of Missouri. If you will remove the supplies at Fort Scott to the interior, and relieve us of the Lane brigade, I will guaranty Kansas from invasion . . . until Jackson shall drive you out of St. Louis."

Captain Prince, in command at Fort Leavenworth, wrote Lane September 9th: "I hope you will adopt active and early measures to crush out this marauding which is being enacted in Captain Jennison's name, as also [in] yours, by a band of men representing themselves as belonging to your command." When General Hunter took charge of the department in November the brigade, according to the report of Assistant Adjutant-General C. G. Halpine, was "a ragged, half-armed, diseased, mutinous rabble, taking votes whether any troublesome or distasteful order should be obeyed or defied. . . . To remedy these things mustering officers were sent to remuster the regiments of Lane's brigade. . . . Had the department, as previously, been without troops from other states, there is every probability that a general mutiny . . . would have taken place instead of the partial mutinies which have been suppressed." The thieving, foot-pad, devastating expedition of Lane's brigade did much to incite animosities and reprisals, whose ghastly work sent a thrill of horror through the country.

Lane made a furious harangue at Leavenworth October 8th in defense of his campaign. He wrote President Lincoln the next day: "I . . . succeeded in raising and marching against the enemy as gallant and effective an army, in proportion to its numbers, as ever entered the field. Its operations are a part of the history of the country. . . . Governor Charles Robinson . . . has constantly, in season and out of season, vilified myself and abused the men under my command as marauders and thieves." He suggested the formation of a new military department out of Kansas, the Indian Territory, and portions of Arkansas, with himself as commander, and not less than ten thousand troops at his disposal. He would resign his seat in Congress and accept the military appointment. In case the department should not be created, he saw only calamities ahead. "I will . . . be compelled to leave my command," he continued, "quit the field, and most reluctantly become an idle spectator of the great struggle, and witness, I have no doubt, the devastation of my adopted state and the destruction of its people."

In November Lane returned to Washington and at once entered upon fresh military schemes. He projected an expedition, which he would lead in person from Fort Leavenworth into Arkansas and the Indian Territory — representing the movement as the result of conferences between himself and General Hunter. With this understanding, he obtained for it the approbation of President Lincoln and the War Department. Friends in Kansas sent on to Washington resolutions applauding his military genius, and urging that the most ought to be made of it. Lane, said the "Leavenworth Conservative" "has every quality of mind and character which belonged to the historical commanders. . . . There are no obstacles in his path, and to him a difficulty is simply a thing to be overcome." Refugee Indians at Fort Leavenworth, driven from the territory by disloyal tribes, concurred in these sentiments. "General Lane is our friend," said two chiefs with sesquipedalian names in a communication to "Our Great Father the President of the United States." "His heart is big for the Indian. He will do more for us than any one else. The hearts of our people will be sad if he does not come. They will follow him wherever he directs. They will sweep the rebels before them like a terrible fire on the dry prairie." Lane unfolded his plans, shaped evidently by the recent experiences of his brigade, to General McClellan. He proposed to extirpate disloyalty in Missouri and Arkansas. If conciliatory methods should not be successful, he would employ the most violent. "Sir, if I can't do better I will kill the white rebels, and give their lands to the loyal blacks!"

General Hunter received communications from the War Department in January, 1862, announcing that a Southern expedition, consisting of eight or ten thousand Kansas troops and four thousand Indians had been decided upon, and implying the existence of a definite, mutual understanding that Lane should have the chief command. These communications took Hunter by surprise, and in his perplexity he wrote General Halleck, who had succeeded General Fremont in command of the Western Department, for information : —

"It seems . . . that Senator J. H. Lane has been trading at Washington on a capital partly made up of his own senatorial position, and partly of such scraps of influence as I may have possessed in the confidence or esteem of the president, said scraps having been 'jayhawked' by the Kansas senator without due consent of the proper owner. . . . I find that 'Lane's great Southern expedition' was entertained by the president under misrepresentations ; . . . that said 'expedition' was the joint design of Senator Lane and myself. . . . Never to this hour has he consulted me on the subject, directly or indirectly, while the authorities at Washington have preserved a similar indiscreet reticence. . . . Thus I am left in ignorance, but . . . I think it more than probable that the veil of mystery has been lifted in your particular case."

Some weeks before receiving Hunter's letter, which was written February 8th, 1862, rumors reached Halleck that Lane would be commissioned brigadier-general, and he immediately forwarded a remonstrance to headquarters. "I cannot conceive a more injudicious appointment," he wrote General McClellan. "It will take twenty thousand men to counteract its effect in this state, and, moreover, is offering a premium for rascality and robbery." President Lincoln indorsed upon Halleck's communication, which was of considerable length, and touched various topics — "an excellent letter; though I am sorry General Halleck is so unfavorably impressed with General Lane." Concerning the "expedition" Halleck had no information aside from current rumors. Yet this unofficial hearsay sufficed to rouse his indignation. "I protested" . . . he wrote Hunter February 13th, "against any of his [Lane's] jayhawkers coming into this department, and said positively that I would arrest and disarm every one I could catch."

Lane reached Leavenworth January 26th in high spirits. But on the next day he met a sudden and stinging rebuff. Without waiting for interview or explanation, without intimating to Lane what was impending, Hunter issued an order announcing his purpose to command the "expedition" in person. The unexpected turn of affairs nonplused Lane. He sent a telegram to Representative John Covode: "See the president, secretary of war, and General McClellan, and answer what I shall do." There was nothing to do except to retire or take a subordinate position. He succeeded, however, in breaking up the expedition. "I have been with the man you name," Covode telegraphed. "Hunter will not get the men or money he requires. His command cannot go forward. Hold on. Don't resign your seat." Lane followed Covode's advice and returned to Washington after addressing a public letter to the legislature, which had passed complimentary resolutions: "I have been thwarted in the cherished hope of my life. The sad yet simple duty only remains to announce to you and through you my purpose to return to my seat in the United States Senate."

Lane's military intrigues reached their final stage in his appointment July 22d, 1862, as "Commissioner for Recruiting in the Department of Kansas." He proceeded to organize regiments, completely ignoring the state authorities in whose hands the laws and the constitution placed the whole business. At this time he began to enlist colored men — probably the pioneer movement in that direction — protesting that "a nigger can stop a bullet as well as a white man." But Lane's scheme did not altogether succeed. Governor Robinson, who proposed to stand upon his constitutional rights, declined to commission the officers whom Lane had appointed. The secretary of war telegraphed that if the state executive did not issue the commissions the War Department would. "You have the power to override the constitution and the laws," was the unconciliatory response; "but you have not the power to make the present governor of Kansas dishonor his own state."

Another feature in the singular tangle was a formidable effort to crush Governor Robinson, whom the Lane politicians found intractable and difficult to manage. In the autumn of 1861 these gentry made an abortive effort to displace him on the ground that, by the provisions of the constitution, the term of state officers expired January 1st, 1862. There was an election, but the courts pronounced it illegal.

The failure of this first personal assault lent additional violence and venom to the second. January 20th a resolution of inquiry concerning the sale of certain state bonds was offered in the legislature. The bonds in question had no quotable market value, and a sale was effected only through negotiations — evidently not ruled by the severest business maxims — with the Interior Department, which held, in trust, Indian funds for investment. It appeared that bonds to the amount of ninety-five thousand six hundred dollars were delivered, upon which the sum of fifty-five thousand dollars was paid; that while the sale was effected at eighty-five per cent., only sixty per cent. reached the state treasury, notwithstanding the law declared that nothing less than seventy per cent. should be accepted. Here was a palpable violation of the law, and the official upon whom it could be fastened, especially if he happened to be the governor, would fare badly. It is now well understood that the whole movement, which proceeded from Lane, was aimed at Robinson. The prosecution had no wish to harm the auditor and secretary of state who went down in the fight.

Though the committee of investigation appointed by the House of Representatives discovered no evidence connecting the governor with the negotiation, they resolved to include him among the inculpated officials. They ventured their case on chances that the progress of the trial might bring out criminating facts.

An intensity of excitement, unsurpassed even in the stormiest territorial days, convulsed the legislature when, on the 13th of February, the committee of investigation reported resolutions impeaching the auditor, the secretary of state, and the governor. On the next day a vote was reached, the resolutions passed unanimously, and there followed cheers long and loud. Why these law-makers applauded it would be difficult to say. They had not read the voluminous report upon which the resolutions were alleged to be based. If it were true that the executive had brought disgrace upon the state and ought to be driven from office, that would be poor cause for any outbreak of jubilation. When at a later stage specific articles of impeachment against the governor came before the House the unanimity gave way, and seven representatives are on record as voting against them. So far as Robinson was concerned the prosecution broke down, and he was almost unanimously acquitted, though a majority of the Senate belonged to the Lane faction.

That a rank growth of general freebooting should have sprung up in Kansas during the war was no more than might have been expected. The border naturally attracts men adapted to shine in this calling, and the territorial period afforded admirable training for the wider field of spoliation opened by the war for the Union. Early in the struggle an organization appeared known as "Red-legs," from the fact that its members affected red morocco leggings. It was a loose-jointed association, with members shifting between twenty-five and fifty, dedicated originally to the vocation of horse-stealing, but flexible enough to include rascalities of every description.

At intervals the gang would dash into Missouri, seize horses and cattle — not omitting other and worse outrages on occasion — then repair with their booty to Lawrence, where it was defiantly sold at auction. "Red-legs were accustomed to brag in Lawrence," says one who was familiar with their movements, "that nobody dared to interfere with them. They did not hesitate to shoot inquisitive and troublesome people. At Lawrence the livery stables were full of their stolen horses. One day I saw three or four Red-legs attack a Missourian who was in town searching for lost property. They gathered about him with drawn revolvers and drove him off very unceremoniously. I once saw Hoyt, the leader, without a word of explanation or warning, open fire upon a stranger quietly riding down Massachusetts Street. He was a Missourian whom Hoyt had recently robbed." The gang contained men of the most desperate and hardened character, and a full recital of their deeds would sound like the biography of devils. Either the people of Lawrence could not drive out the freebooters, or they thought it mattered little what might happen to Missouri disloyalists. Governor Robinson made a determined, but unsuccessful effort to break up the organization. The Red-legs repaid the interference by plots for his assassination, which barely miscarried.

In the destruction of Lawrence August 21st,

1863, the irregular, predatory hostilities of the border reached a shocking climax. The causes which brought about that event were various, and have been in the main already indicated — the campaign of Lane's brigade, the depredations of Red-legs, enmities and exasperations dating back to the settlement of Lawrence in 1854, as well as ordinary bushranging motives of plunder. "Jennison has laid waste our homes," was the declaration of more than one Missourian on the day of the massacre, "and the Red-legs have perpetrated unheard-of crimes. Houses have been plundered and burned, defenseless men shot down, and women outraged. We are here for revenge — and we have got it!"

Quantrill, who led the raid, once lived in Lawrence — a dullish, sullen, uninteresting knave, giving no promise of unusual bushranging genius. Just before the war opened he was driven from town in consequence of some misbehavior, and cast his lot among Missouri guerrillas. The stimulus of the great conflict developed in him unexpected capacities for marauding. He was eager to cross swords with Lane. "I should like to meet him," he said. "But then there would be no honor in whipping him. He is a coward. I believe I would cowhide him."

In 1862 and the earlier months of 1863 several of the smaller Kansas towns along the Missouri line — Aubrey, Shawnee, and Olathe — were sacked by ruffians under Quantrill's lead. Governor Thomas Carney, who succeeded Governor Robinson January 1st, 1863, was uneasy, and vainly importuned the War Department for more troops. In May he visited the Southern border, where he found everything in confusion, and the whole region defenseless. There was no money in the state treasury. April 6th, 1862, Lane and eight of his friends addressed a communication to the secretary of war and the secretary of the treasury, protesting "against the payment of the money due to the State of Kansas for expenses in organizing volunteer troops for the service of the United States," and were able to stop it. In the emergency Governor Carney raised one hundred and fifty mounted men for police duty, and paid expenses out of his own pocket.

That Quantrill meditated striking a blow at Lawrence some time was well known. There were alarms, citizens organized for defense, and kept a sharp lookout for the ruffian, but the bushrangers did not appear when they were expected, vigilance relaxed, and a fatal sense of security followed panic.

Quantrill's preliminary movements were not wholly enveloped in mystery. Intelligence that great activity prevailed among his forces, and that he was planning a dash into Kansas, reached federal headquarters at Kansas City, Mo., but no attention was paid to it. Had scouts been dispatched to exposed towns and warned them of danger the raid would have failed.

Late on the afternoon of August 20th Quantrill, with perhaps one hundred and seventy-five mounted men, crossed the Missouri line into Kansas. In Aubrey, five miles distant, there was a federal force of one hundred dragoons commanded by Captain J. A. Pike. It was not until half-past seven in the evening that the tardy scouts brought in news of the guerrillas' whereabouts. Captain Pike dispatched couriers to Kansas City, thirty-five miles distant, who arrived at half-past eleven o'clock. Couriers might have reached Lawrence, a ride of forty miles, about midnight, and in that case the bushrangers would have encountered a warm reception. Or had Captain Pike instantly started in pursuit, hanging upon their rear, dogging their movements with menace if not attack, Lawrence would have been saved.

It was nearly sunrise when Quantrill reached a little swell of the plain about a mile eastward from the doomed town. Not a whisper of his approach had reached it. Yet though the surprise promised to be complete, the cowardly raiders hesitated — declined to go farther. A discussion ensued, which was ended by Quantrill's avowal that he should go into Lawrence whatever his men might do. This declaration revived their fainting courage.

The bushrangers advanced within half a mile of

the town, halted again, and called the roll. Two horsemen, dispatched on a reconnaissance, rode through the principal street, and returned with the report that the village was asleep. A strange fatality of success attended the movements of the guerrillas. They rode "leisurely from their hiding-place in Missouri through the federal lines, and almost within shooting distance of a federal camp in the day-time," says H. E. Lowman in his "Lawrence Raid"; "then just as leisurely made their way over forty miles of traveled road through Kansas settlements in the night, and halted — called the roll in the early dawn within pistol-shot of the houses of residents of Lawrence, and yet no warning voice . . . rang through her quiet streets — ' Quantrill is coming.' "

There was a wild charge upon the village. The flying column of one hundred and seventy-five men riding with perfect horsemanship, yelling like demons, emitted one continuous, death-dealing volley as it dashed along. " I can still see the raiders," said an eye-witness of the scene years after the fatal morning, " as they stormed into town with their broad-brimmed hats — much like those which cowboys wear on the plains — with their unshaven beards and long hair, their dirty, greasy flannel shirts — coatless, and carrying no weapons except side-arms."

While skirmishers instantly and completely enveloped the village, the main body pushed on to seize the Eldridge House, a substantial brick building four stories high, which could have been successfully defended by a dozen armed and resolute men against the attacks of horsemen whose heaviest ordnance was revolvers. But weapons for the citizens there were none. A fussy, over-confident mayor had locked them up safely and inaccessibly in the arsenal. At the hotel resistance was apparently anticipated. The bushrangers drew up in front of it — surveyed it curiously, doubtfully. Presently a window was flung up, a white sheet displayed, and Quantrill summoned. Surrender speedily followed upon condition that the inmates of the hotel, who were mostly strangers, should be protected. A gong was sounded through the halls to collect them for convoy to the Whitney House, where Quantrill had established his headquarters. Mistaking the clangor for a signal of attack the ruffians hastily fell back. But finding their fears without foundation, and all likelihood of concerted resistance at an end, they broke up into small companies, scoured the town in literal and hearty obedience to the order — " Kill every man and burn every house."

Then began a scene that cannot be matched on the border, crimsoned as it is with blood — a scene far surpassing Dutch Henry's Crossing and Marais des Cygnes in scope of death-dealing passion — a scene which, like the massacre of Enniscorthy, "swallowed up all distinct or separate features in its frantic confluence of horrors." Then began a terrible exhibition of what is best and worst in human nature — rapacious cupidities of successful pillage; cowering, palsied panic; courage that defied and cursed the villains to their faces; flight, aimless and headlong or watchful and stealthy; pitiless revenge stung by memory of wrongs still fresh and rankling; affection that freely and gladly braved death; pistol-shots; the clatter of horsemen riding furiously; the groans of the dying, and the roar of conflagration. With few exceptions the bushrangers seemed to be dehumanized and transformed into the image of devils. The divine nature of love and mercy, if it ever existed, passed away, and the fiendish nature took its place. Stores, banks, hotels, and dwellings they rifled and then set them on fire. Citizens of the town were hunted like wild beasts and shot down indiscriminately. They pursued Red-legs with particular earnestness, and showed them no mercy when captured. Nor did they neglect to search attentively though vainly for Lane and the thrifty chaplain of his brigade. But the wrath of the raiders burned without nice distinction or qualification against all the male inhabitants of Lawrence, of whom one hundred and eighty-three fell victims in the butchery.

The heroism and fertility of resources shown by women of Lawrence on this day of blood are worthy of mention. At no other crisis of Kansas history does their service come into such bold and brilliant relief — of which only an instance or two can be set down here. Four wretches, crazed with drink, rode to the Whitney House, swearing they would shoot some one — it did n't matter much whom. A young woman offered herself, remarking, " They might as well kill me " — an act of daring that temporarily arrested their murderous designs. Another woman fairly magnetized a brace of ruffians, and saved her husband's life by charm of manner and tact of conversation. A third, whose husband was particularly obnoxious to the bushrangers, and whom they were anxious to catch, gave him opportunity to escape by noticing that the leader of the gang detailed to shoot him and burn his house wore a flower in his hat. " Good morning," she said cheerfully; " you have come to see my flowers " — the front yard was full of them. " They are fine," he said, looking about with evident admiration. " They are too d—d pretty to be burnt. I 'll shoot the man that touches them. March on ! "

When the work of butchery and destruction was finished Quantrill took a lunch at the Whitney House, and ordered the bushrangers to retire. " Ladies," said he, politely lifting his hat and bowing, " I now bid you good morning. I hope when we meet again it will be under more favorable circumstances ! "

It was a sickening scene from which the guerrilla chief galloped away — the town in flames, the principal street lined with corpses, many of them so charred and blackened that they were at first mistaken for negroes. "In handling the dead bodies," said one of the survivors, "pieces of roasted flesh would remain in our hands. Soon our strength failed us in this terrible and sickening work. Many could not help crying like children."

Early in the forenoon the bushrangers were retreating toward Missouri, freshly mounted on stolen horses, and heavily accoutred with spoils. Between nine and ten o'clock citizens who survived the butchery began to rally, and a small company under the lead of Lane, who happened to be in town, gave chase. The pursuers, whose numbers were slenderly recruited as they advanced, overtook Quantrill about noon near Brooklyn, halted, got into line, were counted, and found to number thirty-five men. They were mounted on beasts of every sort — mules, half-trained colts, and slow-paced draft-horses, as well as animals of higher grade. Nor were their weapons less various than their steeds. Lane put Lieutenant J. K. Rankin in command, who attempted to execute a flank movement by way of Prairie City and cut off Quantrill's retreat into Missouri. The little company was only fairly in motion when a courier rode up with the message — "Major Plumb is yonder with two hundred and fifty men and sent me to notify you." "Tell the major that Quantrill is just beyond us on the prairie, and that we shall attack him at once."

The enemy were less than a mile away, and Lieutenant Rankin ordered a charge upon the rearguard. Possibly half of the intervening space had been traversed, when the lieutenant found himself almost alone. As each trooper had a gait and speed of his own, the company was scattered at irregular intervals along the line of advance, and from a military point of view did not present a very formidable appearance.

Major Plumb's force divided, one company moving upon Quantrill's rear, and the other upon his flank. Lieutenant Rankin, seeing that little could be expected from his thirty-five stragglers, joined the former company, which had ridden within striking distance of the bushrangers, and ordered a charge, but the valiant troopers declined to make it. Soon Lane came up and repeated the command, — with no better result. Major Plumb shortly arrived with his division, and there was still opportunity to ride down the marauders. The federal commander hesitated and missed his opportunity. Pursuit continued into Missouri, reprisals were made, and three or four border counties, in obedience to General Thomas Ewing Jr.'s famous order No. 11, largely depopulated — but the desperadoes escaped.

When the full extent of the massacre dawned upon the survivors, there rose a frantic reaction toward revenge. Woe to the man within reach upon whom suspicion of confederacy with the marauders might fall. Had the troops who brought them to bay on the prairies fully appreciated the enormity of their crimes, possibly the hideous knowledge might have strung their courage up to the fighting point. However that may have been, the spectacle of sons, brothers, fathers, neighbors, slaughtered with every aggravation of cowardly brutality — of a town completely wrecked and given over to the torch — kindled the dead coals of desperation and revenge. There was a luckless wight — Jake Callew by name — against whom lay suspicions of playing the spy in the interest of Quantrill — suspicions vague, indirect, unevidenced, but sufficient to rouse a mob that would listen to no appeals deprecating violence, or pleading for delay.

"The sea enragèd is not half so deaf."

The mob seized Callew and arraigned him before an extemporized court. A verdict was rendered that the evidence did not prove his guilt. "You have heard the verdict," said the judge, addressing the frenzied rout. "Now, gentlemen, what will you do with the prisoner?" "Hang him," was the quick response. Preparations for the gibbet went on apace. It occurred to somebody that the doomed man might need the consolations of religion. Among the spectators a clergyman was discovered. "You had better make your peace with God for you don't stand much chance with this crowd," said the clergyman. "You need n't trouble yourself about my soul," the unappreciative sinner replied. "How do you like that, old fellow," broke in the hangman as he gave a tug at the rope and swung the poor wretch into eternity!

The destruction of Lawrence did not allay the feuds among Kansas officials. Lane's relations with Governor Carney ran through the entire gamut of variation from friendship to hostility, from hostility to confidential intimacy. He still struggled for absolute control of the military patronage of the state, and generally carried his point. Carney determined to make an end of this discreditable business — a senator of Kansas usurping the functions of the governor of Kansas. "No governor with a proper self-respect," he wrote President Lincoln . . . could or would tolerate such interference. What other loyal state has been thus humiliated ? . . . Kansas stands alone. I claim for her that she shall be the equal of the proudest of them. . . . I ask the revocation of the power conferred on J. H. Lane as recruiting commissioner." This letter Governor Carney followed up by an interview with President Lincoln, at the conclusion of which he addressed the following note to Secretary Stanton, dated Washington, May 28th, 1864: "Please see and hear the governor of Kansas with Judge Williams and Mr. Vaughn. Will we not, at last, be compelled to treat the governor of Kansas as we do other governors about raising and commissioning troops? I think it will have to be so." Governor Carney delivered this note in person to Secretary Stanton who read it, tore it in two, and said angrily — "Tell the president that I am secretary of war." Carney turned on his heel. "Wait," said Stanton, in a milder tone. "What do you want?" An understanding was reached, and henceforth the governor of Kansas was to be treated like other governors.

After the Lawrence raid Kansas experienced no general upheaval until the attempted invasion of General Sterling Price, who led a daring expedition, in the autumn of 1864, from Arkansas across the State of Missouri, living upon the country through which he passed, remounting his cavalry with fresh horses, threatening St. Louis, then deflecting toward Jefferson City, and pushing on to the Kansas line before his advance was successfully arrested. Great alarm prevailed. October 8th Governor Carney called out the entire militia. Ten thousand six hundred men responded, and were mostly concentrated in the neighborhood of Kansas City — a gallant, but undisciplined force. The battles at Lexington, along the Little Blue and the Big Blue, demonstrated their inability to cope with Price. The arrival of General Pleasanton on the 22d with seven thousand cavalry and eight pieces of artillery put a new face upon the campaign. On the next day the battle of Westport was fought, and the bold raiders turned southward in confusion. Their retreat scurried along the border, bending into Linn County, zigzagging toward Fort Scott, then turning eastward and southward until it crossed the Arkansas.

The expedition of Price was the last Confederate foray into Kansas. A long series of Missouri invasions closed with his retreat across the Arkansas. Bushrangers, jayhawkers, Red-legs, who played so prominent and so protracted a part on the stage of local history, now make a leisurely exit.

The first five years of Kansas history after admission to the Union were years of intrigue, confusion, alarm, and guerrillaism. With the wounds of the territorial struggle unhealed, with a heavy percentage of the population under arms, with the streams of immigration almost completely dried up, it was not possible that Kansas should make material or social progress while the war for the Union continued. The forces of repair and development were unequal to the waste.

The man who figured so largely in Kansas affairs during the rebellion did not long survive its close. When the Republican party broke with President Johnson, Lane declined to join in the attack upon him. This step gave offense to former friends. "So far as I am concerned," he said in the Senate April 6th, 1866, "I propose to-day and hereafter to take my position alongside the president." His course disposed Republican senators to investigate discreditable rumors about him that filled the air. Charges of corruption in connection with Indian contracts had been made vaguely in the public prints against some unnamed senator. "I propose to fill up the hiatus," wrote the Washington correspondent of the Boston "Commonwealth," "and let the public know . . . that the charge refers to Senator James H. Lane." Governor Carney, whose relations with Lane were now on a confidential footing, happened to be at his lodgings when the mail arrived containing a copy of the " Commonwealth " — which he read and then handed to Carney. "Oh that's nothing," said Carney, cheerfully. "You have been charged with about everything on the face of the earth. That does n't amount to much." "Does n't amount to much!" Lane repeated in a very excited and tragic manner.

The next morning Carney returned and found Lane in a pitiable plight — half-clad, his hair erect and bristling, his small, sunken, snaky eyes burning like live coals, his "sinister face, plain to ugliness," figured over with desperation, and raving that two sunshine friends whom he suspected of treachery must be sent for at once, the one to receive a challenge, the other a cowhiding. The gentlemen present — Perry Fuller, the Indian trader in whose government contracts Lane was accused of having pecuniary interest, Major Heath, and Governor Carney — bestirred themselves to refute the newspaper charges. Major Heath wrote a corrugated oath denying that Lane ever had financial transactions with Fuller of greater magnitude than house-renting, and Fuller signed it. Then something must be done about the Senate. Lane felt that he could not take his seat again without a personal explanation. As he was incapable of doing the work himself in his distraught condition, Carney and Heath, who did not then know all the facts, wrote out a short speech, pronouncing the "imputation conveyed by innuendo and indirection in the Boston 'Commonwealth' . . . a baseless calumny." On the following day — May 29th — Lane read this speech from manuscript in the Senate, and shortly afterward returned to his lodgings. "The speech," he said, "was just the thing. It was one of the happiest little efforts of my life."

June 11th Lane obtained leave of absence for ten days, subsequently prolonged until the close of the session, to visit Kansas, where such was the hostility which grew out of his alliance with President Johnson, he met a cold and hostile reception. Old acquaintances passed him on the street without recognition, and political conventions denounced him. It was a reception far different from what had awaited him in other days. "When Lane," said the "Leavenworth Daily Conservative" January 28th, 1862, "touches this soil, which his own courage, his own strategy, his own unconquerable perseverance saved for freedom, a glorious halo surrounds his head, a sublime inspiration fills his eye, a splendid glow lights up his countenance!"

After Lane's personal explanation in the Senate Carney made a visit of some days to New York. Upon his return to Washington he met Senator Doolittle, chairman of the Senate committee on Indian affairs, who showed him the copartnership papers of the Indian traders, Fuller & Co., in which Lane's name appeared, and a canceled check on E. H. Gruber & Co., of Leavenworth, which proved that he had received twenty thousand dollars from the concern.

Spending a few unhappy days in Kansas — doubly unhappy in the case of one so eager for the applause of men, so ambitious

"To live on their tongues and be their talk," —

Lane set out for Washington. He reached St. Louis on the 19th of June. There he met Governor Carney, and the whole situation was discussed — the fatal papers in Senator Doolittle's possession, and the exasperation of Republican congressmen. "Do you think," he asked, "that I had better resign? Do you suppose Johnson would give me a foreign mission? Could I be confirmed?" No light of hope appeared, "freaking gloom with glow." Lane returned to Leavenworth, where on the 1st of July he placed the pistol in his mouth and discharged it. Though the bullet passed through the brain, such was his vitality, he survived ten days.

No more unscrupulous soldier of fortune ever posed before the public than James H. Lane. He possessed in large measure the qualities that find a congenial and successful field in border turmoils. Of a slight and wiry figure, he had remarkable physical endurance. When removed from leadership of the overland "Northern army" in 1856, he set off immediately from Nebraska for Lawrence. Riding night and day, he arrived at his destination alone, and without apparent fatigue. His half-dozen companions, including Captain Samuel Walker and Old John Brown, all gave out by the way.

Lane was a confusion of passions grossly but not wholly ignoble. "Nobody can study his face," says Mrs. Ropes in her vivacious "Six Months in Kansas," "without a sensation very much like that with which one stands at the edge of a slimy, sedgy, uncertain morass." Conscienceless and with little confidence in the truth; selfish, grasping to the last degree, though at times and by spasms alive with seeming generosity and public spirit; watching the vanes of popular sentiment and veering with them, though occasionally showing unexpected boldness and obstinacy of opinion; attracting men and managing them consummately; able to pay heaviest obligations in the cheap coin of promises; indomitably persistent; cowardly and courageous by turn; a merciless enemy, but faithful to friends where personal interest did not require their sacrifice, Lane belonged to the basest, most mischievous class of politicians.

As a stump speaker he had no equal on the border. "I heard him at Nebraska City in 1856, before a hostile audience," says T. W. Higginson, "and if eloquence consists in moving and swaying men at pleasure I never saw a more striking exhibition of it." Lane's oratory faithfully reflected the character of the man, in which elements of chaos and lunacy were bound up with extraordinary astuteness and knowledge of human nature. It owed little to elocutionary grace. His manner was strained, angular, and dramatic, while his voice vibrated between shouts and blood-curdling whispers. Neither weight of thought, nor subtilty of logic, nor elevation of sentiment, nor exceptional range of vocabulary, appeared in his oratory. Lane was an unlettered man. In his hands rules of grammar fared badly. His knowledge came from observation rather than from books. Types can do only scant justice to oratory that is essentially personal, and hence his speeches lose in print. Skillful adaptation to time and place; sure tact in humoring the prejudices and firing the passions of an audience; unmeasured invective; an intensity of utterance that sometimes reached the verge of frenzy; grotesque, extravagant, ringing turns of phrase, and what, in the absence of a better word, is called magnetism, seem to be the capital elements of Lane's singularly effective speech.

That the harm which such a man does to a commonwealth must largely exceed the service goes without saying. Lane's energy, enthusiasm, and eloquence were serviceable in the territorial struggle, but even then these admirable qualities had a serious offset in his restless jealousy, intrigue, and rashness. The free-state cause would not have been safe in his hands an hour at any critical juncture. But if the evil was checked and mitigated at first by the necessities of the situation, when Lane reached the United States Senate and gained the ear of the administration, then his wretched policies and ambitions had ample sea-room — policies and ambitions that debauched the political morals of the commonwealth and drew upon it a grievous train of calamities.

CHAPTER XIV.

AD ASTRA.

It is often difficult, some one has said, to manage the future of an heroic action — a problem no more formidable for individuals than for states. An exceptional, brilliant past demands a present and a future that shall not be out of harmony or fall into anti-climax. Kansas has a significant and memorable history; the territorial struggle converted a wilderness, which had little claim upon the interest of mankind, into historic ground.

But now we reach a different epoch. From the date of settlement until the close of the war for the Union, though in the later stages it broke down into discreditable political intrigue and murderous bushfighting, the history of Kansas pursued a single theme. The war for the Union caught up and nationalized the verdict of the territorial broil.

In the large influx of colored people from the South in 1878-79 there was indeed a striking after-piece of the border conflict. Out of the unsettled condition of affairs in the South, out of the frictions and hardships unavoidable in a radical reconstruction of society, an extensive colored exodus sprang. Reports were rife that in Kansas — a name glorified in their minds as having some vague connection with emancipation — better homes, larger opportunities, kindlier treatment, awaited them than could be expected elsewhere. A colored convention, attended by delegates from fourteen states, met at Nashville, Tennessee, May 7th, 1879, and advised colored people of the South to " emigrate to those states and territories where they can enjoy all the rights which are guarantied by the laws and constitution of the United States." The excitement, fanned by outrages and demagogues, became intense. Notwithstanding the conciliatory efforts of Southern planters and the warnings of prominent colored leaders, who opposed migration as a remedy for grievances, not less than forty thousand negroes reached Kansas in every stage of destitution. These fugitives relief societies took in charge; provided with shelter, clothing, and food; organized into new colonies, or distributed among the older communities. On the whole, they seem to have improved their circumstances by the flight, though at the expense of much temporary discomfort. It was dramatically befitting — a fact not destitute of pathetic and poetic suggestion — that Southern negroes, in the extremities of reconstruction, should have turned their eyes toward the state where the first blow was struck for their freedom.

The people of Kansas in 1865 dropped the sword and grasped the plow. "A happy nation," says Ruskin, "may be defined as one in which the husband's hand is on the plow and the housewife's on the needle." Though embarrassed from 1864 to 1870 by Indian hostilities, in which at least a thousand citizens lost their lives and much property was destroyed; though scorched by occasional droughts; though visited in 1874 by plagues of locusts which desolated large districts, devouring fruits, vegetables, and grains with inexhaustible voracity, so that the familiar story of destitute, starving Kansas was heard once more, yet few American commonwealths have ever made so much material progress in twenty years.

This progress appears the more remarkable when we consider the geographical notions current fifty years ago, not to mention those that Senator Green, of Missouri, avowed so late as the Lecompton debate. Fifty years ago no agricultural future was thought possible for Kansas. It belonged to that vast Mediterranean tract, the greater part of which Irving thought would "form a lawless interval between the abodes of civilized man, like the wastes of the ocean or the deserts of Arabia. . . . Here may spring up new and mongrel races, like new formations in geology, the amalgamations of the débris and abrasions of former races civilized and savage; . . . the descendants of wandering hunters and trappers; of fugitives from the Spanish and American frontiers; of adventurers and desperadoes of every class and country, yearly ejected from the bosom of society into the wilderness."

Irving's prophecy went wide of the mark. No mongrel races, the detritus of neighboring civilizations, overrun Kansas. The wastes have disappeared or are disappearing. And recent writers do not hesitate to pronounce the Great American Desert a myth.

Little was done, as has been said before, to test the material resources of Kansas until the close of the Rebellion. The Indians, it is true, dabbled in agriculture. They succeeded in raising slender crops of corn, beans, and pumpkins. Rev. Thomas Johnson and other missionaries tried ineffectually to deepen their practical interest in the soil. During the territorial period political interests compelled a paramount attention. When the war for the Union broke out there followed a still greater diversion from farm industry. "One half of our entire population, between the ages of eighteen and forty-five," Governor Robinson wrote September 1st, 1862, "is in the army."

The population of Kansas in 1865 was 135,807. In the two succeeding decades the increase reached nearly a million souls, an immigration scarcely precedented in volume. A corresponding agricultural development followed, which placed Kansas, according to the census of 1880, seventeenth on the list of states in value of farm products, and eighth in value of live stock. In 1884 the wheat crop was 48,050,431 bushels against 25,279,884 in 1880. The corn crop rose from 101,421,718 bushels in 1880 to 190,870,686 in 1884. Other branches of farm industry advanced proportionally during the years 1882–84, so that in 1884 Kansas ranked among the foremost states in agricultural products.

Meteorological changes have accompanied the settlement of Kansas. However the fact may be explained, whatever agency the sudden and extensive agriculture or the planting of artificial forests, which, including fruit-trees, were estimated in 1884 at 171,810 acres, may have exerted, the amount of annual rain-fall, according to the foremost Kansas authority in such matters, Professor Snow, of the State University, shows an increase of five inches in Eastern Kansas during the last twenty years compared with a like pre-settlement period. In this augmented precipitation the western third of Kansas has shared, but so moderately as to promise little for agriculture. Apparently successful farming in that region must await the introduction of some practicable system of irrigation.

The creation of a great state in the wilderness of Kansas since 1865 is mainly a feat of the railroad. "If this invention," said Emerson, "has reduced England to a third of its size by bringing people so much nearer, in this country it has given a new celerity to *time*, or anticipated by fifty years the planting of tracts of land." Without the adventurous forecast and push of railway corporations, which drew public attention to the resources of Kansas and put them within reach, its settlement, like that of older states, would have stretched over a much longer period. By a system of advertising which skillfully seized upon avenues of communication — newspapers, pamphlets, traveling agents, national and international exhibitions — these corporations greatly abridged the ordinary course of events. Railways now penetrate every part of the state, —

"And thatch with towns the prairies broad."

At the last national census Kansas had reached the ninth place among the states in railway mileage. January, 1885, the amount of main track exceeded four thousand miles.

Certainly Kansas is assured of whatever starward energy may reside in numbers or in material prosperities. That their tendency is not altogether ennobling and uplifting social philosophers have been careful to point out. Matthew Arnold ventures his hope for the future on remnants in Israel who have not bowed the knee to Baal. Carlyle sneers at political economy, and disparages Americans in particular as a generation of dollar-hunters.

> " Oh, better far the briefest hour
> Of Athens self-consumed whose plastic power
> Hid beauty safe from Death in words or stone;
> Of Rome, fair quarry where those eagles crowd
> Whose fulgurous vans about the world had blown
> Triumphant storm and seeds of polity;
> Of Venice, fading o'er her shipless sea,
> Last iridescence of a fading cloud;
> Than this inert prosperity
> This bovine comfort in the sense alone!"

Mere bigness will not do much for a state or nation except in politics, where heavy weights tell. Holland, with limited area and population, is the mother of illustrious statesmen, soldiers, and scholars, and at one time championed the cause of freedom for the world. But while industrial and numerical progress does not necessarily imply progress in culture, yet it lays broad foundations upon which culture may build. It enlarges the scope of possibilities. The outcome of a splendid material development will turn on the question whether high moral, intellectual, æsthetic, and idealizing forces mingle in it, —

> "And set our pulse in tune with moods divine."

Kansas is not wanting in these superior forces. The New England colonists, though feebly influenced by motives of technical theology, gave immediate attention to the establishment of a church. October 1st, 1854, Rev. S. Y. Lum preached at Lawrence the first sermon delivered to white men in the territory. The Pioneer Hotel served as a meeting-house. "A few rough boards were brought for seats," Mrs. Robinson wrote, "and with singing by several good voices among the pioneers the usual church services were performed. . . . The people then, as on many succeeding sabbaths, were gathered together by the ringing of a large dinner bell." Plymouth Congregational Church was organized October 15th, with seven members, and is the oldest in Kansas. Other denominations began work in the territory at an early day. But as the religious history of the commonwealth exhibits little that is exceptional, it will not now be set forth at large. To home missionaries — to their patient, self-denying, heroic and sometimes perilous service — Kansas is heavily indebted. The State had 2046 church organizations in 1884, with a membership upwards of 185,000.

Educational matters have awakened strong interest in Kansas and exhibit praiseworthy progress, though the expectations of the Senate Committee on Education for 1858-9 have not as yet been realized. "It should be the aim of the educators of Kansas," said the optimistic committee, in a report recommending that the schools should be supplied with Webster's dictionaries, "to make this territory a model state in American literature. In this new territory we have all the requisite elements for building up a system of universities, colleges, schools, and seminaries of learning unequaled by any other on the globe.

Your committee believe it is the province of the people of Kansas to inaugurate an educational system which shall perfect the English language as well as English literature." It may have been sympathy, more or less conscious, with these liberal expectations that induced the territorial legislature in the sessions of 1855-60 to incorporate eighteen universities and ten colleges! Out of these twenty-eight institutions, twenty-five have perished — a mortality unparalleled in the history of education.

Governor Reeder commended the subject of schools to the legislature assembled at Pawnee, saying, with admirable point, "It is always better to pay for the education of a boy than the punishment of a man." The first territorial legislature, which was more modest in the matter of universities than most of the legislatures that followed, since it incorporated only three, provided for the establishment of schools in each county, "which shall be open and free to every class of white citizens," and directed that half the fines paid into county treasuries should be applied to their support. When the legislature fell into the hands of the free-state men in 1857, they reconstructed and liberalized the school system, and created the office of territorial superintendent. Yet, as a matter of fact, almost nothing was done under territorial laws until 1859. January 1st, 1859, not more than five school districts had been organized in Douglass County which was better circumstanced in this matter than the other counties. But before June, thirty additional districts were organized. And during this period considerable educational machinery was set up in the rest of the territory.

In Lawrence private schools began at an early date. "You have laid out grounds for a college," Mr. Lawrence wrote Governor Robinson, November 21st, 1854, "and will have a good one, without doubt, in due time; but in the first place you must have a preparatory school." On the 16th of January, 1855, a private school — the earliest in the territory of any kind — was opened in the Emigrant Aid building. It continued fourteen or fifteen weeks, with an attendance of twenty scholars. From its close, three terms of private school, for three months or less, comprised all the educational facilities of Lawrence until the 30th of March, 1857, when a select school of larger pretensions was opened. It continued for two years, with C. L. Edwards as principal, and was called the "Quincy High School," in honor of Josiah Quincy, of Boston. "A school is now in progress under the Unitarian Church, with two teachers and about fifty scholars," said a letter-writer April 17th, 1857.

In the spring of 1857 Mr. Lawrence gave ten thousand dollars to the city of Lawrence, the income of which should be devoted to school purposes. Originally a memorial college seems to have been in mind. "You shall have a college," he wrote Rev. Ephraim Nute, of Lawrence, December 16th, 1856, "which shall be a school of learning, and at the same time a monument to perpetuate the memory of those martyrs of liberty who fell during the recent struggles. Beneath it their dust shall rest. In it shall burn the light of liberty, which shall never be extinguished. . . . It shall be called the 'Free State College,' and all the friends of freedom shall be invited to lend a helping hand." The dream had a touching, though accidental and shadowy realization. No free-state college was ever built, but in making excavations for the main building of the State University workmen disinterred the remains of a dead soldier.

For a time the income of the ten thousand dollars was applied to the support of the Quincy High School. This fund attracted the attention of religious denominations, among which no less than three — Presbyterians, Congregationalists, and Episcopalians — lured by hopes of obtaining it as a nucleus for endowment, attempted the establishment of a college in Lawrence. The Presbyterians were first in the field, secured a site, and laid the foundations of a college building. In the spring of 1859 the "Circular of the Lawrence University" appeared, announcing that an "Institution of Learning of the first class has been

chartered and established at Lawrence, Kansas.
... The institution will open on the 11th of
April next [1859], and continue for a term of
three months." In the faculty "eminent teachers" and "distinguished educators" were found,
so that the institution confidently promised to furnish the "culture and discipline essential to success and eminence in any walk of life." But the
undertaking did not prosper. Denominational
feuds hurt it, and failure to get possession of the
Lawrence fund completed its ruin. "We did not
feel justified as a board," wrote the secretary of
the trustees to Mr. Lawrence, "to commence a
university in Kansas at the present time without
the benefit of your fund." In 1860 the Congregationalists took up the enterprise and proposed
to build a "Monumental College." An act of
incorporation was procured, a board of trustees
elected, and a subscription paper circulated. The
subscription paper met with some success. Money
and material to the amount of four thousand dollars, town lots, twenty acres of land in Lawrence
and twelve hundred elsewhere were pledged, provided thirty thousand dollars should be raised
before January 1st, 1861. That sum could not
be secured, and the effort failed. Finally the
Episcopalians took the business in hand. They
effected an organization, chose trustees, and solicited funds to complete the "Lawrence University." Governor Robinson writes May 22d, 1861,

that the "Episcopal College trustees" have purchased the site and basement of the building commenced last year by the Presbyterians, and are anxious to secure the Lawrence fund. But they did not get the money, and accomplished little beyond a partial completion of the unfinished building.

The much-sought ten thousand dollars fell at last to the State University, as did the assets of all the contemplated colleges in Lawrence that preceded it, and had decisive influence in determining where it should be placed. "The legislature has passed a law," Governor Robinson wrote Mr. Lawrence February 23d, 1863, "locating the State University at Lawrence, on condition that fifteen thousand dollars shall be paid into the treasury in six months, and forty acres of land given to the University. If these conditions are not complied with, then the University is [to be] located at Emporia. . . . It was with great difficulty that the location was secured here, and nothing saved us but the inducements of your fund."

The school system of Kansas does not require elaborate exposition in this place. In addition to primary and intermediate schools, the state supports three higher institutions, which are in successful and progressive operation, the Normal School at Emporia, the Agricultural College at Manhattan, and the University at Lawrence. Seven religious denominations have established colleges or universities which constitute an important factor of educational work in the state. Among Kansas teachers, it is due them to say, a commendable alertness, enthusiasm, and ambition prevail. Their work gives evidence that the very highest mission of education is not wholly unappreciated. That mission cannot be accomplished by processes, however admirable, of drill and acquisition alone. Recognizing the fact that moral and sentimental problems are by no means the least important for a community; that the first order of citizenship is impossible without the service of the impassioned imagination to body forth living, vivid conceptions of ethical and æsthetical realities, the ideal education creates vitalized intelligence, alive and responsive to whatever is nobly said or done.

In the ministry of physical environment, which, in its higher forms, is a perennial source of æsthetic, idealizing, poetic inspirations for communities as well as individuals, Kansas at once has drawbacks and advantages. Expanses of rolling prairie, flattening on the western border into level plains, sparingly watered with brooks and rivers, unbroken by great mountain ranges, without the shadows, recesses, and deep seclusions of primeval forests, exposed and bare to all the garish sunshine of the year, have obvious limitations of scenic power. Yet there are compensations. Some phases of beauty shine in magnificent exhibition.

There may be seen gorgeous splendors of cloud-glory; lustrous starlight and moonlight in comparison with which northern heavens seem faded and withdrawn; the winter greenery of wheat fields; the faint, delicate blush of maple buds that sometimes give signs of life in February; the brilliant bloom of wild crab-apple and Judas trees, greeting the spring; expanses of landscape rich with half tropical vegetation, figured with infinite interplay of light and shade, —

> "Vast as the sky against whose sunset shores,
> Wave after wave the billowy greenness pours."

It only remains to note the eager, restless, progressive spirit which distinguishes Kansas. This spirit has appeared and is appearing variously. It is exhibited in the great and as yet unsettled temperance agitation, which amended the organic law of the state by the introduction of a prohibitory clause; in the admission of both sexes to the State University from the date of its foundation; in the service of women as county superintendents of schools and as university regents and professors; in literary and art circles, which form an interesting feature of various towns; in the Woman's Social Science Club, an organization that embraces Kansas and Western Missouri, and holds semi-annual meetings for the discussion of social, domestic, hygienic, and literary topics. Such an aggressive and ambitious temper, which has the nerve to venture, to experiment, if need be, at the expense of tradition and precedent, promises effectual defense against enervating influences — against the insidious lethargy of fierce summer heats and that "bovine comfort" of broad and teeming acres which Lowell deprecates.

The history of Kansas which began three decades ago with a wilderness, with the fence and skirmish that preluded a tremendous civil war, closes with a great commonwealth rich in the material and immaterial things essential to life.

BIBLIOGRAPHY.

THE following publications have been of service in the preparation of this volume. The list does not include newspaper files, nor does it include to any considerable extent pamphlets and magazines:—

Agriculture, Biennial Reports of the State Board of. Topeka, Kansas.
Arnold, I. N. Life of A. Lincoln. Chicago, 1885.
Bartlett, D. W. Contested Elections in Congress, 1834-65.
Bowles, Samuel. Across the Continent. Springfield, 1865.
Boynton, C. B. A Journey through Kansas. Cincinnati, 1855.
Brevier, R. S. History of the 1st and 2d Missouri Brigades from Wakarusa to Appomattox. St. Louis, 1879.
Brewerton, G. D. A Rough Trip to the Border. New York, 1856.
Briggs, C. W. Reign of Terror in Kansas. Boston, 1856.
Britton, Wiley. Memoirs of the Rebellion on the Border. Chicago, 1882.
Brown, G. W. Reminiscences of Old John Brown. Rockford, Ill., 1880.
Burke, W. S. A Military History of Kansas Regiments. Leavenworth, 1870.
Canfield, J. H. A History of Kansas [in Berand's School History of the United States]. Philadelphia, 1884.
Clarke, J. F. Anti-Slavery Days. New York, 1884.
Colt, Mrs. M. D. Went to Kansas. Watertown, N. Y., 1862.
Copley, Josiah. Kansas and the Country Beyond. Philadelphia, 1867.

Curtis, G. T. Life and Letters of James Buchanan. New York, 1884.
Debates, Political, between Lincoln and Douglas. Columbus, 1860.
De Bow's Review. New Orleans.
Democratic Review, The. New York.
Dictionary, U. S. Biographical. Kansas edition, 1879.
Douglas, S. A., Life of. New York, 1860.
Doy, Dr. John, The Thrilling Narrative of. Boston, 1860.
Edwards, J. N. Shelby and his Men. Cincinnati, 1867.
Emerson, R. W. Miscellanies. Boston, 1884.
Executive Documents, 33d Congress, 2d Session. Nos. 1, 31, 45, 73.
———, 34th Congress, 1st and 2d Sessions. Nos. 4, 23, 28, 33, 53, 66, 106.
———, 34th Congress, 3d Session. Nos. 1, 2, 5, 7, 10, 34, 45, 60, 111.
———, 35th Congress, 1st Session. Nos. 2, 8, 11, 12, 17, 21, 22, 80, 103, 111, 114, 118, 128.
———, 35th Congress, 2d Session. Nos. 37, 46, 66, 96.
Fisk, John. American Political Ideas. New York, 1884.
French, B. F. Historical Collections of Louisiana.
Gihon, J. H. Governor Geary's Administration in Kansas. Philadelphia, 1857.
Gladstone, T. H. Kansas; or, Squatter Life and Border Warfare in the Far West. London, 1857.
Gleed, C. S., Editor. The Kansas Memorial. Kansas City, 1880.
Globe, Congressional, The. Washington.
Gordon, J. W. An Argument designed to show the Origin of the Troubles in Kansas. Indianapolis, Ind., 1856.
Greeley, Horace. The American Conflict. Hartford.
Greene, Max. The Kansas Region. New York, 1856.
Greg, Josiah. Commerce of the Prairies. Philadelphia, 1850.
Griswold, Wayne. Kansas, her Resources and Developments. Cincinnati, 1857.
Hakluyt, Richard. The Principal Navigations, Voyages, Traffiques, and Discoveries of the English Nation. London, 1599.
Hale, E. E. Kansas and Nebraska. Boston, 1854.
Higginson, T. W. A Ride Through Kansas. [1856.]

Hinton, R. J. The Rebel Invasion of Missouri and Kansas. Chicago, 1865.
History of the Expeditions of Captains Lewis and Clark. Philadelphia, 1814.
Holloway, J. N. History of Kansas. Lafayette, Ind., 1868.
Holst, Herman von. The Constitutional and Political History of the United States. Chicago.
Hughes, T. H. The Struggle for Kansas [in Ludlow's History of the United States]. London, 1862.
Hugo, Victor. John Brown. Paris, E. Dentu, 1861.
——— Letters on John Brown. New York, 1860.
Hutchinson, C. C. Resources of Kansas. Topeka, 1871.
Hutchinson, William. A History of Lawrence. 1859.
Hyatt, Thaddeus, The Prayer of, to James Buchanan in behalf of Kansas. Washington, 1860.
Impeachment Cases. Lawrence, Kansas, 1862.
Information for the People. Two Tracts for the Times. Boston, 1855.
Irving, Washington. Astoria.
——— Tour on the Prairies.
Journal of the Missouri Senate, 1858–59.
Kansas, History of the State of. Chicago, 1883.
Kansas State Rights. An Appeal to the Democracy of the South. Washington, 1857.
Lays of the Emigrants, as sung by Parties for Kansas on the Days of their Departure from Boston. Boston, 1855.
Louisiana, History of. From the French of M. Le Page du Pratz. London, 1774.
Lowman, H. E. The Lawrence Raid. Lawrence, Kansas, 1864.
"Lynceus," Letters of, for the People on the Present Crisis. 1853.
Magazine, The Kansas. Topeka.
Massachusetts Emigrant Aid Company. Boston, 1854.
Meline, J. F. Two Thousand Miles on Horseback. New York, 1868.
Miscellaneous Documents [Senate], 34th Congress, 1st and 2d Session. Nos. 17, 32, 49, 58, 80.
——— [Senate], 34th Congress, 3d Session. Nos. 17, 48.
——— [H. R.], 34th Congress, 1st and 2d Sessions. Nos. 3, 42, 82, 90, 100, 101, 103, 119, 120.

Miscellaneous Documents [H. R.], 34th Congress, 3d Session. Nos. 12, 13, 38, 49.
—— [Senate], 35th Congress, 1st Session. Nos. 140, 165, 194, 204, 206, 228, 232, 242.
—— [H. R.], 35th Congress, 1st and 2d Sessions. Nos. 37, 39, 40, 41, 43, 44, 50, 60, 80, 95, 103, 104, 120, 124.
—— [Senate], 36th Congress, 1st and 2d Sessions. Nos. 16, 23.
—— [H. R.], 36th Congress, 1st Session. Nos. 6, 34.
—— [Senate], 37th Congress, 3d Session. No. 29.
New England Emigrant Aid Company. Boston, 1854.
New Haven Memorial, The, to the President. Boston, 1857.
Orville, J. V. History of American Conspiracies. New York.
Parker, N. H. Kansas and Nebraska Handbook. Boston, 1857.
Phillips, Wendell. Orations, Speeches, Lectures, and Letters. Boston, 1884.
Phillips, W. A. The Conquest of Kansas. Boston, 1856.
Pike, Major Z. M. An Account of Expeditions. Philadelphia [1808].
Rebellion Record, The. New York.
Redpath, J. The Public Life of Captain John Brown. Boston, 1860.
—— The Roving Editor. New York, 1859.
—— and Hinton, R. J. Handbook to Kansas. New York, 1859.
Register, The Kansas Annual.
Reports [Senate], 33d Congress, 1st Session. No. 15.
—— [H. R.], 33d Congress, 2d Session. Nos. 36, 37.
—— [Senate], 34th Congress, 1st and 2d Sessions. Nos. 34, 198, 282.
—— [H. R.], 34th Congress, 1st and 2d Sessions. Nos. 3, 181, 200, 275.
—— [H. R.], 34th Congress, 3d Session. Nos. 173, 186, 179, 184.
—— [H. R.], 35th Congress, 1st Session. No. 377.
—— [Senate], 35th Congress, 1st Session. No. 82.
—— [Senate], 36th Congress, 1st Session. No. 278.
—— [H. R.], 36th Congress, 1st and 2d Sessions. Nos. 255, 665, 104.
Richardson, A. D. Beyond the Mississippi. Hartford, 1867.

Robinson, Mrs. S. T. L. Kansas; Its Exterior and Interior Life. Boston, 1856.
Ropes, Mrs. H. A. Six Months in Kansas. Boston, 1856.
Sanborn, F. B. The Life and Letters of John Brown. Boston, 1885.
—— Life of John Brown [in Orcutt's History of Torrington, Conn.]. Albany, 1878.
Scribner's Statistical Atlas. New York.
Seward, W. H., The Works of. Boston.
Smithsonian Reports, 1869.
Stephens, A. H. The War between the States.
Stringfellow, B. F. Negro Slavery no Evil.
Sumner, Charles, The Works of. Boston.
Ternaux — Compans, H. Voyages, Relations et Mémoires publiés. Paris.
Thoreau, H. D. A Yankee in Canada, with Anti-Slavery and Reform Papers. Boston, 1866.
Three Years on the Kansas Border. New York, 1856.
Tice, H. J. Over the Plains and on the Mountains. St. Louis [1871].
Tomlinson, W. P. Kansas in 1858. New York, 1858.
Transactions of the Kansas Historical Society. Topeka, 1881.
Tuttle, C. R. Centennial History of Kansas. Madison, Wis.
War of the Rebellion, The. A Compendium of the Official Records. Washington.
Webb, R. D. Life and Letters of Captain John Brown. London, 1861.
Webb, Thomas H. Information for Kansas Immigrants. Boston, 1857.
Wilder, D. W. The Annals of Kansas. Topeka, 1875.
Wilson, Henry. The Rise and Fall of the Slave Power. Boston.

INDEX.

Abbott, J. B., 88, 179, 199, 242.
Abolitionists, the early, 15.
Atchison, D. R., 24, 25; designs in Kansas, 56; course of in the Wakarusa War, 97, 98, 100; at Lawrence May 21, 1856, 121, 122, 123, 124; appeals of to the South, 173, 174, 188, 189; conference of with Governor Geary at Franklin, 200, 201.
Atchison, town of, 28.
Atkins, Representative of Tennessee, 232.

Babcock, C. W., 95, 96.
Bayard, J. A., on Emigrant Aid Company, 33; on the Topeka movement, 77; on the Lecompton Constitution, 223.
Beecher, H. W., 165.
Bell, John, 9, 23.
Benjamin, J. P., 75.
Benton, T. H., 7, 11.
Biggs, Senator, of North Carolina, 231.
Black Jack, battle of, 154-156.
Blood, James, 132, 143, 148, 185, 199.
Blue Lodges, 41.
Bourgmont, M. de, 20.
Branscomb, C. H., 34.
Branson, Jacob, 86, 87; arrest and rescue of, 88, 89.
Brindle, General William, 230.
Brooks, P. S., 129.
Brown, John, speech of at Lawrence, 100, 101; relation of to Kansas history, 137; character and theories of, 138-141; raid of upon the Pottawatomie, 142-154; fight of at Black Jack, 154-156; foray upon St. Bernard, 156, 157; releases Pate, 159-161; narrow escape of from capture, 171; at Lawrence, September, 1856, 199; declaration of to Captain Snyder, 244; letter of to A. A. Lawrence, 251; interview of with Governor Robinson, 252; raid of into Missouri, 252-255.

Brown, John Carter, 30.
Brown, John, Jr., 141, 142.
Brown, R. P., 72, 73.
Buchanan, James, 210, 211, 230.
Buford, Jefferson, 105, 106, 125.
Bulkley, Harrison, 87.
Bull Creek, 190, 198.
Bushnell, Horace, 31.
Butler, A. P., 8, 97, 105.
Butler, Rev. Pardee, 79-82.
Byrd, J. H., 65.

Cabot, Dr. Samuel, Jr., 30, 166.
Calhoun, John, 221, 229, 230.
Calhoun, J. C., 4.
Callew, Jake, 295, 296.
"Candle-box" election returns, the, seizure of, 229, 230.
Carney, Governor Thomas, 271, 273, 287, 297, 298; confidential relations of with Lane, 299-302.
Caskie, John S., 8.
Cass, Lewis, on the Compromise of 1850, 1; presents the Topeka memorial to the Senate, 74, 75; denounces Sumner's speech, 128.
Cato, Judge S. G., letter to Governor Shannon on the Pottawatomie raid, 152; course of toward free-state prisoners, 202; a mandamus of, 219.
Census, first territorial, 43; second territorial, 212.
Chase, S. P., 9, 10, 12.
Choate, Rufus, 13.
Church, Lieutenant J. R., disperses John Brown, Jr.'s company, 141, 142, 147.
Clarke, G. W., raid of in the Southeast, 239, 240; arrest of, 248, 249.
Clay, Henry, 1.
Cline, Captain, 190.
Coates, Kersey, 50.
Coleman, F. N., 86, 87.
Committees, Eastern Aid, operations of, 164.
"Commonwealth," the Boston, 299, 300.

330 INDEX.

Compromise, the, of 1850, 1, 11.
"Conservative," the Leavenworth, 278, 301.
Constitutional Convention, the, at Topeka, 70, 71; at Lecompton, 211, 220-226; at Minneola and Leavenworth, 261; at Wyandotte, 263, 264.
Convention, the, at Salt Creek Valley, June, 1854, 27; at Lawrence, June 27, 1855, 63; August 14-15, 63, 68-69; at Big Springs, October 5, 64-68; at Topeka, September 19, 69; at Leavenworth, November 14, 83, 84; at Topeka, July 4, 1856, 131; at Lecompton, July, 1857, 215; at Topeka, July, 216; at Grasshopper Falls, August, 216, 217; at Lawrence, December, 225-228.
Conway, M. F., 54, 90, 104.
Cooke, Colonel P. St. George, 171, 192, 193, 194, 198, 199, 200.
Coronado, 17-19.
Court, Squatter, 242-244.
Covode, John, 281.
Crittenden-Montgomery bill, the, 234.

Davis, Jefferson, 135, 265.
Debates of 1850 and 1854, comparison of, 4.
De Bow's Review, "An Appeal" in, 175, 176.
Deitzler, G. W., 60.
Democratic party, the, changes of in nomenclature, 263.
Democratic Review, 49, 60, 106, 234.
Denver, J. W., appointment of as acting governor, 228; familiarity of with the border, 229; letter of to President Buchanan, 231; visit of to the Southeast, 250, 251; refusal of to remove from Lecompton, 259; vetoes bill for a Constitutional Convention, 259; resignation of, 260.
Dixon, Archibald, amendment of to the Kansas-Nebraska bill, 3.
Dodge, A. C., bill of for the organization of Nebraska, 2.
Donaldson, Marshal J. B., proclamation of, 118; at Topeka, July 4, 1856, 133, 134.
Doolittle, Senator, 302, 303.
Douglas, S. A., Chairman of Senate Committee on Territories, 3; statement of to Senator Dixon, 3, 4; relation of to the Compromise of 1850, 5, 6; qualifications of for leadership, 6; debates of with Lincoln, 8, 9; burnt in effigy, 14; on the Emigrant Aid Company, 33; on the convention at Big Springs, 68; attacks the Topeka Memorial, 74, 75, 76; denounces Sumner, 129; on the slavery clause of the Lecompton Constitution, 222.
Dow, Charles M., 86.
Doyle, James P., 145, 147.
Dred Scott decision, The, 210.
Dunn Bill, the, 107.
Dutch Henry's Crossing, massacre at, 142-154; consequences of the raid upon, 176, 190.

Easton, affray at, 72, 73.
Edwards, C. L., 314.
Elections, territorial, November, 1854, 40; March 30, 1855, 43-49; October 5, 1857, 218; December 21, 1857, and January 4, 1858, 225, 228-230.
Eldridge, S. W., 172, 179, 180.
Elmore, Rush, 133, 134, 222.
Emerson, R. W., 164, 310.
Emery, J. S., 104.
Emigrant Aid Company, 29-33; towns founded by, 34; rumors concerning on the border, 39, 40.
English Bill, the, 235, 236.
English, W. H., 14, 235.
Everett, Edward, 9, 23.
Examiner, the Christian, 232.

Famine of 1860, the, 271.
Fort Orleans, 20.
Fort Saunders, capture of, 182.
Fort Scott, 238, 239; expedition of Captain Walker to, 248, 249; attacked by Montgomery, 249, 250; Denver's visit to, 250, 251.
Fort Titus, capture of, 182-185.
Franklin, attacks upon, 179-182.
Free-State party, the, 63, 64, 216-218, 225-228, 262, 265, 266.
Fuller, Perry, 300.

Geary, J. W., appointment of as governor, 197; succors Lawrence, 198-201; efforts of to reform the judiciary, 202, 203; proclamation of for a day of thanksgiving, 203; interview of with Governor Robinson, 204; assault on, 205, 206; letter of to A. A. Lawrence, 207; resigns, 208.
Gihon, J. H., on the second territorial legislature, 205.
Gladstone, T. H., 117, 128, 268.
Green, J. S., on Emigrant Aid Company, 33; member of conference committee on the Lecompton bill, 235; opposes the Wyandotte Constitution, 264.
Grinnell, Moses H., 31.

Hale, Edward Everett, 31.
Halleck, General H. W., 279, 280.

INDEX. 331

Halpine, C. G., Report of, 276.
Hamilton, Charles A., 244-246.
Hammond, Senator of South Carolina, 231, 236.
Harlan, James, 75.
Harris, James, testimony of on the Pottawatomie raid, 150.
Harvey, J. A., 192, 193, 201.
Heiskell, W. A., letter to Governor Shannon on the Pottawatomie raid, 150, 151.
Hickory Point, Jefferson County, skirmish at, 201, 202.
Higginson, T. W., 303.
Houston, Samuel, 9, 23.
Houston, S. D., 55.
Howard, W. A., 108, 114, 235.
Howe, Dr. S. G., 30, 169.
Hoyt, Major, D. S., murder of, 182.
Hughes, Representative of Indiana, 212.
Hughes, Thomas, 148.
Hunter, General David, 276, 279-281.
Hunter, R. M. T., 235.
Hutchinson, William, 185.
Hyatt, Thaddeus, 168, 169.

Indian chiefs, opinions of concerning Lane, 278, 279.
Investigating Committee, the Congressional, 108, 145, 146.
Irving, W., on the "Great American Desert," 307, 308.
Iverson, Alfred, 232.

Jayhawking, note on the origin of the word, 240.
Johnson, Andrew, remarks of upon John Brown, 146.
Johnson, Rev. Thomas, 53, 308.
Johnston, Colonel J. E., 170, 200.
Jones, S. J., 87, 88; arrests Branson, 88; appeals to Missouri and Governor Shannon, 90, 91; on the Wakarusa treaty, 99, 100; makes arrests in Lawrence, 108, 109; attempted assassination of, 109, 110; at Lawrence, May 21, 1856, 122, 123, 125, 126, 127; assails Secretary Stanton, 219; advice of to McLean, 229, 230.
Judiciary, the territorial, 202, 203.

Kansas, territorial boundaries, 17; a part of the Louisiana purchase, 19; migrations across, 22; an Indian reservation, 22; an arena for experiments in popular sovereignty, 23; Southern opinion of, 231, 232; admission of to the Union, 266; character of the struggle for, 265, 266; social condition of in the territorial period, 268-270; drouth in, 270; "exodus" of negroes to, 305, 306; Irving on, 307, 308; Indian troubles in, 307; agricultural development of, 308, 309; meteorological changes in, 309, 310; indebtedness to railroads, 310; religious progress of, 311, 312; educational history of, 312-318; natural scenery of, 318, 319; spirit and temper of, 319, 320.
Kansas-Nebraska bill, 2, 3; its revisions, 4; Southern views of, 7, 8; arguments for, 6-8; argument against, 10, 12; review of the debate on, 12, 13; consequences of the passage of, 13, 14.
Kickapoo, 28.

Lane, J. H., 63; at Big Springs, 64, 65; President of the Topeka Constitutional Convention, 70; elected senator under the Topeka movement, 74; in charge of the Topeka memorial to Congress, 75, 76; collision with Douglas, 76, 77; second in command during Wakarusa War, 92; speech at Franklin, 99; "Northern army" of, 169, 170; expedition of against Fort Saunders, 182; marches to Lecompton, 193, 194; operations of in Jefferson County, 201; election of to the United States Senate, 272; campaign of in 1861, 274-278; "Great Southern Expedition" of, 279-281; declarations of to General McClellan, 279; appointment of as Commissioner for recruiting, 281, 282; downfall and death of, 298-302; character and influence of, 302-304.
Lawrence, Amos A., 30, 35, 49, 61, 92, 104, 166, 197, 199, 251; efforts of for the release of Governor Robinson, 195, 196; Letter of to Governor Robinson, 314; bequest of to the city of Lawrence, 314; letter of to Rev. E. Nute, 315.
Lawrence, founding of, 34, 35; siege of in the Wakarusa War, 91; attack upon, May 21, 1856, 118-128; condition of in the summer of 1856, 179, 180; destruction of by Quantrill, 285-296; schools and colleges at, 314-317.
Leavenworth, 28; election riot at, 72; Emory's regulators in, 188.
Leavenworth Constitution, 259-261.
Lecompte, S. D., charge of to the grand jury of Douglas County, 111, 112; letter of to J. A. Stewart, 123; con-

332   INDEX.

troversy of with Governor Geary, 203.
Lecompton, 28; panic at, 186, 187; reconnaissance upon, 192-194; affray at, 206, 207; free-state demonstration at, 221.
Lecompton Constitution, the, 211, 212, 220-225, 227-230; in Congress, 232-236.
Legislature, territorial, first session of, 53, 54-58; second session of, 205; extra session of, 227, 228; third session of, 257-259; fourth session of, 262.
Lewis and Clark, expeditions of, 21.
Lexington, Mo., Convention, 24.
Liberator, the, 29, 31.
Liberty township, skirmish in, 238, 239.
Lincoln, A., debates with Douglas, 8, 9; relations of with Lane, 274; indorsement of on Halleck's letter, 280; letter of to Secretary Stanton, 297.
Lines, C. B., 165.
Little, Marshal, 242-244.
Log Cabins, 102, 268.
Long, Major H. S., 21.
Lowman, H. E., 289.
Lowrey, G. P., 90, 95, 96.
Lum, Rev. S. Y., 311.
"Lynceus," 24, 25.

McClellan, General G. B., 279, 280.
McGee County, frauds in, 218.
McIntosh, Lieutenant James, 109, 110.
McLean, L. A., 229, 230.
Marais des Cygnes Massacre, 244-246.
Mason, James M., 129.
Massachusetts Legislature, the resolutions of, 163.
Medary, Samuel, 261.
Minneola, 258, 259.
Missouri Compromise, 3, 7, 11-13.
Missouri Legislature, action of in reference to troubles in the Southeast, 252-255.
Missouri River, the, embargo on, 166, 167.
Missouri, Western, population of, 24, 25; squatters from, 26.
Montgomery, James, 240, 241; attempt of to kill Hamilton, 244; attacks Fort Scott, 249, 250.
Morrow, Robert, 172.

Native American Suffrage, 41, 42.
Nute, Rev. E., 316.

Oliver, Mordecai, apology of for his constituents, 39; investigations of concerning the Pottawatomie raid, 146.
Osawatomie, 34; pillage of, 162; battle of, 190, 191.
Osceola, Missouri, sack of, 275.
Overland immigration, 167, 172.
Oxford, frauds at, 218.

Parkville Luminary, the, 47.
Pate, Captain H. C., 152, 153; surrenders at Black Jack, 155, 156; released by Colonel Sumner, 159, 161.
Pawnee, 53.
Phillips, William, 49, 50, 188.
Phillips, W. A., 164.
Pierce, Franklin, election of as president, 2; dispatch of to Shannon, 119; declarations of concerning the free-state movement, 195, 196; releases Governor Robinson, 196.
Pike, Captain J. A., 288.
Pike, Lieutenant Z. M., 21.
Plumb, P. B., 294.
Plymouth Church, 312.
Polk, Senator of Missouri, 233, 234.
Pomeroy, S. C., 126, 172, 195, 196, 272.
Popular Sovereignty, first appearance of in politics, 7; constitutionally exercised when, 8, 9.
Pottawatomie Massacre, the, 142-154, 162, 176, 190.
Prairie City, skirmish at, 153, 154.
Presidential Election of 1856, the, 209.
Preston, Colonel W. J., 171, 172.
Price Raid, the, 297, 298.
Pugh, George E., 75.

Quantrill, W. C., 286-294.

"Red-legs," the, 284-286.
Redpath, James, 170.
Reeder, A. H., 37, 38; canvass of returns of the March election, 1885, 49-52; visits Washington, 52; breaks with the legislature, 55, 56; removal from office, 58; character of his administration, 58; at Big Springs, 65-68; elected senator under the Topeka movement, 74; attempted arrest of, 113, 114.
Reid, J. W., 190, 191, 200, 238.
Republican party, the, organization of in Kansas, 262, 263.
Robinson, Charles, 33, 34; letters to A. A. Lawrence, 35, 49, 61, 62, 92, 93, 104, 199, 203, 204, 314, 317; urges M. F. Conway to resign his seat in the territorial legislature, 54; scheme of counter-moves, 59; secures Sharpe's rifles, 60; an abolitionist, 64; elected

INDEX. 333

governor under the Topeka Constitution, 71; consulted by Branson rescuers, 89, 90; in command during the Wakarusa War, 92; speech at Franklin, 99; Atchison on, 100; plans for a visit to the East, 114, 115; arrested at Lexington, Mo., 116; experiences of at Leavenworth, 116, 117; letter to the Topeka Legislature, 132; Missourians on the plans of, 174; interview of with Governor Geary, 204; favors voting, 217, 218; accompanies Governor Denver to the Southeast, 250; interview of with old John Brown, 252; leadership of, 266; message of to the state legislature, 271; relations of to Lane, 272; letter of to General Fremont, 275, 276; reply of to Secretary Stanton, 282; impeachment of, 282-284.
Robinson, Mrs. S. T. L., 89, 164, 184, 196, 312.
Rodrigue, Aristides, 185.
Ropes, Mrs. H. A., 304.

Sanborn, F. B., 154.
Saunders, Fort, capture of, 182.
Sedgwick, Major John, 183, 185, 186.
Selby, Minerva, testimony of concerning the Pottawatomie raid, 151.
Seward, W. H., on the Compromise of 1850, 6; character of, 10; on the consequences of the Kansas-Nebraska bill, 16; member of conference committee on the Lecompton bill, 235; calls up the bill for the admission of Kansas, 266.
Shannon, Wilson, 79, 83, 84; reception at Shawnee Mission, 82, 83; calls out the militia, 91; visits Lawrence, 98; speech at Franklin, 99; letter of to the president, 119; orders the dispersion of the Topeka Legislature, 130; on the Pottawatomie raid, 152; proclamation of June 4, 1856, 158; negotiations of at Lawrence, 185, 186; removal of, 187; on governing Kansas, 187.
Sherman, John, 108, 114, 235.
Sherman, William, 145, 147, 150, 151.
Shore, Captain S. T., 154, 155.
Silliman, Professor Benjamin, Sr., 31.
Slave-Code of the first territorial legislature, 56-58.
Smith, Gerrit, 140, 141.
Smith, General P. F., 189, 192, 203.
Smith, Samuel A., 232, 233.
Snow, F. H., 309.
Snyder, Captain Eli, 245, 246.
Southeast, the, 237, 238, 241.
Spooner, W. B., 30.

"Squatter Sovereign," the, 111, 121, 167.
Stanton, E. M., 274, 282, 297.
Stanton, F. P., appointment of as territorial secretary, 211; his apportionment of the territory, 212; rejects the Oxford and McGee returns, 218; assailed by Sheriff Jones, 219; calls an extra session of the legislature, 226.
Stearns, G. L., 31.
Stephens, A. H., on the Compromise of 1850, 5; on the nativity of the immigrants, 43; member of conference committee on the Lecompton bill, 235.
Stewart, governor of Missouri, 252, 253.
Stringfellow, B. F., slave-colonization project, 27; on the plans of free-state men, 39; appeal of, to the South, 173, 174.
Sumner, Charles, 9; 128, 129.
Sumner, Colonel E. V., 93; disperses the Topeka Legislature, 131-135; on Shannon's proclamation, 158; releases Pate, 159-161; disbands Whitfield's command, 161.
Swift, F. B., 202.

Tecumseh, forays into, 178.
Thayer, Eli, 29, 30.
Thorpe, Jim, 47-49.
Tissenet, M. du, 19.
Titus, Colonel H. T., 121, 183, 184, 186, 200.
Toombs bill, the, 107, 108.
Topeka, 34; freebooting in the vicinity of 178, 179; destruction of ordered by Secretary Woodson, 192.
Topeka Constitution, the, 71; in Congress, 74-77; character of the movement, 77, 78.
Topeka Legislature, the, 74; dispersion of, 129; third session of, 204, 205; fourth session of, 214; session at Lawrence, 257; final adjournment of, 258.
Townsley, James, 143-145, 148.
Tweed, W. M., 13.

Updegraff, Dr. W. W., 190.

Wakarusa War, the, 91-100.
Walker, Mathew, 174.
Walker, R. J., appointed governor, 210; speech of at Topeka, 213; watches the state legislature, 214; rejects the Oxford and McGee returns, 218; makes a tour of Lecompton, 219, 220; departure of from Kansas, 226.

INDEX.

Walker, Samuel, on the winter of 1855-56, 102, 103; consulted by Colonel Sumner, 132; captures Fort Titus, 182-185; encounter of with a free-state mob, 186; interview of with Colonel Cooke, 193; seizes "candlebox" election returns, 230; expedition of to Fort Scott, 247-249.

Webster, Daniel, 5, 13.

Weiner, Theodore, 143, 148.

White, Rev. Martin, 142; on the Pottawatomie raid, 151, 152; driven from the territory, 176, 177; shoots a son of John Brown, 190; resolution of in the territorial legislature, 206.

Whitfield, J. W., 40, 41, 110, 157, 161, 200.

Wigfall, senator of Texas, 264.

Wilkinson, Allan, 145, 147.

Williams, H. H. 142, 143, 147, 249.

Williams, J. M. S., 30.

Wilson, Henry, 216.

Women, hardships of, 103; heroism of, 292.

Wood, S. N., 89, 90, 108, 109.

Wood, Captain T. J., 202.

Woodson, Daniel, acting governor, 83, 189; letter to Colonel Sumner, 130, 131, 134; orders the destruction of Topeka, 192; correspondence of with the "State Central Committee," 194, 195.

Wyandotte Constitutional Convention, 262, 263, 264; in Congress, 264, 265.

American Commonwealths.

EDITED BY

HORACE E. SCUDDER.

A series of volumes narrating the history of such States of the Union as have exerted a positive influence in the shaping of the national government, or have a striking political, social, or economical history.

The commonwealth has always been a positive force in American history, and it is believed that no better time could be found for a statement of the life inherent in the States than when the unity of the nation has been assured; and it is hoped by this means to throw new light upon the development of the country, and to give a fresh point of view for the study of American history.

This series is under the editorial care of Mr. Horace E. Scudder, who is well known both as a student of American history and as a writer.

The aim of the Editor will be to secure trustworthy and graphic narratives, which shall have substantial value as historical monographs and at the same time do full justice to the picturesque elements of the subjects. The volumes are uniform in size and general style with the series of "American Statesmen" and "American Men of Letters," and are furnished with maps, indexes, and such brief critical apparatus as add to the thoroughness of the work.

Speaking of the series, the *Boston Journal* says: "It is clear that this series will occupy an entirely new place in our historical literature. Written by competent and aptly chosen authors, from fresh materials, in convenient form, and with a due regard to proportion and proper emphasis, they promise to supply most satisfactorily a positive want."

The series, so far as arranged, comprises the following volumes: —

NOW READY.

Virginia. A History of the People. By JOHN ESTEN COOKE, author of "The Virginia Comedians," "Life of Stonewall Jackson," "Life of General Robert E. Lee," etc.

Oregon. The Struggle for Possession. By WILLIAM BARROWS, D. D.

Maryland. By WILLIAM HAND BROWNE, Associate of Johns Hopkins University.

Kentucky. By NATHANIEL SOUTHGATE SHALER, S. D., Professor of Palæontology, Harvard University, recently Director of the Kentucky State Survey.

Michigan. By Hon. T. M. COOLEY, LL. D.

Kansas. By LEVERETT W. SPRING, Professor of English Literature in the University of Kansas.

IN PREPARATION.

Tennessee. By JAMES PHELAN, Ph. D. (Leipsic).

California. By JOSIAH ROYCE, Instructor in Philosophy in Harvard University.

Connecticut. By ALEXANDER JOHNSTON, author of a "Handbook of American Politics," Professor of Jurisprudence and Political Economy in the College of New Jersey.

Pennsylvania. By Hon. WAYNE MCVEAGH, late Attorney-General of the United States.

South Carolina. By Hon. WILLIAM H. TRESCOT, author of "The Diplomacy of the American Revolution."

New York. By Hon. ELLIS H. ROBERTS.

Missouri. By LUCIEN CARR, M. A., Assistant Curator of the Peabody Museum of Archæology.

Massachusetts. By BROOKS ADAMS.

Others to be announced hereafter. Each volume, with Maps, 16mo, gilt top, $1.25.

PRESS NOTICES.

"VIRGINIA."

Mr. Cooke has made a fascinating volume — one which it will be very difficult to surpass either in method or interest. If all the volumes of the series ["American Commonwealths"] come up to the level of this one — in interest, in broad tolerance of spirit, and in a thorough comprehension of what is best worth telling — a very great service will have been done to the reading public. True historic insight appears through all these pages, and an earnest desire to do all parties and religions perfect justice. The story of the settlement of Virginia is told in full. . . . It is made as interesting as a romance. — *The Critic* (New York).

It need not be said that it is written in a fascinating style, and animated by a spirit of strong love for the author's native State, and pride in its history. It should be said further that it brings out many an obscure or forgotten bit of history, and makes real an epoch which is familiar to very few. — *New York Evening Post.*

No more acceptable writer could have been selected to tell the story of Virginia's history. Mr. Cooke is a graceful writer, and thoroughly informed in reference to his subject. . . . He has mastered his subject, and tells the story in a delightful way. — *Educational Journal of Virginia* (Richmond, Va.).

"OREGON."

The long and interesting story of the struggle of five nations for the possession of Oregon is told in the graphic and reliable narrative of William Barrows. . . . A more fascinating record has seldom been written. . . . Careful research and pictorial skill of narrative commend this book of antecedent history to all interested in the rapid march and wonderful development of our American civilization upon the Pacific coast. — *Springfield Republican.*

There is so much that is new and informing to the reading world embodied in this little volume that we commend it with enthusiasm. It is written with great ability and in a pleasing style, a vein of humor rippling along its pages and imparting an agreeable and appetizing flavor to the varied descriptions. . . . The book is worthy of careful perusal by all who claim to be intelligent concerning the rich and progressive country beyond the Rocky Mountains. — *Magazine of American History* (New York).

"MARYLAND."

In the choice of Mr. William Hand Browne as an author for a trustworthy and graphic account of the rise and development of Maryland, the editor of this valuable series of historical volumes has made a very strong point. Mr. Browne's familiarity with the political and material development of the Province as well as the State has enabled him to produce a work of more than usual excellence. . . . Much that has been hitherto obscure is now presented to the reader in a clear light. The book is well written in simple, straightforward, vigorous English, and is a substantial contribution to the history of America. — *Magazine of American History.*

In every way an admirable and most useful contribution to American history. . . . Mr. Browne has done his work with rare skill, thoroughness, and the moderation that of all things befits historical writing. His narrative, he tells us, has been written almost entirely "from the original manuscript records and archives." He has certainly made the subject his own, and the result is a volume of such interest that the reader cannot afford to skip a line. — *New York Graphic.*

"KENTUCKY."

Professor Shaler has made use of much valuable existing material, and by a patient, discriminating, and judicious choice has given us a complete and impartial record of the various stages through which this State has passed from its first settlement to the present time. No one will read this story of the building of one of the great commonwealths of this Union without feelings of deep interest, and that the author has done his work well and impartially will be the general verdict. — *Christian at Work* (New York).

Professor Shaler has prepared a succinct, well-balanced, and readable sketch of this "pioneer Commonwealth." Himself a native of Kentucky, he writes with the natural affection which a man of loyal impulses feels for his State, and yet with no apparent bias. . . . The volume is in every way a worthy addition to a series which possesses unique value and interest. — *Boston Journal.*

A capital example of what a short State history should be. — *Hartford Courant.*

HOUGHTON, MIFFLIN & CO., BOSTON, MASS.

American Men of Letters.

EDITED BY
CHARLES DUDLEY WARNER.

A series of biographies of distinguished American authors, having all the special interest of biography, and the larger interest and value of illustrating the different phases of American literature, the social, political, and moral influences which have moulded these authors and the generations to which they belonged.

This series when completed will form an admirable survey of all that is important and of historical influence in American literature, and will itself be a creditable representation of the literary and critical ability of America to-day.

Washington Irving. By CHARLES DUDLEY WARNER.
Noah Webster. By HORACE E. SCUDDER.
Henry D. Thoreau. By FRANK B. SANBORN.
George Ripley. By OCTAVIUS BROOKS FROTHINGHAM.
J. Fenimore Cooper. By PROF. T. R. LOUNSBURY.
Margaret Fuller Ossoli. By T. W. HIGGINSON.
Ralph Waldo Emerson. By OLIVER WENDELL HOLMES.
Edgar Allan Poe. By GEORGE E. WOODBERRY.
Nathaniel Parker Willis. By HENRY A. BEERS.

IN PREPARATION.

Nathaniel Hawthorne. By JAMES RUSSELL LOWELL.
William Cullen Bryant. By JOHN BIGELOW.
Bayard Taylor. By J. R. G. HASSARD.
William Gilmore Simms. By GEORGE W. CABLE.
Benjamin Franklin. By JOHN BACH MCMASTER.

Others to be announced hereafter.

Each volume, with Portrait, 16mo, gilt top, $1.25.

"WASHINGTON IRVING."

Mr. Warner has not only written with sympathy, minute knowledge of his subject, fine literary taste, and that easy, fascinating style which always puts him on such good terms with his readers, but he has shown a tact, critical sagacity, and sense of proportion full of promise for the rest of the series which is to pass under his supervision. — *New York Tribune.*

It is a very charming piece of literary work, and presents the reader with an excellent picture of Irving as a man and of his methods as an author, together with an accurate and discriminating characterization of his works. — *Boston Journal.*

It would hardly be possible to produce a fairer or more candid book of its kind. — *Literary World* (London).

"NOAH WEBSTER."

Mr. Scudder's biography of Webster is alike honorable to himself and its subject. Finely discriminating in all that relates to personal and intellectual character, scholarly and just in its literary criticisms, analyses, and estimates, it is besides so kindly and manly in its tone, its narrative is so spirited and enthralling, its descriptions are so quaintly graphic, so varied and cheerful in their coloring, and its pictures so teem with the bustle, the movement, and the activities of the real life of a by-gone but most interesting age, that the attention of the reader is never tempted to wander, and he lays down the book with a sigh of regret for its brevity. — *Harper's Monthly Magazine.*

It fills completely its place in the purpose of this series of volumes. — *The Critic* (New York).

"HENRY D. THOREAU."

Mr. Sanborn's book is thoroughly American and truly fascinating. Its literary skill is exceptionally good, and there is a racy flavor in its pages and an amount of exact knowledge of interesting people that one seldom meets with in current literature. Mr. Sanborn has done Thoreau's genius an imperishable service. — *American Church Review* (New York).

Mr. Sanborn has written a careful book about a curious man, whom he has studied as impartially as possible; whom he admires warmly but with discretion; and the story of whose life he has told with commendable frankness and simplicity. — *New York Mail and Express.*

It is undoubtedly the best life of Thoreau extant. — *Christian Advocate* (New York).

"GEORGE RIPLEY."

Mr. Frothingham's memoir is a calm and thoughtful and tender tribute. It is marked by rare discrimination, and good taste and simplicity. The biographer keeps himself in the background, and lets his subject speak. And the result is one of the best examples of personal portraiture that we have met with in a long time. — *The Churchman* (New York).

He has fulfilled his responsible task with admirable fidelity, frank earnestness, justice, fine feeling, balanced moderation, delicate taste, and finished literary skill. It is a beautiful tribute to the high-bred scholar and generous-hearted man, whose friend he has so worthily portrayed. — *Rev. William H. Channing* (London).

"JAMES FENIMORE COOPER."

We have here a model biography. The book is charmingly written, with a felicity and vigor of diction that are notable, and with a humor sparkling, racy, and never obtrusive. The story of the life will have something of the fascination of one of the author's own romances. — *New York Tribune*.

Prof. Lounsbury's book is an admirable specimen of literary biography. . . . We can recall no recent addition to American biography in any department which is superior to it. It gives the reader not merely a full account of Cooper's literary career, but there is mingled with this a sufficient account of the man himself apart from his books, and of the period in which he lived, to keep alive the interest from the first word to the last. — *New York Evening Post*.

"MARGARET FULLER OSSOLI."

Here at last we have a biography of one of the noblest and the most intellectual of American women, which does full justice to its subject. The author has had ample material for his work, — all the material now available, perhaps, — and has shown the skill of a master in his use of it. . . . It is a fresh view of the subject, and adds important information to that already given to the public. — REV. DR. F. H. HEDGE, in *Boston Advertiser*.

He has filled a gap in our literary history with excellent taste, with sound judgment, and with that literary skill which is preëminently his own. — *Christian Union* (New York).

Mr. Higginson writes with both enthusiasm and sympathy, and makes a volume of surpassing interest. — *Commercial Advertiser* (New York).

"RALPH WALDO EMERSON."

A biography of Emerson by Holmes is a real event in American literature. . . . He has brought Emerson himself so near, and painted him for us with a pencil so loving and yet so just, that it will remain with many of us a question which shall be hereafter most dear to us, the man whom the artist thus reveals, or the artist himself. — *Standard* (Chicago).

Dr. Holmes has written one of the most delightful biographies that has ever appeared. Every page sparkles with genius. His criticisms are trenchant, his analysis clear, his sense of proportion delicate, and his sympathies broad and deep. — *Philadelphia Press.*

"EDGAR ALLAN POE."

Mr. Woodberry has contrived with vast labor to construct what must hereafter be called the authoritative biography of Poe — a biography which corrects all others, supplements all others, and supersedes all others. — *The Critic* (New York).

The best life of Poe that has yet been written, and no better one is likely to be written hereafter. This is high praise, but it is deserved. Mr. Woodberry has spared no pains in exploring sources of information; he has shown rare judgment and discretion in the interpretation of what he has found; he has set forth everything frankly and fairly; and he has brought to bear upon the critical part of his work a keen instinct, a well-informed mind, a sound judgment, and the utmost catholicity of spirit. — *Commercial Advertiser* (New York).

"NATHANIEL PARKER WILLIS."

Prof. Beers has done his work sympathetically yet candidly and fairly and in a philosophic manner, indicating the status occupied by Willis in the republic of letters, and sketching graphically his literary environment and the main springs of his success. It is one of the best books of an excellent series. — *Buffalo Times.*

The work is sober, frank, honest, trustworthy, and eminently readable. — *The Beacon* (Boston).

A delightful biographical study. — *Brooklyn Union.*

HOUGHTON, MIFFLIN & CO., BOSTON, MASS.

American Statesmen.

A Series of Biographies of Men conspicuous in the Political History of the United States.

EDITED BY

JOHN T. MORSE, JR.

The object of this series is not merely to give a number of unconnected narratives of men in American political life, but to produce books which shall, when taken together, indicate the lines of political thought and development in American history, — books embodying in compact form the result of extensive study of the many and diverse influences which have combined to shape the political history of our country.

The series is under the editorship of Mr. JOHN T. MORSE, JR., whose historical and biographical writings give ample assurance of his special fitness for this task. The volumes now ready are as follows: —

John Quincy Adams. By JOHN T. MORSE, JR.
Alexander Hamilton. By HENRY CABOT LODGE.
John C. Calhoun. By DR. H. VON HOLST.
Andrew Jackson. By PROF. W. G. SUMNER.
John Randolph. By HENRY ADAMS.
James Monroe. By PRES. DANIEL C. GILMAN.
Thomas Jefferson. By JOHN T. MORSE, JR.
Daniel Webster. By HENRY CABOT LODGE.
Albert Gallatin. By JOHN AUSTIN STEVENS.
James Madison. By SYDNEY HOWARD GAY.
John Adams. By JOHN T. MORSE, JR.
John Marshall. By A. B. MAGRUDER.
Samuel Adams. By JAMES K. HOSMER.

IN PREPARATION.

Henry Clay. By Hon. CARL SCHURZ.
Martin Van Buren. By HON. WM. DORSHEIMER.

Others to be announced hereafter. Each biography occupies a single volume, 16mo, gilt top. Price $1.25.

ESTIMATES OF THE PRESS.

"JOHN QUINCY ADAMS."

That Mr. Morse's conclusions will in the main be those of posterity we have very little doubt, and he has set an admirable example to his coadjutors in respect of interesting narrative, just proportion, and judicial candor. — *New York Evening Post.*

Mr. Morse has written closely, compactly, intelligently, fearlessly, honestly. — *New York Times.*

"ALEXANDER HAMILTON."

The biography of Mr. Lodge is calm and dignified throughout. He has the virtue — rare indeed among biographers — of impartiality. He has done his work with conscientious care, and the biography of Hamilton is a book which cannot have too many readers. It is more than a biography; it is a study in the science of government. — *St. Paul Pioneer-Press.*

"JOHN C. CALHOUN."

Nothing can exceed the skill with which the political career of the great South Carolinian is portrayed in these pages. The work is superior to any other number of the series thus far, and we do not think it can be surpassed by any of those that are to come. The whole discussion in relation to Calhoun's position is eminently philosophical and just. — *The Dial* (Chicago).

"ANDREW JACKSON."

Prof. Sumner has, . . . all in all, made the justest long estimate of Jackson that has had itself put between the covers of a book. — *New York Times.*

One of the most masterly monographs that we have ever had the pleasure of reading. It is calm and clear. — *Providence Journal.*

"JOHN RANDOLPH."

The book has been to me intensely interesting. . . . It is rich in new facts and side lights, and is worthy of its place in the already brilliant series of monographs on American Statesmen. — Prof. MOSES COIT TYLER.

Remarkably interesting. . . . The biography has all the elements of popularity, and cannot fail to be widely read. — *Hartford Courant.*

"JAMES MONROE."

In clearness of style, and in all points of literary workmanship, from cover to cover, the volume is well-nigh perfect. There is also a calmness of judgment, a correctness of taste, and an absence of partisanship which are too frequently wanting in biographies, and especially in political biographies. — *American Literary Churchman* (Baltimore).

The most readable of all the lives that have ever been written of the great jurist. — *San Francisco Bulletin.*

"THOMAS JEFFERSON."

The book is exceedingly interesting and readable. The attention of the reader is strongly seized at once, and he is carried along in spite of himself, sometimes protesting, sometimes doubting, yet unable to lay the book down. — *Chicago Standard.*

The requirements of political biography have rarely been met so satisfactorily as in this memoir of Jefferson. — *Boston Journal.*

"DANIEL WEBSTER."

It will be read by students of history; it will be invaluable as a work of reference; it will be an authority as regards matters of fact and criticism; it hits the key-note of Webster's durable and ever-growing fame; it is adequate, calm, impartial; it is admirable. — *Philadelphia Press.*

The task has been achieved ably, admirably, and faithfully. — *Boston Transcript.*

"ALBERT GALLATIN."

It is one of the most carefully prepared of these very valuable volumes, . . . abounding in information not so readily accessible as is that pertaining to men more often treated by the biographer. . . . The whole work covers a ground which the political student cannot afford to neglect. — *Boston Correspondent Hartford Courant.*

Frank, simple, and straightforward. — *New York Tribune.*

"JAMES MADISON."

The execution of the work deserves the highest praise. It is very readable, in a bright and vigorous style, and is marked by unity and consecutiveness of plan. — *The Nation* (New York).

An able book. . . . Mr. Gay writes with an eye single to truth. — *The Critic* (New York).

"JOHN ADAMS."

A good piece of literary work. . . . It covers the ground thoroughly, and gives just the sort of simple and succinct account that is wanted. — *Evening Post* (New York).

A model of condensation and selection, as well as of graphic portraiture and clear and interesting historical narrative. — *Christian Intelligencer* (New York).

"JOHN MARSHALL."

Well done, with simplicity, clearness, precision, and judgment, and in a spirit of moderation and equity. A valuable addition to the series. — *New York Tribune.*

"SAMUEL ADAMS."

Thoroughly appreciative and sympathetic, yet fair and critical. . . . This biography is a piece of good work — a clear and simple presentation of a noble man and pure patriot; it is written in a spirit of candor and humanity. — *Worcester Spy.*

A brilliant and enthusiastic book, which it will do every American much good to read. — *The Beacon* (Boston).

HOUGHTON, MIFFLIN, AND CO., BOSTON, MASS.

www.ingramcontent.com/pod-product-compliance
Lightning Source LLC
Chambersburg PA
CBHW030315240426
43673CB00040B/1179